Life
Lessons

Life Lessons

B RUCE G RAHAM

F REE R EIN P RESS

2022

GPM Publishing
FreeRein Press

Pen & Ink Illustrations by Kevin Ritchie with permission

First hardcover edition, 2022
ISBN: 979-8-9857865-0-7

First paperback edition, 2022
ISBN: 979-8-9857865-1-4

1 3 5 7 9 10 8 6 4 2
First Printing

This book is dedicated to my grandson,

Stanley Andrew Maness

For what is the life of a man, if it is not interwoven with the life of former generations by a sense of history.

—Cicero 106–43 B.C.E.

Table of Contents

INTRODUCTION

The stories in this book are tales of people in my family that have been passed down from one generation to the next. These stories were told to me in bits and pieces over my lifetime. Some of the people I knew directly; however, all had a great impact on me. Later in life, when I began to reflect on these family members and their lives, it came to me that all of them were remarkable in their own way. I realized there were lessons to be learned from their lives and experiences, both good and bad. I researched the stories for accurate historical times, places, and events that correlate to the individuals who feature in them. I have attempted to revive people's personalities and make them come alive instead of chronologically describing every event of their lives. I have emphasized several seminal events and the outcomes of keen decisions made when facing a crossroads in life that determined their futures and exemplified their personalities. Many of the stories highlight my own personal experiences with some of these people and how they affected my life.

Entire books could be written about some of these fascinating individuals. However, to include all of them, I have told the most salient anecdotes in their lives that highlight the most poignant lesson to be taken away from each person's experience. These people were active in many important parts of American history. Each person can serve as a front-row personal account of the events that unfolded in the United States during that time.

Each chapter has a moral, and each individual has a story behind him or her. Although these people lived in the past, their stories remain viable because human nature does not change over time. Problems of the human condition stay the same. There are issues that we all must face in the present and in the future. These stories can serve as an inspiration, a guidepost to life, and a warning that could benefit anyone.

The stories depicted here paint a broad picture of many aspects of American life. Each person's life is different, with different dilemmas that needed to be faced and dealt with. These stories are of high adventure, love, interpersonal relationships, gaining wisdom, war, building and succeeding in a business, sports, the counterculture, drug and alcohol abuse, the profession of medicine, crime, Christian redemption, firsthand accounts with Harry Truman and many other world leaders to name just a few.

These people left a legacy that is woven into my life and others' lives. I feel that certain features of this family are uniquely present in the American character. Independence, self-reliance, and at times great courage are commonplace among this group, and these traits have been passed down from one generation to the next.

1.

Happy Jack

The Homestead Act passed by the U.S. government in 1862 gave 160 acres of free land to any U.S. citizen who was willing to build on and use the land for five years. This was done to entice people to settle on lands previously thought undesirable because of location, lack of water, or topography. Jack Graham and his new wife, Elizabeth, built a sod house on the prairie and began to farm the area.

The date was September 1868 in Phillips County, northwestern Kansas, close to the Nebraska line. John W. Graham—whom most people called Jack—was repairing the fence of his corral that held several horses and two cows. Hearing the advance of horses, he looked up and saw a group of people in an open wooden wagon racing toward his house and waving their hands in the air with urgent gestures. They appeared frantic and fearful. The wagon pulled up to the corral, and the occupants jumped out. All began talking at once. Jeffrey Knudsen, his wife, his three young children, and his younger brother Eric were Graham's nearest neighbors. The Knudsen family lived eight miles away. It was hard to discern what they were talking about, but Jeffrey began speaking, out of breath. Speaking with a thick foreign accent, he told Jack that Chief Tall Bull and the Cheyenne were now at war with the United States and were killing every white person they could find. Jeffrey said breathlessly, "I'd guess the tribe to be more than two hundred warriors!" He went on to tell that every settlement between the Republican and Solomon Rivers had been destroyed, an area of nearly three hundred square miles. The Knudsens had barely gotten out alive. However, their house and all their belongings had been burned. They said the Cheyenne were close behind them on horseback.

It was early evening, and the sun was about to set. The Knudsens were recent immigrants from Sweden and had only one single-shot rifle with minimal ammunition. Jack had been on the frontier for some time and knew how dangerous it could be. He was well armed, as the Knudsens knew. Jack had served in the Civil War and, along with occasional scrapes with Indians, had seen his share of combat. He knew Tall Bull was a very capable, fearsome, and ruthless war chief who was the leader of the Dog Soldier Society. These warriors were the most aggressive, organized, and powerful of the Cheyenne tribe. Jack knew the chances of survival for those gathered at his homestead were slim if the whole war party descended on them at once. However, he would exact a heavy price if it did.

Jack had one of the new Spencer repeating rifles. They were very expensive but could be lifesaving in bad situations. He took the rifle out of its case, which had been hidden from sight, and loaded it with shells.

He had prepared for a situation like this before returning to the frontier. Jack then gave orders to the group. They gathered as many food stores and water as they could to prepare for a potential siege. He stationed each man at a window with a rifle, ready to defend the occupants of the sod house.

Jack gave Jeffrey Knudsen his military Springfield single-shot musket that he had used in the Civil War along with instructions on how to use and reload it. Jack told Jeffrey to aim a little low because of the rifle's past tendency to shoot over the heads of its targets. He also instructed him to lead a rapidly moving target by about a foot. Jack told Jeffrey he should be able to get off two to three shots per minute after the first firing of the gun. Jeffrey took the musket, aimed it out the window, moved it from side to side, and then held it by his chest. He seemed confident in its use since the older gun that he owned was not much different in its reloading, though much less accurate and effective than the Springfield. Jack then gave Eric a double-barrel shotgun and instructed him in its use. Jack also gave each man a box of shells and firing caps.

Jack stood outside the house and took a long look at the surrounding horizon. He saw nothing but miles and miles of open prairie and the setting sun, with no sign of the Cheyenne. Jack was the last person to enter the house, which was made entirely of sod except for the doorway, windows, and beams in the roof. Those inside barricaded the door with extra wood planks. The Knudsen family became less fearful upon seeing Jack's efficient manner and calm leadership in the present chaotic and dangerous situation.

The sun slowly set, but there were still no signs of Indians. Each person was vigilant at his or her post, guns at the ready. Later, the night became filled with strange forebodings. Signal arrows shot across the horizon, and campfires flickered on the distant hills. Coyotes, or Indians impersonating coyotes, howled unseen in the dark. Jack ordered all lamps to be extinguished. The sounds of coyote yips and howls came closer to the house, but those inside still could see nothing but darkness. The inhabitants of the sod house were restless and anxious. The women tried to comfort the children by telling Bible stories. Jack's wife, Elizabeth, recited the Twenty-Third Psalm. Jack heard birdcalls and twittering close to the house, although he knew birds didn't call at night.

Jeffrey Knudsen looked over to Jack with obvious concern and asked, "Do you think the Indians are out there?"

"Oh, yes, they're there all right. We just can't see them yet. I figure it shouldn't be too long before we can, though. Keep your eyes open."

The horses became restless in the corral, running from one end to the other. Jack still couldn't see anything beyond the moving animals. He told the men to hold their fire until he gave the command. He quickly glanced at the two other defenders, noting that sweat was pouring down their faces. Otherwise, they seemed to be holding up well.

Jack thought, "Just show yourself so I can get a shot." He knew the Indians were out there in the dark. He didn't know where or how many, but he was sure they were there. Jack could feel that it would be just a short time before the Indians attacked, and then all hell would break loose. He remembered many stories of Tall Bull being especially fierce, never taking any prisoners, and taking a special delight in torture, even of women and children. He remembered what some old scouts on the frontier had told him: When being overrun by Indians, keep a bullet in the chamber of your gun for yourself and for any loved ones. Jack tried to put those thoughts out of his mind for the time being. He took a deep breath and slowly exhaled, trying to relax and focus on accuracy as he peered into the dark. He wanted to be ready.

The commotion and chaos in the corral increased, with dust rising in small, billowing clouds. One horse reared up and let out a loud whinny. Suddenly, out of the darkness, Jack saw eight or ten dark figures running toward the house and gave the order to fire. The occupants of the house fired their guns in rapid successive bursts, but no one got a clear shot. Everyone kept firing. The figures in the dark returned fire. Bullets whizzed through the windows, breaking the glass into large shards that hit the dirt floor. Everyone stooped as low as possible to avoid being hit by the incoming barrage. The children were flat on their bellies on the dirt floor crying, with Mrs. Knudsen lying over them for protection. Tufts of sod and dirt puffed out inside the house, depleting the energy of the bullets fired at them and filling the air inside the house with dust. The men kept firing, especially Jack, who had the advantage of a repeating rifle that could fire seven rounds rapidly without reloading.

Several screams of pain were heard outside by the corral. The noise from the gunfire was deafening in the enclosed space of the sod house, but the men barely noticed. They were now totally focused on aiming their rifles and firing. Their fear and apprehension were now gone, replaced by a focused determination to protect themselves and the others. They could hear the Indians' loud, terrifying war whoops in the moonless night. They could see fleeting glimpses of shadows running in the dark and the dust. Jack knew that if he could hit a target anywhere on the body, it would result in a devastating injury, if not immediate death, because of the large .52-caliber rifle shells he was firing at a relatively short range. This type of rifle was frequently used to bring down large buffalo.

Something hit the door with a sudden, violent thud. Just as Jack heard the loud impact against the door, he looked over and saw Elizabeth, his bride, in a military stance holding a Colt .45 revolver in her right hand, aiming straight as an arrow at the door. She was in a side stance to give the assailant the smallest possible target. Her left hand was on her hip, and she appeared steady, calm, and determined. Jack had been about to tell her to do just what she had done by her own instinct. At that moment, he knew he had married the right woman. He felt confident that she would prevent anyone from coming through that door alive while he and the other two men were fending off attacks from outside the house. The door held tight, thanks to the extra planks nailed across it.

Jack then heard footsteps on the roof. He glanced up to the rafters and could see a small amount of dust coming from above with each slow step. He didn't know how many, but he knew they were there. He quickly swung his rifle up and aimed at the ceiling where the dust was coming from. He shot several volleys. This shocked and alarmed the occupants of the house, who had not realized that their assailants were now on the roof. Jack could hear commotion and movement from above, which stopped abruptly after a loud thud. He then swung his rifle around and saw a clear shot close by the window. He fired several times, not knowing if he had hit his mark because of the darkness and the fleeting quickness of his target. He then reloaded his seven-shot Spencer repeating rifle.

The nearest military fort was Fort Hays, nearly one hundred miles away. They knew they could not expect help anytime soon. Mrs. Knudsen held her crying children tightly in the dark. She began singing

Swedish songs while rocking them, although her singing was barely audible over the deafening noise of the ongoing gunfire. After a prolonged period of firing, Jack ceased to see any movement of human or animal outside.

"Hold your fire!" Jack instructed. Suddenly, all was quiet. They all listened intently but heard nothing. No firing came from outside the house, no screaming or war whoops, and the animals in the corral were strangely silent. As quickly as the violence and chaos had begun, it had now stopped. Jack lifted his head above the windowsill for a better look but saw nothing but the dead, silent darkness of the prairie—no movement by any attackers or his animals in the corral.

The other men also looked intently out into the darkness but saw nothing. The Knudsens looked at Jack for further orders. He instructed them to keep quiet and vigilant. Jack said, "We might get another attack at any time, and the next one may be worse. We're not out of this yet."

Hours passed, and the total silence continued. Jack no longer heard any bird or animal calls, which he took as a good sign. The night seemed endless, as they did not know when the next attack might come or if the main war party would come next. The children were whimpering but holding up extremely well, all things considered. Jack thought these were tough little kids, and Mrs. Knudsen seemed to be a very good mother. He also thought that the inexperienced Swedish men had proved to be fairly decent soldiers. They had kept their wits about them in the middle of the attack. He thought, "Maybe there is some Viking blood still left in them," and chuckled to himself at the idea. Jack was pleased with his little army, but he wondered how long the silence would last.

Jack asked the occupants of the dark house, "Is everyone all right?" Jeffrey Knudsen replied in his thick Swedish accent, "Yah, we are all fine." Jack expected a second attack soon. He crawled across the floor to avoid being shot at through the windows and went to each of the other men's posts by the windows. He checked everyone's ammunition, and all were well supplied. Jack spoke some encouraging words and said, "Keep a knife by your side just in case." He had prepared as much as he possibly could for life on the frontier, and it had paid off, at least so far.

The sod house was terribly hot and poorly ventilated. It reminded Jack of the glass factory where he had worked years ago as a child. He had nearly forgotten what it was like after spending so much of his life out west on the frontier.

Jack thought, "I'd rather be fighting for my life out here in freedom than slowly dying in that dungeon they called a glass factory, always on the verge of starvation. I've had a good life and if it's time to meet my maker, then let his will be done. But if I'm goin down, I'm goin down swingin."

The air seemed almost too thick to breathe. A fine dust permeated the air, stirred up by the recent battle. Everyone was coughing, and all were sweating profusely in the near total darkness of the small enclosure. It felt as if they were in a dungeon with no option for escape. They had the frightening thought that there were hundreds of people outside this little house who wanted them all dead, and the enemy would do their best to kill every last person within. The Knudsens knew several families that had not been as lucky as they and had been overrun by the Indians. They grieved at the thought of their friends' and neighbor's fate. They all realized that they were not yet out of trouble, but at least they had a fighting chance, especially with an experienced commander in Jack Graham.

Everyone was praying for the sun to rise so they could emerge from this miserable dense darkness. No one had any idea of the time or how long it would be until dawn. Hours upon hours passed, and the darkness seemed to go on forever. Jack knew that the more time passed, the greater the chance that the Indians would not return. However, if they did return for a daylight attack, it would be in force with large numbers. He hoped that would not be the case. He kept his thoughts to himself and continued to encourage the rest of the group. All of the Knudsens felt grateful that a man such as Jack Graham was around, although they never said so. Everyone just kept silent, trying to breathe and not cough, waiting for the sunrise.

Elizabeth walked around, bent over to avoid being seen through the broken windows. She gave everyone a cup of water and an encouraging smile. She seemed steady and confident. Jack was amazed at how well she had carried herself in such a dire situation, especially with no prior experience. Jack was proud of his diminutive new wife for withstanding the rigors and dangers of frontier life. She had left a safe, protected life in Chicago, Illinois. Growing up in Scotland as a child, she certainly had not had any experience with Indians. Throughout their new life on the frontier, Elizabeth had never complained. Jack concluded that he had married one tough little lady.

Dawn's light slowly began to peek through the shattered windows of the small sod structure. The light gradually brightened through the house and immediately lifted everyone's spirits. The dark night had seemed like an eternity. Now, all felt a glimmer of hope, especially with no evidence of a second attack. The Knudsens had held up well, and the children were now quiet.

Jack looked out the broken window and saw nothing suspicious. All was quiet. He got up from his kneeling position at the window and walked toward the barred entrance. He unbarricaded the door and slowly walked out of the house. His gun was fully loaded and ready.

Elizabeth told Jack, "Please be careful."

"I will. I'm taking it real slow and easy."

Jack looked around and again scanned the horizon. The horses were gone, but the two cows were still there. Jack looked down in front of the door and saw a large pool of blood. There were drag marks from two legs in the dust extending away from the house along with a trail of blood. Beside the pool of blood, he found a Cheyenne war club. He picked it up and kept it as a memento.

He could not imagine how someone could have lost so much blood and lived. He knew this all too well from his relatively recent experience in the Civil War. He found more blood on the other side of the corral. He surmised that one Indian had been killed and the body dragged away by the others, and another may have been seriously wounded near the corral. Jack thought he might have hit more but just didn't know for sure. There could be blood on the roof where he had shot at one of the attackers, but he wouldn't bother investigating since it really didn't matter at the moment.

As he looked around, the others came out of the house. They were relieved to be out of the hot, claustrophobic sod room and to breathe fresh air without inhaling dust. Jeffrey Knudsen asked Jack, "Do you think they're going to come back?"

Jack looked at Jeffrey's dirty, sweaty face and said, "I don't think so. I think we're going to be all right." Knudsen wiped the sweat off his face with his arm, looked across the wide horizon along with Jack, and said, "Thank God!"

Jeffrey and his brother Eric smiled at each other and then shook Jack's hand. "Thank you for saving us!"

Jack replied, "We saved each other. None of us could have survived this alone. You were good soldiers."

The group they had battled was likely a scouting raiding party, with the main group of warriors heading east toward the town of Long Island, Kansas. They later found out that the U.S. Seventh Cavalry had intercepted the war party and turned it away before the town could be attacked. The Grahams and the Knudsens felt lucky to be alive. The Knudsens moved south and eventually resettled in Lindsborg, Kansas. To this day, Lindsborg has a large population of people of Swedish descent.

J ack Graham had a hard life, but he never thought of it that way. He was always energetic and positive in his outlook. His parents had emigrated to America from Northern Ireland by way of Scotland. They initially lived in Boston, Massachusetts, where his father was a foreman at the shipyards. He was killed at the shipyard by a blow to the head from a heavy tool wielded by a member of a gang of Irish thugs. There was long-standing animosity between Northern and Southern Irish people that had not been left behind in the old country.

Jack was nine years old when he went to work in the glass factory after his father's death. In that era, there was no government assistance, and the Grahams had no other family members to help. Jack became the main provider of the family, supporting his mother and two younger siblings. He worked long, hard hours in the factory. He would arise at 5:00 a.m., eat some porridge or oatmeal that his mother prepared, and walk to work by 6:00 a.m. He carried bread and cheese for lunch. He worked ten hours a day, going home by 4:00 p.m. When he got home from work, he did family chores to help his mother and two younger siblings. His dinner consisted of beans and toast with occasional potatoes. They obtained some vegetables, usually onions and turnips, every two to three days and small portions of meat every two to three weeks that were usually cooked in a soup. Jack was continually hungry, but he never complained. He knew that his mother was doing the best she could under difficult circumstances.

Glass factories were very hot and poorly ventilated. The glass required melting in furnaces for its manufacture. The making of glass objects required expertise and was all done by hand. Jack started as an apprentice but became a very adept glass worker by the age of ten and was then considered a craftsman. The managers of the factory and the other adult workers were not friendly. They were not abusive but just seemed not to care about Jack and never engaged in conversation with him. They simply gave him instructions on what to do and what not to do. He was scolded if he did not perform to their standards or wasn't quick enough in completing a task. There were other children working in the factory, but he was the youngest. When he tried to speak to the other children, they were told to stop wasting time and to get back to work.

He never went to school because times were hard and money scarce.

He envied some of the other boys in his tenement neighborhood who went to school and had free time to play. He frequently looked out the windows of his house and saw other children running around and having fun. He wanted to join the other boys in the street to play ball and other games but couldn't because of his responsibilities. However, he knew many more boys like him who were poor and had to work.

Jack felt a great responsibility to support his mother and siblings as "the man of the house," even at such a young age. His mother was very kind and always told Jack she was proud of him.

When Jack was ten, the family moved to Pittsburgh, Pennsylvania, where he got a job in another glass factory. This job paid higher wages and had slightly better working conditions. His mother became a housecleaner, but he made more money than she. Eventually his mother remarried and had another son. His new stepfather was a mild-mannered, kind man who did odd jobs as a laborer. The family struggled financially to make ends meet. Although their new apartment in Pittsburgh was slightly larger than the previous one, it was still in a dilapidated building in a rundown part of the city. The air was filled with smog and smoke from area factories and the extensive use of coal for heating and cooking in family homes. A faint stench of garbage was always present because of the poor systems of waste removal in crowded areas of the city as well as the extensive use of horses for all forms of transportation and the resulting animal waste. Because of these conditions, epidemics of lung and intestinal diseases were common. Childhood mortality was quite high.

In 1848, when Jack was thirteen, free land became available on the western frontier in the Kansas territory. Although this was technically Native land that had been given to the eastern tribes that had been resettled there, immigrants in wagon trains were allowed to travel through the area to the West Coast. However, many of these people settled in Kansas and other territories before they reached their destination. Within twenty years, the U.S. population had doubled. Masses of poor people with a limited future headed west for a better life.

The family decided to move after saving all of their money. They faced significant risks, and the move was potentially dangerous, but they thought the opportunity was worth it. They wanted desperately to chart their own destiny, work for themselves, and own their own land. If they were not allowed to settle in Kansas, they planned to go farther west to Oregon. Jack was thrilled to escape from the glass factory and exhilarated about the prospect of a new life. The family traveled by paddlewheel riverboat down the Ohio River to the Mississippi and then up the Missouri River to Kansas City and then to Westport, close to the Kansas border.

They outfitted for the remaining trip to Kansas at the town of Westport, which was the primary staging area for all western overland migration. West of this town, there was no real civilization until travelers reached the West Coast or Santa Fe. The family were able to buy a Conestoga wagon and an ox to pull it. They bought a horse and other necessities for life on the frontier. Jack thought the wagon, the largest he had ever seen, looked more like a big boat than a wagon. These wagons were so large that they were nicknamed "prairie schooners."

Westport was a bustling place, filled with all sorts of people preparing to travel west. It was the jumping-off point for the westward expansion of America and was far different from the cities of the East. Families like Jack's were preparing for a long journey to Oregon, California, or Santa Fe for a new life. Gold had just been discovered in

California, and thousands of men were planning to strike it rich by traveling to those gold fields. Jack saw rough-looking frontiersmen dressed in buckskin coming from the West to sell furs, occasionally with an Indian woman in tow. The Indians walking around the dirt streets were the first he had ever seen. They were not what he had expected. Most were wearing a mixture of white and Indian apparel. Conspicuously absent were the feathered war bonnets that he had heard about in stories and magazines. They didn't look particularly fierce in their present state. Occasionally he saw patrols of soldiers whose duty was to guard the frontier. He knew that Fort Leavenworth was not far away, just upstream on the Missouri River. He passed saloons with crowds of noisy, rowdy men outside. Jack was slightly frightened to see so many drunk men out of control, many of whom were armed with pistols on their hips. Jack's mother told him to stay away from places like that, as saloons were dangerous in more ways than one. He believed her but didn't quite understand.

The wagon was packed to the brim with articles of life and family members. Jack's stepfather and mother rode in front and held the reins to drive the ox, while he rode the horse. His three siblings were in the back of the wagon. Jack was excited that he was able to ride the horse. He had never done this before, but he picked up the technique quickly. Fortunately, the horse was docile and well behaved. He rode bareback since they didn't have enough money to buy a saddle. They signed up with a wagon train, of which most of the travelers were going much farther west on the Oregon Trail. They planned to split off from the group when they reached their destination. Until then, they would be much safer traveling in a group led by an experienced wagon master and a scout.

Jack's family eventually settled in Marshall County, north-central Kansas. Large herds of bison still roamed the area, along with antelope, deer, and elk. Wolves and coyotes were ever present. The air was clean, and the sky was bright blue. The grass was above the knees. They could see for miles over rolling hills to the horizon. The prairie reminded Jack of a green ocean with miles and miles of grass rippling in the wind like waves. Large cottonwood trees were scattered along the streams and ravines. His present new world was a far cry from the industrial, smoke-filled cities of Pittsburgh and Boston. Jack hadn't known this world existed. All of his senses were in shock from this new land, but for the better. The clean, subtle scent of grass was everywhere instead of the smell of smoke and the always underlying smell of garbage in the industrial cities of the East. Every day in this new environment, Jack would get up and be excited about whatever came during the day. No more hot, gloomy factory. No more unfriendly factory managers. No more rigid work schedules. He was free!

Jack loved it, even though the farm work was hard. He and the rest of the family built a sod house. They began tilling the soil and planting crops. When he had free time away from the farm chores, he loved to take long, fast rides on his horse across the prairie. He became an excellent horseman riding bareback. He managed the care of his horse and livestock at an early age. He loved the farm animals, especially his horse. The entire family's attitude began to change to optimism for the future, an optimism that slowly brought happiness. Everyone seemed to smile and talk more. The most dramatic change was in his stepfather, who previously had been quiet and at times sullen but now became a lively and talkative man. Even at his young age, Jack realized what a little bit of freedom and independence could do to someone's personality and outlook on life. He knew it was well worth the risks and rigors of the frontier.

Soon after their arrival in Kansas, Jack came into the house and told his mother that his skin hurt. His mother looked at his red and blistered skin and said, "You have had too much sun; you need to wear a broad-brimmed hat when you go outside." Jack didn't know what a sunburn was. He had never spent so much time outdoors.

Wild game was plentiful, and in time the family was able to buy a .50-caliber single-shot buffalo rifle and a .22-caliber single-shot pistol for small game. Jack became an expert hunter. The rifle was quite heavy, and the recoil was painful. He placed a fur pad on the butt of the gun to soften the kick. Jack was told that Indians were around, but he had never seen any. He was told to stay away from them if he ever saw them. One of the men on the wagon train told him, "The only time you will see an Indian is when they want you to see them. They will usually stay away from white people unless they want something from you."

On one of his hunts, he shot a buffalo. He thought he had hit his mark well, but the buffalo kept running across the prairie and over several hills. Jack chased the wounded animal on his horse for nearly a mile. He came to the crest of a hill, where he saw the dead buffalo a quarter mile away. Leaning over the carcass were four Indians who were already starting to butcher the beast. Jack was shocked at the sudden sight of a group of real Indians and nearly lost his breath. They were not at all like the Indians he had seen in Westport—they appeared much more fierce. He was initially at a loss. Then, without much thought, he raised his hand as a sign of peace. The Indians seemed menacing. They stopped and looked at Jack, motionless and without expression. He couldn't tell if they were Sioux or Cheyenne. He knew they were not

Pawnee by their hairstyle. The Pawnee were generally more friendly to whites. Jack turned his horse around and galloped back home as fast as he could. He wasn't going to dispute the ownership of the buffalo. He wasn't about to take any chances with the Indians. There were plenty of other buffalo around.

Ammunition was scarce and expensive, so he had to make every shot count. He became an excellent stalker of game and learned great patience as well as the art of camouflage. The family grew to depend on the wild game that Jack brought in to supplement their otherwise meager diet. Because of his improved nutrition, with added protein in his diet, Jack grew several inches and put on forty pounds. He actually became fairly broad-shouldered and muscular. Jack had never felt so healthy in his life, and he now had more energy than ever before. He noted that he could now easily lift heavy objects that he had previously struggled with. He was able to perform heavy farm work, go hunting, and skin and prepare the meat, all in a day's work with energy to spare at the end of the day. Jack sold the hides of animals he shot, mainly buffalo, in the nearest town to earn extra money for the family. He had never been so happy in his life. He felt a freedom and an independence that he had never experienced before. Jack concluded that he was in heaven. He also realized that there could be great danger in this "heaven."

When Jack was sixteen years old, he took a job at a nearby cattle ranch. His younger brothers were growing up and could now take over the farm work that he had been doing. The cattle business was just starting in the state. It would later become a huge industry for all of the plains states. He became one of the cowboys, driving cattle to the nearest newly made railhead in south-central Kansas.

Jack made a conscious decision: "From here on out, I'll most likely be on my own away from my family. I better grow up right now and become a man." He didn't realize that he had already grown-up years before at a young age.

Jack was the youngest and newest of the group and became the butt of many practical jokes from the older cowboys. The jokes were never malicious, but rather a rite of passage that they had all experienced. The mild teasing would show the rest of the crew what kind of stuff Jack was made of. Jack always had a smile on his face and was polite in spite of his rough company. He knew that the cowboys were hard on the exterior but good, hardworking men underneath. He admired their toughness and courage, which was frequently tested, whether it be turning a stampede or fighting off outlaws and Indians. The food was nothing special, consisting mainly of salted pork, beans, coffee, and hard bread, which they called "hardtack." The cowboys ate only two meals per day, as lunch was not a regular meal in those days. After dinner, they turned in under the stars on their blankets in a circle around the campfire. They got wet when it rained, having only a canvas tarp to lay over themselves. They would hopefully dry out in the saddle the next day. Cold, wind, and heat all had their problems, but they did their jobs despite the conditions.

As the least experienced cowboy, Jack had to ride "drag," which was in the rear. This was the least desirable position because of the dust and dirt raised by the cattle herd in front of him. Dirt and grit got into everything: food, bedroll, clothing, and between his seat and the saddle.

Jack wore a large pale-yellow bandanna over his nose and mouth while riding. His eyes, however, were frequently irritated by the dust.

There was little chance for bathing on the prairie. All the cowboys suffered the same conditions, but Jack fared much worse because of the drag position. At one point, the cattle drive had to cross a small river that was waist deep. The cattle and horses were able to ford the river with guidance from the cowboys. Jack saw some of the cowboys actually jump into the river and quickly get back in the saddle to wash off some of the dust and grit. One of the cowboys carefully rode up alongside Jack without Jack being aware of his presence. The cowboy slowly raised his leg and gave Jack a big shove off his saddle and into the river. All had a big laugh. The cowboy said, "You need a bath, son." Jack had just been thinking that he would love to jump in the river and clean up, so he was glad someone had forced him in. Jack never complained. Cowboy life was still better than working in a glass factory.

Jack proved himself useful to the main group because he was an expert marksman and hunter. The cowboys were amazed at Jack's accuracy with a rifle at great distances. They saw Jack take a bead on a buffalo that looked like a black dot on the horizon and take it down with a single shot. Jack told them, "You get good at something if your next meal depends on it." He was occasionally ordered to obtain fresh meat for the group by shooting wild game. The cook would then fix something special that all the men loved. It was hard to beat buffalo and elk steaks compared to the usual hardtack, salted pork, and beans. The entire crew was quite appreciative of Jack's hunting skills.

The cook was an old, scruffy, bearded cowboy who took Jack under his wing. He had a disheveled appearance and wore a broad, floppy hat. None of the cowboys knew his real name. They all just called him

Cookie. He liked to chew tobacco and whittle with a pocketknife, making small wooden figurines when he wasn't fixing food. Cookie gave Jack occasional snacks from the chuck wagon because he figured Jack was a growing boy and didn't want to "stunt his growth." Cookie and Jack often talked after dinner. Cookie had a lot of life experience on the frontier. He told stories of his life and the unspoken rules of being a cowboy. Cookie said, "If it's a job, do it. Put your back into it. Never complain or whine. If it's a horse, take good care of it. If you get bucked off and it hurts, hide it, then dust yourself off and get back on again. If it's a fence, mend it; if it's a load, truck it. If it's a punch, duck it, then finish it. If it's a lady, treat her like a queen."

Cookie said, "Tough times don't last, but tough people do. So, make the best of the bad times." It seemed that Cookie had a simple solution for just about everything. None of the cowboys ever messed with him because he controlled the amount and distribution of food. Overall, Cookie was a rough but kind man with much practical wisdom and good humor.

Jack could ride a horse as well as or better than the older cowboys. He also was a better shot with rifle or pistol than any of the others. However, he didn't know how to throw a rope to pull in a cow. He had not mentioned this to Mr. Farrow, the trail boss, when he was hired, thinking it might result in his not getting the job. Cookie spent many hours after dinner instructing Jack in throwing a rope and practicing with him. They started with stationary objects and then practiced throwing at cattle from horseback. Jack was a quick learner and impressed not only Cookie but the rest of the cowboys as well. Cookie said, "That's the good thing about being so young; you're not set in your ways, and you learn quicker than older folks." Once, while Jack was practicing throwing at a tree stump, he felt a rope encircle him and pull tight around his body. He turned around, and the whole crew broke out in laughter because one of the cowboys had lassoed Jack. Jack laughed as well, realizing it was just good-natured fun.

Jack didn't remember his father well and had never had a close relationship with his stepfather, although they got along well. Cookie and the trail boss, Mr. Farrow, became mentors to Jack over the years. He always looked up to the two, who proved to be good examples for him through the rest of his life.

The trail boss was William Farrow. He was tall, with broad shoulders and a military bearing. He had chiseled features and wore a long mustache, as was common at the time. He had a weathered appearance from his long years on the frontier. He was a no-nonsense person who rarely smiled. He was fair and honest with his cowboy employees and gave compliments if a job was done well. In his younger days, he had been on expeditions to the Far West with John Fremont and Kit Carson. Now he was in the cattle business, which he believed was the big business of the future. He had a steady, firm hand and knew what he was doing. All of the cowboys respected him. Cookie said, "When the chips are down and times are tough, you definitely want Mr. Farrow around." He ran the outfit like a ship's captain, guiding the herd across a lonely, dangerous ocean of grass. Any dissension or slacking off on the job was not tolerated, since it could be dangerous for the entire group so far away from civilization.

One of the duties of the cowboys was to take turns watching the herd at night. They guarded against animal predators or anyone who wanted to steal the cattle. On horseback, they would slowly move around the herd, singing songs or just talking out loud to settle and reassure the cattle. The worst thing that could happen was a stampede, which was extremely dangerous for both men and cattle. The cowboy's job was to avoid anything that would spook the cattle. This was especially difficult when there was thunder and lightning. During these times, two or three cowboys would take night watch to prevent a stampede.

Mr. Farrow told the cowboys what to expect on each stage of their journey and their objectives. One day, he told the men to be extra vigilant because they were going through Indian country. The next day, the cowboy in front of Jack turned around and pointed toward the hills flanking the herd on one side. Jack noted several deer running rapidly over the ridgeline toward the herd, only to veer off quickly when they saw the men. This happened several more times, not only with deer but with many other animals. He saw flocks of prairie chickens and other birds fly over the ridge as if startled by something beyond the hills. It was a very unusual sight, and Jack didn't know what to make of this strange animal behavior. He called out to one of the nearby cowboys, "What's going on with all those animals?" There was no response. Jack was uneasy and didn't know what to think. No one was telling him anything.

Finally, one of the cowboys rode up to Jack and said, "Something is behind those hills scaring those critters towards us."

"What could that be?"

"Well, it could be a wolf pack or coyotes, or it could be humans. Mr. Farrow did say we were coming into Indian country."

A wave of concern flashed through Jack with instant fear. "What if it is Indians?"

"I'm sure Mr. Farrow knows what's going on. It's hard to miss all of them critters coming over the hills at us. At present, there is nothing we can do anyway. Just keep your eyes open and your gun handy."

Jack thought, "Mr. Farrow must have a plan, so I'm just going to take it easy." He felt anxious and kept staring at the hills and ridgeline to his right. This continued for over forty minutes, with various animals intermittently fleeing over the tops of the hills.

As the herd turned around a large group of hills, it was met by fifteen to twenty Indians in a line directly in front of it. These riders were motionless as they stared at the herd of cattle and cowboys before them. They appeared without expression, like a line of statues blocking the advance of the herd. The cowboys stopped the herd, and Mr. Farrow and five of the cowboys rode up to the Indians. Cookie and the chuck wagon drove up next to Jack. Cookie was silent and just stared at the Indians. He took out a monocular spyglass and gave it to Jack. When Jack looked at the group in front of them, he could see that the cowboys were well armed with pistols and rifles. They stopped directly in front of the Indians. Jack then noticed Mr. Farrow moving his arms and hands, communicating with sign language. The Indians looked fierce. They had colored paint, mainly red and black, on their faces. They were menacing in their appearance, and all had bows and arrows. The Indians were well known for their deadly accuracy and effectiveness with arrows. Jack knew that they could bring down large animals such as bison with arrows, let alone a human. They could fire multiple arrows rapidly, making them more effective at short range than a single-shot rifle. Several of the Indians also had long lances. Pieces of scalped human hair were attached to the lances, with more adorning their buckskin shirts. Jack saw through Cookie's spyglass that there was no evidence of Caucasian hair.

Cookie said, "Those scalps are highly valued among them warriors. It's like wearing a medal for bravery. They're always at war with somebody. If not us, then the Sioux or Cheyenne. Or for that matter, anyone who crosses them the wrong way. These plains Indians are a contentious bunch."

Jack continued to monitor events through the spyglass. Many of the Indians had a mohawk hairstyle that was dyed red. This was usually associated with the Pawnee tribe. Cookie took the spyglass from Jack, looked with one eye at the group, and commented, "Yep, it's a Pawnee war party all right. I don't think they're gonna mess with us, though. Otherwise, we would've known it by now. Those Pawnee knew they were scaring them critters towards us. They didn't care if we knew they were there or not. You might say they may have been slowly introducing themselves to us so we wouldn't be too startled when we finally met them."

Mr. Farrow seemed to talk with the Indians for a very long time. Jack didn't see any hostile activity, just a lot of back-and-forth communication. Cookie said, "They're in the midst of bargaining. It takes them longer because it's being done with sign language. Or maybe them Injuns are being a little stubborn. I've seen things like this before. It could go on for hours." Cookie could tell Jack was anxious, so he reassured Jack again: "If something bad was going to happen, it most likely would have commenced by now! So don't you worry yourself."

Jack said, "Mr. Farrow and the Indians seem quite relaxed."

Cookie replied, "Mr. Farrow has done a lot of this before. He knows what he's doin. In fact, he may even have crossed paths with them Injuns before. Maybe they're old acquaintances; you just never know. He's been around these parts a long time."

Just as Cookie finished talking, Jack saw Mr. Farrow and one of the Indians put their palms on their chests and then raise their hands in the air in what Jack took to be a peace sign. Cookie said, "Yep, they're done." Mr. Farrow and his cowboy escort turned their horses around and started riding back toward the herd in a slow gallop.

The Indians had demanded payment for entering their land. Mr. Farrow gave them five head of cattle and some tobacco. This transaction was preferable to risking further trouble. Cookie said, "If those Injuns were Sioux, Cheyenne, or Comanche, we might not have gotten away so easy." The Indians must have realized that attacking such a well-armed group, even though relatively small, would be dangerous for them as well.

Cookie told Jack that if you showed any weakness or fear to the Indians, they would take anything they wanted and likely kill you— "Even the good Injuns." Cookie said, "If you show fear or run away from a wolf, he will come after you and tear you up. But if you stand up to the wolf, show no fear, and don't run, you might have a good chance that he won't attack you. Well, son, humans aren't that much different." Cookie went on, "People from the cities don't realize this, and they get in trouble when they come out here. If you're in a weak position, you need to act stronger than you are, or your life maybe in danger. It's dangerous to travel in a small group out here and darn near crazy to travel alone. Out here in the wilderness, trust no one except your own people, and even with them always keep your eyes open."

Nearly five days had passed since the run-in with the Indians when one night Jack was suddenly awakened by gunfire and a great commotion. He pulled his blankets off, put his boots on, and grabbed his gun. The cattle were stampeding. There was chaos and noise everywhere.

Mr. Farrow was already on his horse and giving orders. A group of cattle rustlers were stealing the cattle and stampeding the herd. Mr. Farrow told several of the cowboys to get their guns, mount up, and follow him. Jack started to jump on his horse. Mr. Farrow said, "Jack, you stay here and help try to hold the cattle in place until we return." Jack was disappointed, but he understood that this was dangerous work. He and the remaining cowboys mounted their horses and began attempting to control the stampede. Jack had heard of cowboys losing their lives while trying to stop a stampede of hundreds of cattle. This was difficult, dangerous work even during daylight.

The noise from the stampede was deafening. The cattle were running so rapidly that Jack's horse was at a full gallop. The front of his broad-brimmed hat flipped up in front, and his yellow bandanna was fluttering in the wind. He could barely see anything in front of him with the darkness and dust all around. He had difficulty getting his bearings and direction. He had only occasional glimpses of his comrades. He yelled at the top of his voice, but he knew it was unheard because of the stampede noise. He felt that he was in a cauldron of chaos in the midst of hundreds of cattle packed together, running as fast as they could.

Jack couldn't remember ever being so afraid, but he knew he had to control his fear and do his duty, or his life would be in danger. The cattle were all around him, jostling him and his horse, pushing him in all directions. He knew he was in a terrible and dangerous position. He realized he needed to be on the edge of the herd, or his life could be at risk. If he were to be knocked off his horse, death by trampling was the probable outcome. Jack held tight to the saddle with one arm while waving a blanket with the other. Suddenly he felt a hard impact from one of the cows against the side of his horse. The horse reared a bit and made a few small jumps. Jack let go of the blanket as he held his reins. He firmly clenched his legs around the horse to let it know that he was in control. Jack was fortunate to have a steady and reliable horse. He managed to move out of the middle of the stampeding herd to the edge of the mass of cattle. This required quite a feat of horsemanship along with some luck. In his new position at the herd's edge, he was much safer and better able to control the stampede. Jack and the other cowboys regained control of the stampede by dawn after traveling many miles, but the rustlers had stolen over eighty head of cattle.

That evening, while sitting by the chuck wagon drinking some recently brewed coffee, Jack asked Cookie, "What's going to happen now?"

"Those rustlers didn't know who they were dealing with," Cookie said. "Mr. Farrow and the boys will probably catch them in an ambush, and it's gonna be really bad for them rustlers."

"How do you mean?"

Cookie replied, "If they don't get shot, they'll be strung up."

Jack was silent. He walked to his bedroll and turned in for the night, exhausted. As he lay under his blanket, he looked up at the stars and thanked God for sparing his life. He had never been so scared before. He realized that this truly was beautiful but dangerous country. He also realized that when danger occurred, it was usually unexpected and happened suddenly. He concluded that he should always be prepared for any emergency at a moment's notice, especially on the frontier, where his life and well-being could depend on it. This learned wisdom of preparedness would be lifesaving in the future.

Two days later, Mr. Farrow and the cowboys who had accompanied him came back into camp with the stolen cattle. Cookie prepared food and coffee, and then the herd was on its way, just as if nothing had happened. Jack was dying to know what had transpired. None of the cowboys talked much about the events while in the saddle all day, riding with the herd. They just seemed to evade Jack's questions.

Cookie later told Jack that sure enough, during the night, Mr. Farrow and the cowboys had surrounded the rustlers, come into their camp, and disarmed them. Mr. Farrow had imposed a punishment that was unusual for the situation. Instead of hanging the rustlers, he confiscated their guns, horses, supplies, and boots. They would be lucky to survive so far from the nearest settlement. However, it would give them a shot if they were fortunate.

Cookie said, "Mr. Farrow must have seen some redeeming quality in them fellers not to have killed them." Frontier justice, whether white or Indian, usually mandated death for an offender. If the spared person survived, he might seek revenge later. Or he might repeat the same of-fenses later with other innocent people, possibly resulting in their death. Cookie said, "Son, there is no civilized law out here, only the law of nature." He continued, "Most of these rustlers out here on the frontier are really bad people who have difficulty living in normal society. That's why they are out here. They have no moral sense to them. They could care less if something is right or wrong. They are like a pack of wolves, only much worse. They prey upon weaker people and take advantage of anyone if the situation is right. They can be worse than an Indian war party. They're extremely dangerous men and can never be trusted. That's why I was surprised to hear that Mr. Farrow let them go. Mr. Farrow never talks to me about things like that, but I trust him to make the right call."

The work was hard, and the pay was marginal, but Jack loved the feeling of being on his own and free, which showed in his good attitude. He enjoyed the comradeship of the cowboys. He became like a younger brother to the rough-and-tumble bunch. Jack was given the nickname "Happy Jack" because of his good nature, easy smile, and gregarious disposition. At the end of the cattle drive, Mr. Farrow gave Jack a bonus over his standard pay and said, "Son, you did a good job in controlling that stampede, and I was impressed with your willingness to go after those rustlers. Courage should always be rewarded." When the cowboys reached town, they spent most of their hard-earned money on drinking, gambling, and women. Jack thought this was a shame and not the prudent thing to do, but he couldn't blame them too much after such a long and strenuous trail.

On later cattle drives, Jack grew into one of the best cowboys of the group. He became a favorite of Mr. Farrow and was placed in the scout position of the cattle drive. The scout determined the direction to take and where to camp, which was a great responsibility. Later, Cookie gave Jack a compliment: "Jack, you have a good and brave heart for someone so young. I think you will fare well."

I n the 1850s, troubled times began between the northern and southern United States. This trouble was particularly evident in the newly admitted state of Kansas. During this time, there was a brutal and bloody guerrilla war between slaveholding Missouri and the free union state of Kansas. Jack was a strong unionist by sentiment. He was definitely against slavery since he felt that he had been like a slave as a young boy working in the glass factory under strict taskmasters. He felt that he had gained his freedom from bondage when he had come to the frontier.

The Civil War began in April 1861 with the attack on Fort Sumter in Charleston, South Carolina. In July 1861, the Union Army suffered a terrible defeat at Manassas, Virginia. Things looked bleak for the Union. Jack felt compelled to aid the Union and do his duty for the country. In October 1861, he enlisted in the Union Army at Fort Leavenworth, Kansas. He was twenty-six years old. He was assigned to Company D, Eighth Kansas Volunteer Infantry.

His initial duties were to suppress Missouri guerrilla fighters, such as William Quantrill, Bloody Bill Anderson, and Frank and Jesse James. He was involved in multiple small battles and skirmishes in Missouri. His regiment was even sent to Fort Kearney, Nebraska, for a short while to suppress a Sioux Indian uprising.

Missouri was a slaveholding state, and many of its residents were aligned with the Confederacy. The local population frequently hid and supplied the rebel guerrillas. Jack's unit was frequently ambushed by guerrilla units, only for the guerrillas to quickly ride away into the vast countryside to safety. Jack was frustrated because the guerrillas wouldn't stand and fight. He wished that Mr. Farrow was a Union cavalry officer and that he were now in the cavalry instead of the infantry. Jack thought that if Mr. Farrow was in command with a few good men, he would make short work of the rebels. On the one hand, Jack could see that the Union cavalrymen were frequently not experienced horsemen and that the horses were not well maintained, resulting in diminished effectiveness against the rebel guerrillas. On the other hand, he noted that the Missouri guerrillas were excellent horsemen with very good, healthy horses. Jack just didn't know how the Union could win unless great changes were to occur.

Jack's unit's main duties were to guard communication centers and railroads. Occasionally they were ordered to burn farms known to have supplied the rebels. There was great frustration among the Union Army because of its inability to control the guerrilla war in Missouri. Initially, if any enemy guerrillas were captured, they were treated as traitors to the country instead of enemy soldiers. Many were shot by firing squads. However, this stopped when Confederate guerrillas started hanging Union prisoners. The frustration of the Union Army general staff was so great that women and children associated with known rebels were frequently taken from their homes and detained in Union-controlled areas. Groups of Kansas militia known as "red legs" caused great destruction to many innocent Missouri civilians' property as well as committing indiscriminate murder. They were not under the direct command of the Union Army and so committed many atrocities. Jack didn't feel good about these developments, but there was nothing he could do. He thought that the red legs were just as bad as the rebel guerrillas. He had the feeling that this was a dirty war, where right and wrong were not clear and sometimes the truth was blurred. He felt that he was in the middle of a huge blood feud on the Kansas-Missouri border, where vendetta, retribution, revenge, and murder were a way of life.

Jack and his unit never liked destroying the civilian farms and towns that had given the rebel guerrillas food and support. Jack said, "It is a terrible thing to be hated by so many of your fellow Americans." He added, "I don't think those people from Missouri will ever get over their bad feelings toward us. They're good Christian people, but they have been led astray by the wrong leaders and the wrong point of view."

In the late fall of 1862, the company was sent to Tennessee. After losing the battles of Shiloh and Corinth, the Confederate Army had retreated from western Tennessee. Jack's regiment joined the Army of the Cumberland under General Rosecrans and headed for Murfreesboro in middle Tennessee, east of Nashville. Their mission was to drive the rebels completely out of the state. These early victories for the Union in the West were the only bright spots at that time in the war. The Confederacy in the East had inflicted several major defeats on Union forces. A defeat in Tennessee would be a profoundly serious setback in the only region where the Union had achieved success.

All of the soldiers in the company knew an important fight was coming. They were strangely looking forward to finally facing the enemy in force. The men had had their fill of chasing Missouri guerrillas who would hit and run, only to ambush them again later.

The men were placed in railroad boxcars in Kansas City to embark on their new objective in Tennessee. Jack knew that the cars were usually used to transport cattle, but the boxcar was unexpectedly fairly clean, all things considered. Substantial amounts of hay served as bedding. Several buckets at the end corners were used as latrines. Although it was early winter and cold, it was tolerable with their blankets and hay to serve as insulation.

Some of the soldiers grumbled about the conditions. In true optimistic form, Jack told them, "At least we're out of the wind and rain, we don't have to eat dust like riding on a cattle drive, and it sure is better than working in a glass factory. You just have to keep these things in perspective." No matter how bad the conditions, Jack always had a positive attitude. The men in his unit were aware of this, and his nickname "Happy Jack" continued in this phase of his life. Jack realized that having a good attitude in the face of hardship and adversity could lighten the load and improve even desperate conditions. He also knew that this attitude could be infectious and improve unit morale and cohesion. He had learned this from his fellow cowboys in the past.

One man pulled out a pipe with tobacco, intending to have a smoke. Jack said, "I wouldn't do that. Any little spark from that pipe onto this hay will cook us like bacon." The man knew Jack was right and put the pipe back into his pack. The other men in his unit all liked Happy Jack and respected his good common sense and easygoing, nonjudgmental nature. They sensed that Jack was wise beyond his years.

After several days, they disembarked in Kentucky to march the rest of the way, since the remaining railways had been destroyed by Confederate raiders. The march to Tennessee was long and hard under cold, rainy conditions. Jack knew that a cowboy always had to take care of his horse because it was his means of transportation. Now, being in the infantry, his feet were his main transportation. He carried several extra pairs of socks and a second pair of shoes in his pack. All of the soldiers except for Jack had cold, wet feet and suffered greatly. He gave an extra pair of socks to his tentmate Sam from Miami County, Kansas, whose skin was "nearly worn off." This was greatly appreciated. The men tried to dry their shoes at night over the campfire but usually were not successful. The company marched over 150 miles to middle Tennessee. Jack again wished that he had joined the cavalry. It is not clear from his letters why he had not done so. He certainly was an excellent horseman. Possibly all of the cavalry positions had been filled; one can only speculate. However, at least he had a tent, and the food was marginally better than it had been during his cowboy days.

Sam was a talkative sort and was the same age as Jack. They got along well and became good friends. Sam's family had migrated to eastern Kansas from Ohio. In Kansas, his family farm had been raided and partially destroyed by proslavery Missouri "ruffians" because of his parents' antislavery views. This had led to Sam's enlistment in the Union Army. Sam had gone to school as a boy, and he taught Jack the fundamentals of reading and writing during their spare time and at night. Jack knew the alphabet but not much else. Sam was very patient in his teaching. Many times, he taught Jack by candlelight in their tent. He helped Jack write letters to his family back home in Kansas. Many of those letters were saved and now have been used to serve as a record of Jack's life and times. The spelling and grammar of Jack's letters are amusing if not comical. However, you can tell the optimistic, almost happy point of view with him, even under adverse circumstances.

Through the long march, Jack always tried to stay upbeat and positive, although everyone was miserable because of the conditions. His attitude had a beneficial effect on the whole company. Jack taught his fellow soldiers songs that he had learned from Cookie and the other cowboys. They sang while marching and around the campfire to keep their spirits up and relieve the boredom. Most of the company was made up of Kansas farm boys who were used to rough conditions. However, none had the experience of outdoor living on the frontier that Jack did. Jack taught the men campcraft from his cowboy days. He showed them how to make a proper fire in wet and cold conditions and how to take care of their tents to prevent rain from leaking in, among other things. His rank was advanced to corporal because of his positive attitude and leadership. At age twenty six he was older than most of his comrades. Both Sam and Jack were good storytellers. They seemed to feed off each other's positive spirit, much to the delight of the other soldiers.

It was late December 1862 when they finally reached the outskirts of Murfreesboro, Tennessee. They set up camp along a small stream called Stones River. There was a cold rain and north wind. At times, the rain turned to icy sleet, freezing the men's facial hair and overcoats.

The men knew the Confederate Army under General Bragg was in the area, but they didn't know exactly where or what the plans were. They stayed in camp for two days, trying to keep dry and regain their strength after the long, grueling march in poor conditions. On the evening of the second day, Jack could hear the ominous sounds of horses, wagons, and marching feet in the distance.

About three hundred yards of open field stretched in front of their camp with the woods beyond. Jack asked permission to take a platoon in reconnaissance beyond the woods. However, his request was denied. Jack told Sam, "I think the whole rebel army is just beyond those woods. I could be wrong, but I can't think of anything else that could make such a noise like that off in the distance." Jack had good instincts regarding such signs and sounds from his experience on the frontier.

Jack felt uneasy all night and was unable to sleep well. He awakened before dawn and walked up to Sam, who was the sentry on guard at the edge of camp. Jack asked if Sam had seen or heard anything unusual.

Sam said, "Not a thing. It's been dead quiet and damn cold. I can't wait to get off duty and get some breakfast; I'm starved."

They talked in the dark, looking out over the black, misty field in front of them. Dawn slowly came. It was cloudy and cold with a mild wind. A heavy winter mist hung over the field like a large gray blanket. Jack and Sam began seeing large numbers of animals running into the field from the woods. Deer, rabbits, raccoons, and squirrels were all fleeing the wooded area en masse.

Sam said, "Isn't that a crazy sight?" Jack knew from his experience on the frontier that something very big was behind the animals, coming through the woods and scaring them out.

"Sound your trumpet!" Jack told Sam.

Sam looked at Jack and said, "Are you sure? If nothing comes of this, we'll be in big trouble for sure."

"Sound it now, or we'll be in worse trouble."

Sam blew loud and clear, a call to arms. The soldiers quickly came out of their tents, grabbed their guns, and formed a battle line. There was a silent pause for several minutes. The soldiers looked around but didn't see anything. They all looked at each other quizzically. Some started grumbling, "What's going on here?" Some thought it was a false alarm.

The commanding officer came up to Jack and asked, "What in the heck are you doing?"

Before Jack could answer, they turned their heads toward the woods and saw an entire brigade of gray-and-butternut-clad soldiers coming at them in battle formation. There were five thousand Confederate soldiers, red battle flags flying, with fixed bayonets marching toward the greatly outnumbered Union line.

Sam, never short of words, said, "Those fellers look like they mean business." The Union company from Kansas had never seen so many Confederates before. It was an awesome and terrifying sight. They all knew they were in for the fight of their lives. They lifted their rifles at the ready.

The officer gave the order to the artillery to prepare for battle. He told the line of infantry, "Load and prepare to fire on my command." The cannons unlimbered, loaded the ammunition, took aim, and began to fire. The cannon fire created large holes in the Confederate line. The rebels began to charge on the double quick. A terrifying loud yell came from the mass of rebel soldiers. The sound of thousands of screaming, enraged men seemed to be coming from everywhere. The Union officer called out in a booming voice, "Steady, boys." He knew that the deafening screams from thousands of rebels could easily unnerve and demoralize his troops. He looked about his Union line and was encouraged. He sensed that their courage was undeterred by the deafening rebel yell.

When the rebel line came into range, the Union officer gave the command, "Ready, aim, fire!" The entire Union line opened up, spreading devastating fire on the rebels. The rebels regrouped, aimed, and fired. Sam, next to Jack, was shot in the chest and went down. Many others fell on the Union line. After several volleys, both Union and Confederate lines fired at will. The Confederates were slowly and steadily coming closer. The Union line was holding well despite undergoing heavy fire and losses. The Union officer viewed the line of his soldiers and was proud of his men for holding firm despite heavy enemy fire. Jack felt the whiz of bullets all around him. He felt a few bullets nick his clothes. He later described the bullets as sounding like a hive of bees buzzing past him continuously. The smoke from the gunpowder of thousands of rifles formed a thick, acrid, dark gray cloud, burning the eyes of the combatants and making the accuracy of fire more difficult.

After some time had elapsed, Jack began to hear firing on both sides and to the rear of his company's battle line. The Union line began to take fire not only from the front but from both sides. This was an ominous sign. The Union regiments on either side had given way and were in retreat. The commander of Jack's company realized that they were now in a deadly crossfire and in jeopardy of being surrounded.

The Union officer gave the order to retreat. The soldiers performed the retreat without panic. A rearguard action retreat was something they had trained to do. One group of soldiers would line up and fire and then retreat, while another group would line up and fire, and so on.

The horses that were hitched to the cannons were killed by gunfire, as were many of the artillery soldiers. Jack's commander ordered him and some other soldiers to push a cannon back to a new position. The ground was very muddy, and a heavy mist was still present along with clouds of acrid gunpowder smoke. The twelve-pound Napoleon cannon weighed around 1,200 pounds. The work of pushing the cannon over muddy fields was backbreaking and exhausting. The amazing feat of pushing the cannon was fueled by pure adrenaline and tenacity in the heat of battle. The wheels of the cannon were sunk nearly a quarter of the way up to the axle in thick mud. It was difficult to gain traction with their feet slipping and sliding in the mud. Periodically Jack or one of the other soldiers would slip and fall face down in the cold, sticky mud. They would quickly recover and start pushing again. Once, when Jack had slipped and fallen, a bullet hit the part of the cannon where he had just been standing, missing him by pure luck.

Jack and the other soldiers pushing the cannon knew how important it was. They put superhuman effort into pushing the heavy cannon through large patches of thick mud, all the while being shot at. Bullets were ricocheting off the barrel and hitting the wheels. Jack felt it was a miracle that none of the soldiers pushing the cannon were hit. The rear guard was doing a good job at fending off the persistent advancing rebels while in retreat. Jack would later say, "Those sesech [secessionists] sure had a lot of pluck." They kept coming despite taking many casualties from the rearguard action.

After pushing the cannon for nearly a mile and being nearly exhausted, the company set up a new Union line. "The rebs are still on us," Jack said. The rebels had reorganized, making a new line, and charged again with bayonets, yelling at the top of their lungs the proverbial "rebel yell." The Confederate soldiers then halted, raised their guns in unison, took aim, and fired a devastating volley at the reorganized Union line. All of the men who had helped push the cannon were hit by the sudden barrage of rifle fire. The ones who were still alive went down, holding their wounds, trying to stop the bleeding, grimacing, and groaning in pain. Jack heard the whiz of bullets pass near his head. He felt several stings on his arms and legs as the bullets superficially grazed his skin and cut his clothing. Jack had a fleeting thought of running away to safety to "save his own hide" but quickly dismissed the idea when he thought of Sam and his other comrades doing their duty for their country. Jack later said that he was too busy with the cannon to worry about being shot or killed. He had important things to do for his comrades who were in peril.

Jack took the initiative and set up the cannon to fire by himself. He had never loaded a cannon before, but he had seen it done. Since there were no artillery soldiers left, he knew he had to take the responsibility, and he didn't have much time.

The screaming rebel horde was bearing down on them rapidly. He placed triple the standard load of canister in the cannon. Instead of one large cannon ball, a cannister shell carried many metal balls and acted as a large shotgun to decimate oncoming infantry. Jack knew there might be a risk of the cannon exploding because of the added charge. He had heard stories of explosions that destroyed improperly loaded cannons and killed all of the soldiers around them, but he felt that they had only one chance to stop the charging rebel line, so he was willing to take it. With no help from anyone, he completed loading the cannon and then stood ready to pull the firing cord. Now the rebels were so close that he could easily see their faces.

The remaining Union infantry quickly lined up, took aim, and fired a full volley. Nearly simultaneously, Jack pulled the firing cord of the cannon with a sudden strong jerk of his arm. There was a deafening explosion with smoke everywhere. The recoil was tremendously powerful and violent, sending the cannon flying backwards through the air. The cannon wheel hit Jack in the chest and drove him into a large tree. He heard his ribs and pelvis crack as loudly as a "tree limb breaking." He lost consciousness for a short time. When he awoke, he raised his head from the ground and saw that all the rebels were gone, devastated by the triple canister and simultaneous gunfire. Hundreds of rebels lay in the muddy field next to the Union line. All of the once proudly waving battle flags were down. The wounded were moaning, asking for help. Many were slowly moving their arms upward while their broken bodies lay in the mud.

Jack's hearing was damaged by the concussion of the blast, and all was silent. He then began having severe chest and hip pain. He began coughing blood and having trouble breathing. The pain was severe. Each breath brought excruciating pain to his chest, to the point that he didn't want to breathe. He felt sure that his life was ending. He remembered the Twenty-Third Psalm, which his mother had taught him. He truly was in the valley of death. However, he would not fear because he knew that the Lord was with him. He would be protected and comforted by the Almighty. This thought seemed to give him strength. He would fight for his life. It was too easy to give up and just slip away into death. Jack felt that something in his subconscious was telling him to keep living because he had a few more things to do on this earth.

Jack was taken to a rudimentary field hospital with fractured ribs and pelvis, head trauma, broken eardrums, and obvious severe lung damage. By the description of the injuries and the medical care available at that time, it is almost a miracle that he survived.

The battle of Murfreesboro or Stones River went on for another day and ended as a Union victory despite the loss the first day. The Confederate Army and General Bragg retreated toward Chattanooga.

Middle Tennessee was now in Union hands. Jack was given a medal for his bravery and for his early attention to and warning of the initial rebel assault.

President Lincoln wrote to Union General Rosecrans, "You gave us a hard-earned victory which had there been a defeat instead, the nation could scarcely have lived over."

Jack spent the next several months in the hospital, where his wounds healed. Prior to being discharged from the hospital, he wrote his brother in Kansas, "I can't wait to get home so we can promenade and do-si-do the girls around the park." Pretty risqué talk for the time, using square dancing as a metaphor for love.

After several weeks, Jack was being pushed in a wheelchair down the hall of the hospital when he heard his name called: "Hey, Jack!" Jack looked in the direction of the greeting, and lo and behold, it was his buddy Sam. Around his chest were bandages tinged with blood.

"Sam, I thought you were dead!"

"I thought I was too, at least for a while. I was knocked out for a time. When I came to, those reb soldiers were trampling all over me. There was a whole bunch of them stepping on my back and head, making me miserable. Those rebs were in a big hurry trying to run down you fellers. They thought I was dead, so I just laid still and let 'em think that so they wouldn't kill or capture me. I laid there all night. I didn't know if I was going to die from my wounds or if I was going to freeze to death. I figured I had an equal chance for both. I felt sure I wasn't going to see the dawn, but sure enough, there was the sun. Later that day, our boys found me. I didn't think I was going to make it, but here I am!"

Jack could tell Sam was a little short of breath and had a slight wheeze caused by a bullet to his lung. Aside from looking a little pale and some weight loss, Sam looked fairly decent. He was his old talkative, happy self. Jack and Sam talked for some time and enjoyed each other's company. Jack was very happy to see his friend again.

At the end of their lengthy conversation, Sam said, "If I don't see you again, look me up after the war. It looks like you and I are going to be out of this mess, at least for a good long time."

While in the hospital, Jack made friends with some fellow soldiers from Chicago. He was honorably discharged from the army in February 1863 and went to Chicago with them. He must have been convinced there were prettier women in Chicago than on the Kansas frontier.

He lived in Chicago for two years and became a fireman. While living there, he met Elizabeth Scott. She was a new immigrant from Scotland by way of Newcastle, England. She was "cute as a bug" and had a lot of "spunk." He was about nine years older than she. Somehow, he convinced her that the Kansas frontier was a "heaven on earth." He was eager to regain the feeling of freedom and independence that he had once experienced as a younger man. He wasn't too keen on big cities since Chicago brought up old bad memories of his youth in Boston and Pittsburgh.

Jack and Elizabeth married and left for Phillips County, Kansas, to start a new life on the frontier. Free land for homesteaders was again hard not to take. They built their sod house and obtained some livestock. They were alone in a vast expanse of prairie, far from any town;

their nearest neighbors, the Knudsens, were eight miles away. It's hard to imagine the sense of isolation and possible loneliness experienced by the couple in this situation. However, they only ever said positive things about life on the prairie, aside from the always present possibility of danger.

Jack and Elizabeth lived in a tent during the construction of their sod house. They were once nearly killed by a huge prairie fire after a long drought had turned the tall grass into dry kindling for any spark to ignite. They managed to save their lives by jumping into a nearby creek. Life was hard and dangerous, though Elizabeth never complained. A true Scot, she was stoic, hardworking, and thrifty. She was also deeply in love with Jack. His pet name for her was "Lady Bug."

After the close call from the Cheyenne Indian attack with the Knudsen family, they both felt that the Kansas prairie was too dangerous a place to raise children. Jack also wished his future children to be educated, something he had never had but always wanted and admired. They both knew that they had been lucky to survive the Indian raid. The frontier was far from stable. Trouble with the Indians was always a possibility and would come when one least expected it. It would be ten more years before the battle of the Little Big Horn began the final decline of Indian warfare on the plains.

The couple moved to Pittsburgh, Pennsylvania, where Jack went back to work in the same glass factory where he had worked as a boy, but under much better conditions and higher pay. He definitely would have preferred to be in Kansas. However, he was willing to do what he felt he should for the benefit of his family. I can't imagine the difficulty for Jack's spirit in leaving the freedom and open spaces to go back to work in the factory that he had been so anxious to leave many years before. This showed that his priorities lay with his family, and he placed his own desires second. Jack and Elizabeth had four children: Ella, Wallace, James, and Harry. All received advanced educations.

After their children's educations were complete, the Graham family moved from Pittsburgh to Highland, northeast Kansas, where Jack and Elizabeth took up farming. They had more money now than when they had homesteaded, and they bought a farm. Elizabeth looked after the family's tight finances. Jack and Elizabeth became widely known in the town and were well liked. The nickname Happy Jack seemed to follow Jack because of his good nature, constant smile, and outgoing personality.

On Jack's return to Kansas, he looked up his old army buddy Sam, who was living in a home for chronically injured soldiers in Fort Scott, Kansas. Sam had never totally recovered from the injury to his chest. He had difficulty breathing, with intermittent lung infections causing occasional fevers and chest pain. He also had a chronic nonhealing wound that discharged bloody fluid periodically from his chest.

Sam said the doctors thought that the bullet had brought some clothing or other debris into his chest, causing the problems of a chronic abscess and infection. The doctors said they couldn't get the bullet or other debris out surgically without killing him. Sam was still his happy self, similar to his old buddy Jack. Jack noted that Sam had lost an extreme amount of weight. His cheeks were sunken, and his arms and legs were like sticks. He was pale, and his hair was thin with patches of baldness. However, he still had his big smile. Jack realized that Sam had been slowly dying since the end of the war.

Sam said, "I don't have it too bad here. I get three squares a day, the nurses are really nice, and I get along with the rest of the boys here quite well. Some of these fellers have it a lot worse than me. The way I see it, it was a dang miracle I made it off that battlefield in Tennessee. I wasn't expecting to live but a few weeks after that, but here I am, still kicking." Sam flashed a big smile.

Jack gently slapped him on the knee and said, "You sure are. You're still kicking."

Sam went on, "I feel good that I served my country and did my duty. That's more than a lot of people can say."

"Yes, sir! You do have a lot to be proud of," replied Jack.

The two old soldiers had a good long visit and a few laughs, remembering their army days. Jack had brought some wool socks as a gift for Sam. Sam said, "Thanks Jack; I can sure use these. I remember the last time you gave me some socks on our big winter march down to Tennessee. You saved my feet from falling off! Yes, sir!"

"It sure is good to see you again, Sam."

"You too, Jack."

The two old men spent the entire afternoon together, talking and reminiscing about old times. Eventually they shook hands and patted each other on the back. They both knew that they would never see each other again. Jack got up and started to walk down the hall. He turned around one last time and waved. With great difficulty, Sam slowly stood up from his bed in an unsteady and clearly painful manner. He finally stood erect, raised his hand to his head, and gave his old friend a military salute. Jack came to attention and returned the salute, holding the position for a long moment while remembering all the things they had been through.

Jack then turned and walked out of the hospital. He walked to his horse and buggy at the side of the hospital and grasped the side of the buggy becoming overwhelmed by emotion. He rested his face on his arm, and tears welled up in his eyes as he took a deep breath. He knew Sam was fully aware of his imminent demise, but he had shown tremendous courage in having a good attitude and standing to salute his old friend despite being in pain. Jack pulled himself together, untied the horse from the hitching post, and climbed into the buggy. He took the reins and in a low, audible voice said, "Goodbye, old friend."

Jack attempted to look up Mr. Farrow, Cookie, and some of his old cowboy friends, but they were long gone by then. The Kansas frontier had been "civilized" by 1891. Gone were the cattle drives, buffalo, and Indians, all replaced by farms and towns. Railroads and highways crisscrossed the landscape, making travel easier and safer. Jack said, "It was an amazement to see such rapid progress." When Jack was a young man, as soon as he was able, he grew a long mustache just like one of his heroes, Mr. Farrow. He kept it for the remainder of his life.

All of Jack's children went on to have good and productive lives. His daughter, Ella, married and had a farm in upstate New York, where his son-in-law was from. Wallace became a successful businessman and, amazingly enough, became the president and owner of the same glass factory where Jack had worked. He became extraordinarily wealthy. James (JW), became a physician and surgeon in Kansas City. Harry became a veterinarian and rancher in Yuma, Colorado. Like their parents, all four children exhibited traits of self-reliance, hard work, independence, and good nature.

After Elizabeth died, Jack moved to Earlsville, New York, to live with

Ella and her husband, William. There again, he became Happy Jack to the townspeople.

Every day, he had coffee in the local café with a bunch of old men, many of whom were Union Army veterans. He was frequently seen in the town square, sitting on one of the benches with his buddies, laughing and telling stories. He always waved at the townsfolk as they passed by and gave them a big smile. He always carried pieces of candy in his pockets. The children of the town loved him and knew just where to go for a little treat and a bit of small talk.

For many years, he marched in a yearly parade of Civil War veterans in New York City. He took great pride in being a member of the Grand Army of the Republic. He used to say that he would walk in the yearly parade until he "Couldn't walk no more." He was in his midnineties on his last march in the parade.

He and Ella spent a lot of time at an orphanage in Earlsville, where Jack told stories of the Wild West, being a cowboy on the frontier, and the Civil War. The children loved him and his stories. My father, Wallace Graham, remembered playing with marbles as a youth while his grandfather, in a rocking chair on Ella's front porch, told stories and jokes. Jack told young Wallace that if he was ever in Tennessee to look around for the eyeball that he had lost down there. Although he had injured his left eye as a child, he never lost his eye in combat. He told young Wallace that if he found it, "You could play marbles with it. It would be quite colorful!" Wallace didn't know quite what to make of that statement. It was most likely Jack using old cowboy humor while seeing marbles looking like blood-shot eyeballs.

Jack sang frequently and loved to waltz with Ella into his nineties.

He believed that life is what you make it. Being content and happy has little to do with adversity in one's life or the amount of money one has. It is maintaining a positive state of mind despite the circumstances. Jack used to quote one of his most admired people, Abraham Lincoln: "Folks are about as happy as they make their minds up to be." As an old saying goes, if life gives you lemons, make lemonade.

2.

All You
Need Is Love

Ella Graham looked into the full-length mirror, styling her long auburn pinned up hair while her mother, Elizabeth, fixed the long white lace dress from the back. Elizabeth was having some difficulty securing the snaps on the high collar despite standing on a footstool. Elizabeth was five feet tall at the most, while Ella stood five feet seven inches. Elizabeth told her to hold still in her thick Scottish brogue. She was preparing for an officer's dance and mixer at Fort Leavenworth, not far away.

Many said Ella was the most beautiful girl in town. She had a sunny disposition like her father, Jack. She was quick to smile and invariably waved and greeted people whom she crossed paths with in the small northeast Kansas town of Highland. She was what some people might call statuesque. Ella moved gracefully with a smooth elegant gait, even though she was somewhat of a tomboy. She had three younger brothers, Wallace, James, and Harry, with whom she was very close. James (JW) was more protective than the others and watched to be sure that Ella was well treated.

Never before had Ella Graham felt so much excitement and anticipation for an upcoming occasion. Her father, Jack, had bought her a lovely white lace dress that was more expensive than most. Her father had taught her how to dance the waltz, among other popular dance steps. She had known how to square dance since she was a child and had fond memories of past fun times; however, tonight would be much more formal. Jack spared no expense for any of his children, despite having only a modest income as a farmer. His children were well educated, had good manners, and were well thought of in the small rural community. Jack doted on them all, but he and his only daughter, Ella, were particularly close.

Ella was better educated than most women of her time in 1897, having attended college and graduated with honors. In addition to keen intelligence and quick wit, she had a kind of charm that allowed her to speak her mind without seeming forward or ill mannered.

She was now twenty-five years old and was starting to feel some concern about ever finding a marriage partner. Most of her friends were married and had children at this age. Though Ella certainly had no shortage of suitors, none had really inspired her interest. Elizabeth and Jack encouraged her to wait for the right man and assured Ella that when it felt right in her heart, she would know she had met the man for her. She was somewhat skeptical but appreciated their advice.

Jack Graham drove Ella and her girlfriend Margaret to the party at Fort Leavenworth in his horse and buggy. It was a beautiful Saturday afternoon. The horse and buggy traveled on dirt roads past tidy, clean farms and along green rolling hills. The corn was high—ripe and ready to pick. The summer smell of freshly cut hay filled the air. The ride, especially beside the bluffs of the Missouri River, was scenic. They could see for miles along the winding river valley, lined with large cottonwood trees with leaves that shimmered silver in the afternoon sun. The unusually large cottonwood and white-barked sycamore trees rose like green cathedral spires from the banks of the river. There were groves of apple trees ripe with fruit on the blufftops. The Missouri River valley seemed like a beautiful oil painting. The blue sky was strewn with white clouds like fluffy pillows. The pink and orange of the late-afternoon sun caused the river to sparkle like colored jewels. The meandering river was bordered by green trees and foliage. The vista was a breathtaking sight for the two women. Soon they could see the fort and people gathering around the pavilion, a large circular structure with white Grecian pillars and an open-air trellis for a roof. White steps led up to the polished hardwood dance floor. Ella could feel her heart racing, and she and Margaret spoke with excitement about the evening to come.

Jack parked his horse and buggy and entered the officer's club for refreshments while the young women walked nervously up the stairs into the pavilion. Ella never showed anxiety, but Jack could tell when she was nervous because she gave her biggest smile. The dance pavilion was beautifully arranged with flowers and colored crepe paper. Around the structure were pre-electric-era gaslights. The venue looked out over the river. In back of the pavilion was a garden filled with boxwood shrubs and various flowers. The well-manicured garden featured white gravel walking paths.

Numerous young people were drinking punch and milling about in the elegant pavilion. Ella looked around and caught a tall, handsome, brown-haired young lieutenant staring at her. He looked into her eyes for a long moment, smiled, and then looked away when Ella caught his gaze. She had the feeling that he had been looking at her for some time. He wore the tight-fitting knee-high brown boots and high-collared jacket that were standard for an officer of the time. Ella turned and scanned the pavilion for Margaret, but she had disappeared into the crowd. She turned back and was startled to see the young officer standing in front of her.

"Good evening," he said. "My name is William Henry." He gently shook her hand and politely bowed his head. She was impressed with his confidence and good manners. They carried on an easy exchange. He told her that he was from upstate New York and had about one more year in the army before he would be discharged.

When they heard the band playing a waltz, Ella looked at William with a big smile. Right on cue, he asked her to dance. She accepted, and they slowly walked out onto the dance floor. He gently took her hands, and they began circling the floor. She noted his smooth, skilled movements and his gentle but firm lead. Her long white lace dress seemed to be floating like a cloud in the wind. She occasionally leaned her head back, enjoying the sensation. William was impressed with her graceful and skilled dancing. In his experience, it was uncommon to find a dance partner so well trained in the waltz who enjoyed it so much without obvious effort. He thought Ella was great fun. After an hour, and many dances, they stopped near the punch bowl and talked again, only this time in a more joking manner, intermittently laughing.

She said, "That was so much fun! You're a better dancer than my dad."

William laughed and said, "I should hope so."

He asked if she would take a walk with him in the garden. As he guided her down the steps from the pavilion to the garden entrance, she picked up the hem of her long dress so as not to trip. The paths were illuminated by gaslights and the moon. It was a lovely evening with a slight breeze. Their conversation continued to flow effortlessly as they ambled along the garden paths. She told him about Kansas, stories of her father's Civil War experience, and about her mother, who had immigrated from Scotland. He told her of the beautiful farm where he had grown up, with clear streams, orchards, and pine trees. Both Ella and William felt at ease and relaxed as they strolled slowly through the garden on this beautiful summer evening. Eventually William escorted her to the officer's club, where she introduced him to her father, Jack Graham. The evening felt far too short, but at its end, William thanked Ella and said good night.

On the buggy ride back to Highland with Margaret and her father, Ella was reserved and seemed to be immersed in pleasant thoughts. She had a slight smile on her face and didn't talk much about the evening except to say that she had had a wonderful time.

As William walked back to his barracks, he couldn't help thinking about the woman whom he had danced with that evening. He was surprised that someone so beautiful had been so pleasant and fun to be with. In his past experience, there had always been some drawback, such as arrogance, silliness, or some quality that quickly made a woman's beauty fade. That did not seem to be the case with Ella, who seemed genuine and without pretension. In short, she seemed like a breath of fresh air in comparison to his previous experiences. She had even seemed to grow more beautiful as the evening went on.

Over the past two years, while in the army, he had been lonelier than he had ever been in his life, being transferred frequently over various parts of the country. He had been looking forward to his discharge so that he could return home to upstate New York, but now, having met Ella, he was having second thoughts about leaving Kansas so soon. Instead, he began thinking of strategies to impress her the next time they met.

The next week, when the townspeople saw Ella and William walking through town, everyone was happy for Ella because William seemed like such a polite young man and had a dashing appearance in his uniform. The couple walked comfortably with one another. They stopped at local shops, where Ella introduced William to the people she had grown up with. William was quite good at small talk and had the ability to put people at ease with his confident, engaging smile and easy laugh. He could always find something in common with whomever he was introduced to because of his broad general knowledge and extensive life experience. He was quick to find humor and interest in the stories of people he met. One might say that William was a real people person.

All of the strategies that William had planned to impress Ella with quickly went out the window, and he reverted to his natural self because Ella seemed to like him just the way he was. They were natural with one another without needing to put on airs or try to impress one another; there was no need for games. They enjoyed each other's company. William thought it was easy and pleasant to be with Ella. Many people have a few rough edges in their personality, small things that can cause irritation, but it was not so with Ella. William thought she was smooth as silk. She just seemed to fit.

Ella was impressed with the way William handled himself among different people of all age groups and walks of life. She was not the only one who was impressed. The whole town was talking about the young man who was accompanying Ella through the streets.

Their strolls grew longer and more frequent over the next few months, extending to a few buggy rides through the countryside. On one of their rides, they planned a picnic. William had a place in mind that he thought would be a perfect spot, one that he had noted on his way to Highland. They traveled east toward Leavenworth in their horse and buggy. Several miles outside town, they came to the spot William had in mind and tied the horse to a nearby tree. They hiked up a hill, picnic basket in hand, to a large, expansive oak tree and placed a large blanket down underneath it. The sprawling branches formed a shady canopy over the area. They proceeded to retrieve sandwiches and lemonade out of the basket they had brought. They were surrounded by tall green grass that waved slightly with the gentle breeze. The spot overlooked a valley filled with tall trees and a rocky stream in the middle. There were pastures and forests in the distance, with no sight of any human presence. The weather was perfect.

After consuming their sandwiches and lemonade, they lay on the large blanket and looked up at the sky. They talked as they stared at the clouds, noticing that the clouds were billowing up high in the atmosphere, indicating the potential for rain. However, neither of them cared whether it rained. They talked of various forms that the clouds seemed to be making, letting their imaginations go with the flow of each other's creative minds. They concluded that neither of them had looked at the sky and the clouds for such a long period of time and in such a relaxed way since they had been children. William gently grasped Ella's hand as they looked at each other, smiling. They laughed at the thought of watching clouds for so long, like children.

After a good laugh, they sat up and noted the stream in the valley below. William asked, "Have you ever been to that stream?"

"No, I can't say that I have." She responded, "I think it's the only stream around here that I haven't been to. You know, when I was younger, I was a bit of a tomboy. My brothers and I would take long hikes to all sorts of places for adventure."

"Do you feel like another adventure to explore the stream?"

She beamed at him and said, "You bet. Let's go exploring!"

They walked hand in hand down the hill through the knee-high grass. When they got to the base of the hill, they entered the shady forest and found a beautiful clear stream. Ella took her shoes off, sat on a small boulder, and put her feet in the water.

"It's cold! It must be spring fed." She gently kicked her feet, making small ripples in the water.

William took his boots off and began wading in the stream. He bent down and overturned a rock. With a lightning-like move, he grabbed something in the water. Ella was curious to see what he had found. He lifted up a small crawdad. Its small legs were rhythmically moving, and its frontal claws were open in defense.

"Do you want some freshly caught lobster?" he asked.

Ella chuckled, looked down next to her feet, and pulled a clam out of the water. "How about an oyster on the half shell?"

They had a good laugh and let their captives go back into the stream. William sat on a boulder next to Ella. He said, "This stream is a lot like a place where I grew up in New York, only a little smaller." They talked about feeling like kids again as they kicked the water with their bare feet. They threw pebbles into the stream, watching the size of each splash. After a long while, they began to notice that the sky was turning dark gray. They put their shoes back on and hiked up the hill hand in hand to pack up the picnic.

When they were halfway up the hill, it began to rain. They looked at each other and laughed. Neither of them cared about getting wet. The warm, gentle summer rain was almost refreshing. In a strange way, they both had a sensation of freedom, a sort of baptism of their free spirits from above. They actually enjoyed the rain as something new and exciting. This was the first time in their lives that they hadn't run for cover while being caught in the rain. They walked slowly up the hill while the rain soaked them, taking their time and still not caring about the rain. When they reached the picnic area, they packed up the basket and blanket. By this time, the rain was coming down much harder, and the raindrops were becoming larger. They were soon soaking wet, and they still didn't care.

William gently held Ella's arm as he pulled her close. She looked into his eyes and smiled as she moved close to him. They were suddenly in each other's embrace. They kissed softly and without inhibition. He slowly backed her up against the tree as the rainwater poured down their faces and bodies. Their bodies were warm together against the rain pouring over them. Ella's long auburn hair came undone and flowed down her back and shoulders. She had never been so excited in her life before. It seemed that their prolonged kiss had taken them to a heavenly place as they embraced each other in the rain. They held each other and wished that this moment and these feelings could last forever. Time seemed to stand still as the rain continued to pour over them. They held each other with the feeling that they were in another world without care.

Eventually they walked hand in hand down the hill to the buggy. Ella was thrilled with the thought that something so exciting was just beginning. In the buggy, she sat close by William's side, locking her arm with his as they rode back to town in the rain.

Ella said, "Isn't this wonderful?" as the rain continued to pour down. William replied, "Yes, it is wonderful."

By the time William pulled the buggy up to Ella's house, the rain had stopped. William escorted Ella to the door. She asked him to have dinner with her family the next day, an invitation he gladly accepted. They couldn't wait to see each other again.

The next day, as dinnertime approached, Jack Graham noticed that Ella was pacing the floor and frequently looking out the window.

Jack reassured his anxious daughter. "Relax, he'll be here soon enough. You know these military men—they're always punctual."

Ella turned and faced her father with the big smile that gave away her anxiety. They each knew what the other was thinking. "Oh, Dad, I think you're really going to like him!"

"I've already met him once before, remember, at the officers' mixer?"

"Oh, yes, of course." She looked out the window again and saw William drive his horse and buggy up to the house and jump out. She noted that he was wearing his uniform again. The last few times they had met, he had been in his civilian clothes. Ella felt her heart pound so hard that she hoped her father couldn't hear it. Jack opened the door before she could get there.

"Well, do come in, Lieutenant," said Jack.

The men shook hands. Jack motioned William into the living room, where they sat down and began talking before Ella could get in a word. William looked at Ella and smiled briefly. Ella's three brothers came in, and William stood and shook hands with all of them. Then they all filed into the dining room and sat down.

Jack talked with William nearly the entire evening. Between bites of food, William and Ella gave each other brief glances and smiles. Both were thinking that they would love to be alone together. Elizabeth immediately picked up on the couple's nonverbal communication and chuckled to herself.

After dinner, Jack and William talked for quite a while. Ella broke into their conversation, saying, "Excuse me, Dad; William is required to get back to the post soon." She showed William to the door as he thanked all of the Grahams for the wonderful evening. The couple walked out to William's horse and buggy. Before William could get in, Ella said, "Let me show you around the farm." They walked hand in hand to the side of the barn, where there was a large vegetable garden.

As soon as they were out of sight of the house, they lunged into one another's arms and kissed long and deeply. They hadn't spoken more than three sentences to each other all evening, but now that didn't matter. Eventually they walked back to the horse and buggy and said goodbye.

As time went on, William became a frequent guest at the Graham household. He was impressed with Elizabeth, Ella's mother. She maintained her beauty despite her age. William felt that this could be an indication of how Ella would age. He loved hearing Elizabeth speak with her Scottish accent. He admired her soft, calm, and confident demeanor, which reminded him of Ella.. However, most of all, he saw the love and affection that Elizabeth had for Jack after many years of marriage and a life filled with hardship.

He respected Ella's father, Jack, who was a decorated Civil War veteran. William loved Jack's easygoing good nature. As time passed, they developed the habit of sitting out on the porch for hours after dinner, having lengthy and good-hearted conversations.

Jack was pleased to hear about William's family in upstate New York. It seemed that they were good people, and William had a good relationship with them. Jack believed that people's relationships with their family could frequently predict their future home life. Jack had a reputation as a real talker, and William found that it was true. The two developed a strong and lasting relationship.

William could see characteristics of both parents in Ella, but the most prominent traits he noticed were Jack's.

William seemed to fit in well with the family. He sensed real quality in all of them. He thought all of the family members were good-looking, outgoing, intelligent, and easy to be with. He was amazed at how well Ella got along with her brothers and the closeness of their relationships. He surmised that this closeness was due to the cohesive sense of love from both parents. Given time, William became like another brother to the other three.

He could definitely see a long-term future with Ella. He felt very fortunate to have met her. He had found a rare and brilliant gemstone in the midst of a beach full of gravel. He realized that women like her were rare, and he was not about to let her go.

Since Ella was so close to her family, it was important to her to have their approval of her new relationship with William. She could tell without asking that Jack liked him a lot. She knew that if he disapproved, he would show it indirectly by his behavior. In a quiet moment when she and Elizabeth were alone, Ella asked, "What do you think of William, Mother?"

"I like him a lot, but it is not what I think that is important. When you are together, I can see that you are quite taken with one another.

He seems to be a serious young man. You have many characteristics in common; however, love is a two-way street. You must be sure that his feelings are the same as yours before you totally commit your mind, body, and soul to him, or else you can be severely damaged. He must seriously express his feelings toward you. Sometimes young men, if they aren't mature, fall in love and don't realize it because they have never been there before and did not intend this to happen. When faced with the prospect of marriage, they may become anxious and end the relationship, only to realize later that they had found their one true love and it was now too late to salvage the relationship. It should be easy to tell within three to four months if he is serious, where his intentions lie, and if he is mature or not. I do like the way he respects your father and your brothers. I also like that he is so polite to me, but most of all, I like that he is polite to you and always shows you respect."

Ella told her brother JW that she had never felt so free and uninhibited as she did with William. She remembered an old poem that concluded with the verse "Now we shall see what the future will bring as we swing freely as one." This seemed to sum up her feelings when she was with William.

One day, William took Ella on a long buggy ride to Fort Leavenworth to visit the place where they had first met. The ride was still beautiful. She again viewed the picturesque Missouri River valley with its large cottonwood trees and the apple trees on the bluffs. They pulled up to the empty pavilion with its white Doric columns. They walked up the steps and onto the wooden dance floor. This time, they were alone and had the entire dance floor to themselves. He took her hand, and they began to waltz around the hardwood floor with the silent music in their heads. After a few twirls, they stopped and began to laugh. He bowed to her, and she curtsied politely as they laughed again. They stepped outside the pavilion and walked hand in hand into the garden. The flowers seemed so much more colorful and vivid now. The deep green boxwood shrubs lining the paths set off the colors even more.

As they walked through the garden, William turned to Ella, looked into her eyes, and asked her to marry him. Without answering, she smiled, and they kissed. This kiss was different than all the others before. William felt her soft lips and thought he wanted to kiss her forever and never stop. He placed his arms around her waist and back and drew her close. She put her arms around his neck with uninhibited conviction. Their bodies were closer together than ever before. Her flat belly was pressed to his, and he felt her breasts against his chest. She wrapped one of her long legs partially around one of his. This was a new and very pleasant sensation. He could tell her trim, well-toned body was relaxed and wonderfully receptive. Both felt as if electricity was coursing through their bodies. They could feel each other's hearts pounding. They had a transcendent feeling, as if they were being transported into the sky. With her face against his shoulder, Ella softly said, "Yes, of course I will marry you."

On their way back to Highland, Ella felt the urge to leap out of the buggy, run around, and jump for joy. However, she composed herself and smiled while talking to her future husband.

After that day, the couple could not stay apart. They longed for one another and could think of nothing else all day. It was difficult to perform their daily activities without their thoughts interfering. Each day they met, their passion for one another increased. They created a fire that was growing and all consuming.

One day, when they were alone together, they looked into one another's eyes. William moved his fingers across Ella's cheek and over her full, rosy lips. He stroked her long, silky auburn hair.

"I have never seen such a beautiful face."

Ella likewise stroked her fingers across his strong, closely shaved jaw and chin. She placed her palm on his cheek and then stroked his hair.

Ella said, "Only you have seen the hidden part of my soul."

When Ella went home, she remembered a chapter in the Bible that was rarely if ever mentioned. She turned in her Bible to the Song of Songs written by Solomon and read the entire chapter. The chapter, written in a beautiful poetic form, was about two young people's love for one another. Her heart began to pound when she realized that the love she and William shared was described so well in the Bible. She knew then that their love was a gift from God. This was something she had been praying for all of her life. She knelt down by her bed, clasped her hands, and gave thanks to the Lord for his clear and obvious blessing.

The couple told Ella's family about their engagement, and they were all overjoyed, especially Jack. Jack shook hands with William and said, "I was hoping this would happen. Congratulations." William wrote to his family in New York about the most wonderful girl from Kansas. He tried to describe her in writing, but nothing he wrote could do her justice. They would just have to meet her. The couple simply could not tolerate a long engagement.

Ella and William were married in a Presbyterian chapel in Leavenworth, Kansas, the month before William was discharged from the army. They subsequently moved to Earlsville, New York, where his family had farmland available for them.

Ella found the land just as beautiful as William had described: rolling green hills with the rounded green Adirondack Mountains in the distance. There were apple and cherry orchards with vineyards of Concord grapes. Maple trees and large, stately white pines were abundant. A beautiful spring-fed stream bordered by low-overhanging pine trees flowed just beyond the orchards. Its water was clear, cold, and drinkable.

The two-story house on the property was painted white and had an expansive porch with a swing and rocking chairs. On one side of the porch was a trellis of climbing white and yellow roses that bloomed extravagantly. Around the base of the porch were beautiful multicolored flowers, pink hollyhocks, purple phlox, and a large patch of daisies, that complemented the white house and the yellow and white roses on the trellis.

As in Highland, Kansas, the townspeople of Earlsville grew to love Ella and William. They would say, "That couple are two birds of a feather," or "They are like two peas in a pod." People said that when the couple showed up, they were a bright spot in the day, as if they brought sunshine with them. Ella and William had the unique ability to lift people's spirits with their mere presence. Most of all, people just loved Ella's big smile.

William went into the accounting business, which he had learned in the quartermaster corps in the army. He also helped out at his parents' farm since his father was getting older.

Ella and William spent many hours caring for children in a local orphanage. Many were in the orphanage because their parents—and sometimes their siblings as well—had died of tuberculosis while being cared for in the nearby sanatorium on the outskirts of town. The couple also assisted in caring for patients in the sanatorium. Occasionally, the parents of children in the orphanage were still alive but were isolated in the sanatorium so as not to spread the disease to their healthy children, but those without parents or family to care for them were sent to this orphanage from all over the state.

Ella and William set up a croquet set and a horseshoe pit in the front yard of the orphanage and spent many hours with the boys and girls playing sports and games. Cards and board games were always popular in the evenings. The couple seemed to become parents to all the children, and the children were always happy to see them show up. Ella was there nearly every day, and both visited frequently in the evenings. It seemed that Ella and William had an automatic family with all of the children.

They took the children to a beautiful nearby lake to swim in the summer. The lake was clear with a sandy bottom. It was flanked by precipitous white-rock cliffs on one side and large white pine trees on the other side. Car-sized smooth granite boulders were scattered around the lake, perfect for sunning or jumping into the water. Ella and William were excellent swimmers and invested much time and effort in teaching the children to swim. They usually brought lunch for the group and sat at picnic tables under the large, expansive branches of the pine trees near the lake. A flattened mat of pine needles served as a natural soft carpet around the picnic area. They would eat a leisurely meal while watching the children run about playing. The children took breaks periodically to eat a bite, then ran off for more fun. In the winter, they took the children skating and sledding.

Ella regularly read to the children from such books as Tom Sawyer, Moby Dick, and The Last of the Mohicans as well as poems by Walt Whitman. The children loved to visit William and Ella's farm. They enjoyed harvesting fruit from the orchards and helped with canning fruit and vegetables.

Ella told the children, "Happiness is like a butterfly, which, when pursued, is always beyond your grasp but which, if you sit down quietly, may alight upon you."

Ella and William were especially close to one girl. Kathryn was eleven years old when they first met her. She seemed much more mature than her age and only occasionally laughed. She was responsible and organized, but Ella thought she detected a deep emotional injury that was not overtly obvious. Kathryn was a pretty girl with brownish-blonde hair and blue green eyes. She was smart and did well in school. She helped the orphanage staff along with Ella and William in caring for the younger children. Outside of school and the orphanage, Kathryn spent most of her time with Ella and William. Unlike most of the children, Kathryn had known and loved her parents before they died. Both her mother and father had died of tuberculosis and subsequent pneumonia in the preantibiotic era. Her father died first after a long, debilitating decline. Her mother began having symptoms a year later. In that era, tuberculosis was not curable, and entire families were frequently wiped out. The only treatment was isolation and avoidance of close contact. Kathryn's mother was sent to the sanatorium in Earlsville to prevent Kathryn from contracting the disease. Kathryn had no other close relatives, so she was placed in the orphanage.

Ella befriended Kathryn's mother, Alice, before Alice died. She did many of the same things for Alice that she did for the children in the orphanage. She brought Alice books to read, and when Alice wasn't feeling well enough to read, Ella read aloud to her. Ella and Alice frequently played cards and had long talks. Ella brought Alice bright flowers from her garden and occasional fruit from her orchard. Alice looked forward to Ella's visits. Ella thought that Alice was a wonderful, kind woman and a good mother. Their friendship grew over time. The two women's personalities seemed to be similar except that Alice was more reserved, much like her daughter, Kathryn. They enjoyed each other's company and became almost like sisters.

Over time, Ella could see the slow deterioration in Alice's condition. Ella tried to be uplifting and positive to Alice but knew the end was coming soon. After leaving the sanatorium, Ella often had to stop the horse and buggy and cry before composing herself to travel back to her farm. She didn't dare show her grief to Alice or Kathryn because she knew she had to remain strong for them. Ella and Kathryn visited Alice wearing face masks to avoid contracting the disease. Alice began having more frequent high fevers, coughing blood and losing weight prior to her final days.

One day, Ella was caring for Alice. She placed a cold washcloth on Alice's feverish forehead and sat her up so that she could take some sips of water. Alice's body was soaked with sweat from the fever and was nothing but skin and bones. Ella could feel the protruding bones of her spine just under her skin as she supported Alice's back. Alice's eyes were dark and sunken.

Alice grasped Ella's hand, looked into her eyes with great intensity, and said, "Listen to me, Ella. I know I am not long for this world. Kathryn has no family. When I go, she'll have no one. I know you are a wonderful person, the way you have taken care of me and brought Kathryn to see me over the past year. Please, please, would you take care of her and make sure that she will be all right? I have total confidence in you. Please—you are my only hope!"

Ella looked into Alice's suffering eyes and said, "Of course; I love Kathryn. She is very special to me and William. I will look after her for her entire life. You can depend on that."

"Thank you, thank you, Ella! I can now feel at ease knowing that Kathryn will be taken care of."

One week later, Alice died. Ella took Kathryn to her mother's funeral. Kathryn stayed at Ella and William's house for a week before returning to the orphanage. True to her word Ella took care of her. Ella became like a second mother to Kathryn. Occasionally, Ella would hear Kathryn crying softly in her room when she stayed overnight. Ella would go to her, hold her gently in her arms, and slowly rock her while singing softly to her until Kathryn was comforted.

It is not clear why Ella and William didn't adopt Kathryn. Possibly it was to avoid showing favoritism because they couldn't adopt all the children, or possibly Kathryn liked the existing arrangement. The administrators of the orphanage knew of the special relationship between Ella, William, and Kathryn and encouraged it. Kathryn helped Ella with the farm, including harvesting honey from the beehives, which the other children were reluctant to do for fear of being stung.

Kathryn got a job at a local shop in town while she was still in high school. She was quiet but definitely not shy. She was a hard worker and highly trusted. During her occasional stays at Ella and William's house, they taught her to dance the waltz. Kathryn marveled at the way Ella and William waltzed so smoothly to the music on the Victrola, as if floating above the hardwood floors of their large, expansive living room. It seemed that this room had been made uniquely for dancing. It pleased Kathryn to see how much Ella and William enjoyed dancing together. Ella would usually do an extra twirl or lean her head back at the end, causing laughter among them all. Kathryn could tell that the couple had a beautiful and unique relationship that she wished she could have with someone someday. When Kathryn was in high school, she stayed at Ella and William's home most of the time.

Kathryn had grown to be a beautiful young woman. Ella and Kathryn frequently went shopping together in town, and most people thought of Kathryn as a beautiful extension of Ella, only slightly more reserved. Kathryn was considered the most eligible single girl in town because she was beautiful, intelligent, kind, and responsible. In addition, Kathryn was associated with Ella and William, who were loved and admired by all.

Kathryn began seeing a young man named Steven, who was four years older than she. He was quite tall, around six feet five inches, moderately thin, nice-looking, and always well dressed. He had a slight slouch in his posture. William always wanted to tell him to straighten up and throw his shoulders back, but he never did. Ella thought he had a somewhat odd haircut, short on the sides, a lot on top, and straight bangs just above his brow.

Steven's family was considered the wealthiest family in town. In fact, he worked at a local bank, which his father owned. He was intelligent if somewhat reserved, yet still quite confident in his demeanor. Kathryn invited Steven to dinner with her, Ella, and William on several occasions. The dinners were always uneventful, and Ella and William did most of the talking. The only real stumbling block in Steven's relationship with Kathryn was that he did not want anything to do with the orphanage or the children, despite Katheryn's repeated requests that he become more involved because it was a big part of her life. Kathryn had the feeling that Steven thought that the orphanage was a lowly place for second-class children, although he never directly said so.

One evening, after a dinner with Steven and Kathryn, Ella said to William as they sat on their porch alone, "Have you ever heard Steven laugh?"

"As a matter of fact, I don't think I have, Ella." Will responded.

Ella continued, "Have you ever seen Steven run or even move quickly at any time?"

"No, I haven't over all of these years that we have known him. For such a young man, he seems extraordinarily old."

Ella asked, "Have you ever had a long conversation with Steven on any topic?"

William replied, "Our conversations consist of him answering my questions. He's not what I would consider a good conversationalist. It's not that he is rude, unintelligent, or quiet. He is just not one to expand the topic of any conversation."

Ella said, "Would you describe Steven as boring?"

"Oh, come on, Ella; he's a nice enough guy. However, now that you mention it, yes!" William laughed.

Ella looked at her husband with a raised eyebrow and a smirk. William shook his head and chuckled.

After several years of dating, Steven and Kathryn began talking of marriage. Kathryn knew Steven was a good, responsible person. She was drawn to his stable life and respected family. Those were two things that Kathryn desperately wanted in her own life. One evening while sitting on the porch after dinner, Kathryn spoke to Ella about marrying Steven. She asked Ella what she thought. Kathryn knew Ella would give her a straight answer.

Ella took Kathryn's hand, looked lovingly at her, and said, "It's not what you say about Steven; it's what you don't say. I don't see one bit of excitement in you or even a slight thrill for him. Your one true love should be a passion, an obsession, someone you can't live without, and someone who will love you back. Once your mind and good judgment have deemed him appropriate, then listen to your heart. There is no sense in living your life without love. If you make the journey of life and don't fall deeply in love, then you haven't lived life at all. You have to try. If you haven't tried, you haven't lived, for love is everything.

"Marriage must be good for your mind and your heart. It must be a combination of the two or it will not succeed and will cause you unhappiness for the rest of your life. It's one of the most important decisions you'll ever make.

"If you marry without love and passion just to fit what your mind says you should do, and not your heart, the marriage will be cold, and in time, you will become bitter and jealous of others who are in love. You'll feel as if you are trapped in a prison. You'll end up having a 'roommate' and not a true husband. Passion is fun and exciting, something that you and a good husband should have for the rest of your lives. Love with passion is a human need that should not be denied.

"If you marry someone because of passion alone against your better judgment, given time, what you knew were your husband's drawbacks will become much greater and magnified. He may leave you destitute with a broken heart or damage the family in some way. He will always be a thorn in your side. You will find yourself trying to make up for or even hide his problems. Never think that by marrying someone, you can change them. That is a mistake many people have made. You need a husband you can be proud of and whom you admire because of his qualities. Someone you know you can always depend on."

Kathryn knew Ella was right. She just didn't have deep feelings for Steven. She was drawn to him because he was safe, stable, and overall, a good person, but that was all.

Kathryn kept to herself and didn't talk much to anybody for nearly a week. During this time, she appeared distracted and at times in deep thought. Once while Ella was walking past Katheryn's room with the door open, she saw Kathryn sitting on her bed staring out the window for a long period of time. Ella noted Kathryn taking long walks alone in the garden and to the stream beyond the orchard. Ella could occasionally see that Kathryn's face was red and puffy from crying, but nothing was said. Ella's heart ached for her because she knew what Katheryn was going through, and there was nothing she could do to help her. Ella realized that Katheryn was potentially giving up a sure life of stability with Steven, something she had desperately wanted all of her life. Ella questioned herself if she had done the right thing by telling Katheryn her opinion of Steven and of marriage in general. However, she knew Katheryn deserved the truth, painful or not. Ella was going to fulfill the promise she gave to Alice long ago by taking care of Katheryn to the best of her ability.

Kathryn eventually broke off the relationship with Steven. She felt terrible but knew it had to be. Understandably, Steven was upset. The majority of the townspeople were disappointed. To outsiders, the young couple had seemed a perfect match. Kathryn almost felt that she was letting everyone down. Ella gave her reassurance and bolstered her confidence. Ella knew that the longer you have a relationship with someone, the more difficult it is to break up despite knowing that it must be. Ella felt deeply for Kathryn and knew the difficulty she was going through. Ella and William did many small things for Kathryn to make her feel loved. Although the breakup was hard, Kathryn was strong and resilient. She moved on emotionally without Steven.

Kathryn had no lack of suitors. She met Robert, who had grown up on a nearby farm and had three brothers. He was outgoing and quite handsome. He was playful and a bit rowdy at times. He had a job in town but also helped his parents on the farm. They occasionally danced together at parties. Kathryn taught Robert the waltz in Ella's large living room. He took her fishing, something she had done in the past with Ella and William. Robert became deeply involved with the orphanage children along with Kathryn, Ella, and William. He brought several baseball gloves that he had borrowed from his brothers to the orphanage with a ball and bat, and he and Kathryn had a lot of fun playing catch and baseball with the children.

Ella thought that she had never seen Kathryn, who was almost always reserved and proper, smile and talk so much as she did when she was with Robert. Robert seemed to bring out the best in Kathryn. Ella felt that Kathryn was like a flower that was opening to full bloom.

Both William and Ella liked Robert very much and thought he was fun to be with. Ella again remembered the ending of the poem she had known so long ago. It did seem that Kathryn and Robert were "swinging freely as one." Kathryn and Robert were eventually married. Ella gave Kathryn a silver brooch that her mother, Elizabeth, had given her. In the center was a thistle, the national flower of Scotland, surrounded by garnets. Kathryn treasured this gift all her life.

Ella and Kathryn sat on the front porch one day, slowly rocking in their rocking chairs. Ella was reminded of her childhood, sitting on the front porch after dinner with Jack back in Highland, Kansas. Ella and Kathryn looked over Ella's extensive flowering gardens. There was an explosion of vibrant colors. Everything was in full bloom. The gardens were well manicured, and each segment had its own color scheme. Vivid red flowers were adjacent to bright yellows and pinks, interspersed with purple. Between the flower beds were paths of white gravel, making each flowered area easily accessible and preventing weed growth. The garden was similar to the garden in Leavenworth, Kansas, where William had proposed marriage to Ella so long ago. Ella had always wanted a garden like it to remind her of that special day and place.

Kathryn looked at Ella, who seemed to be in deep, pleasant thought as she gazed over the beautiful sight before them. Ella then turned to Kathryn and said, "I was thinking that marriage should be like a garden of Eden with a large stone wall surrounding it. All the troubles, confusion, and strife of the world are outside the wall. When one enters the garden, the problems of the world are left behind. While in the garden, you enter another world with your husband. Nothing matters except beauty, love, and your relationship with him. It should be refreshing to your souls when you are together, like drinking clear, cold spring water when you are hot and thirsty."

Ella continued, "A marriage, like a garden, needs great care to become beautiful and to maintain its beauty. In gardening, you must water, care for the soil, remove weeds, and periodically prune for the best results. In a marriage, you must do many things to maintain the beauty of the relationship. You must always be aware of the relationship and how it is doing so that you can care for it properly.

"It is beneficial to always think in a positive way and have an upbeat, cheerful attitude no matter the circumstances. A negative and depressed attitude is like a dark cloud over the garden, blocking sunlight and impairing its growth. Outside the garden walls, there is so much negativity in the world. Hopefully, all of that can be brushed away upon entering the garden.

"One should continue to nurture romance daily by constant reassurance of love and even flirting. It is important to look as attractive as possible. Courtship and attraction should be ongoing, even as you age. True love should never die if properly cared for. However, marriage, like a garden if left unattended and taken for granted, will eventually wither, grow ugly, and die." Ella told Kathryn, "Your relationship with Robert should be treated with great care because it is the most important thing in both of your lives—money, power, or a great job cannot come close to the satisfaction of a loving relationship with Robert.

"You should want your husband to look forward to coming home and entering his garden of Eden, which will refresh and sustain both of you. I do think that love is God's gift to man.

"Just as in the garden of Eden, there is forbidden fruit in life. If one enters into another relationship outside marriage, the garden and the marriage will never be quite the same."

Robert and Kathryn had three children and became wonderful parents. They continued to have a close relationship with Ella and William throughout their lives.

Ella and William had frequent visits and communication from the children of the orphanage after they grew up and moved on. The children also felt strong attachments to Kathryn and Robert, who stayed involved with the orphanage as well. Ella, William, Kathryn, and Robert became mentors to the children throughout their lives. These young adults frequently asked them for advice and opinions on their life issues. Over time, Ella was viewed by the children of the orphanage and the townspeople as a revered and respected queen, with Kathryn as her princess. As time progressed Katheryn and Robert took on more of the duties at the orphanage that Ella and William once had done.

Ella's favorite brother, JW and his family occasionally took summer trips from Kansas City to see Ella and William Henry in Earlsville. As a young boy, my father, Wallace Graham, Ella's nephew, was allowed to spend the summer months with Ella and William. The couple would take little Wally on long walks through the woods and other adventures, similar to their activities with the children of the orphanage.

One night, they took blankets down to the beautiful stream and slept under the sky. My father learned about the stars and constellations, such as Orion's Belt, the Big and Little Dippers, and the Milky Way, as they all lay on their backs looking up at the night sky. Ella and William told Wally stories of the local Iroquois people and old legends of the Northeast. My father remembered chasing fireflies in the darkness and putting them into a glass jar to create a biologic lantern. Ella and William taught Wally to fish from the stream, where they caught perch and smallmouth bass. They occasionally had a fish-fry shore lunch.

One thing Ella and William enjoyed was sitting on their porch holding hands during a summer rain. This brought back strong romantic memories of the time they had been caught in a summer rainstorm during a picnic in Kansas long ago in their youth. It was at that moment that they both knew they were in love and that something thrilling and very special would happen between them in the future. The smell of the new rain on the grass and the view of mist around the property was special and beautiful to them.

My father would see Ella and William holding hands on their long walks down country roads and into the woods. They would kiss frequently, even though such outward displays of affection were somewhat out of the ordinary for the times. My father used to say that he never saw two people so in love, even as they grew older.

William and Ella never had children. I imagine that they would have liked to have them. However, it was probably not meant to be because they probably would not have been so active in the orphanage and sanatorium. They would not have been so close to Kathryn and had such a positive influence on her and other young people's lives if they had had their own children to take care of. The couple spread love and goodwill to everyone they came in contact with. They both died in their nineties, only three weeks apart.

My father learned his interests in gardening, beekeeping, and fishing from his Aunt Ella. He passed those interests along to me. Whenever I tend my garden, pot flowers, plant seedlings, or go fishing, I think of the lovely great-aunt I never knew.

I realized her whole life was one of love, and that is probably all you need.

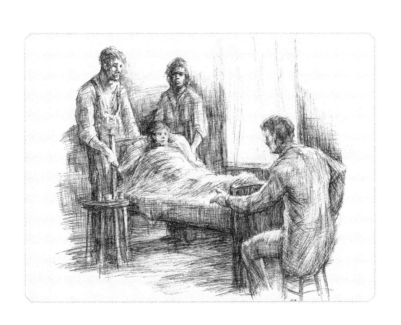

3.

The Wisdom of the Good Shepherd

There was a quick, urgent rap on the door of Dr. JW Graham's house in the late evening. It was a sound he had become familiar with over time, as he was one of only two doctors in the small northeast Kansas town of Highland. Just one year out of his medical and surgical residency, he was very busy. They were the only doctors in nearly a fifty-mile radius. As he opened the door, he saw a panicked ten-year-old boy whose parents he knew well through his medical practice. The boy had run more than four miles from his house. Out of breath and barley able to speak, he told JW that his five-year-old brother had been sick for two days with a high fever and cough. Now, though, he was having difficulty breathing.

Anticipating what he might be confronted with, JW packed his instruments and medicines in his large leather medical bag. He and the boy jumped into his small horse-drawn buggy and raced off to the stricken boy's house.

When the doctor entered the small country home, he saw a slight boy being held in a sitting position by his mother and father. The young boy's shirt was off, and JW noted retractions of the ribs with each jarring and rasping breath. From across the room he could hear the high-pitched wheezing sound of the child's labored breathing. The boy's lips were blue, as were his fingertips. His neck was red and swollen to approximately three times the normal size. His eyes were rolled back, and he was barely responsive. When JW examined the young boy's throat, he found that it was covered with a thick, whitish membrane. He immediately recognized the boy's problem: diphtheria.

The boy was in imminent danger of respiratory arrest unless prompt action was taken. JW knew that an emergency tracheotomy was the only way to save the child's life. He told the parents to boil several gauze bandages, a large towel, and several of his instruments. The parents were instructed to take the child out of bed and place him on the kitchen table since the table was narrower and more elevated and gave JW easier access to the boy's neck. A parlor table was moved next to the kitchen table as a workspace to place the instruments. The sterilized towel was placed on the parlor table, with the gauze and instruments laid on top of it. It was the middle of the night, and there were no electric lights in those days, so two lanterns were placed next to the tables. JW strapped a reflecting mirror to his head for better lighting. He took his coat off and rolled up his sleeves. He thoroughly washed his hands and then immersed them in a solution of carbolic acid from a bottle that he had brought. In the era prior to antibiotics, carbolic acid was known to reduce the risk of infection. JW did not use any narcotics since they could have depressed the boy's already impaired respiratory status. The child was already basically unconscious from hypoxia, or lack of oxygen. The parents laid the boy on the table, and JW approached the child and cleaned his neck with the carbolic acid solution.

Without hesitation, JW told the parents to hold the boy down while he slowly injected a local anesthetic into his neck. With a scalpel in his bare hand, he made a horizontal incision through the tense, inflamed skin and subcutaneous tissue of the neck over the child's airway. There was much more bleeding than usual because of the inflammation of the tissues caused by the disease. JW had to temporarily disregard the bleeding to gain rapid access to the blocked airway. The blood flowed over the child's neck and onto the floor. He could tell the parents were worried, and he calmly reassured them as he exposed the boy's trachea. The distraught parents had great difficulty watching the bloody procedure. They looked away and concentrated on holding their young son tight so he wouldn't move and disrupt what JW was doing. The parents thought this doctor surely had nerves of steel.

JW had performed a tracheotomy on a cadaver but never on a living patient. This was much more difficult. Even though the parents were holding the boy firmly, he couldn't be held completely still. Many critical structures were inches away, such as the carotid arteries, jugular veins, and numerous critical nerves affecting complex body function, which if damaged could cause immediate death or permanent severe injury. Complicating matters further was the fact that the anatomy was distorted by the inflammation and swelling. The excessive bleeding, let alone the poor lighting in the dimly lit kitchen, was obscuring adequate localization of the obstructed airway. But because of his excellent knowledge of anatomy, JW could feel and retract vital structures while finding the trachea.

JW located the trachea and successfully opened it with a scalpel. He placed a small metal breathing tube into the opening, carefully avoiding the thyroid gland adjacent to it. A gush of air came out, and to everyone's relief, breathing rapidly ensued. JW clamped the bleeding points with artery forceps and tied them off with fine silk sutures. He then strapped the tracheostomy tube around the neck to secure it in place. The boy's blue discoloration subsided quickly. The wound was partially closed, and the open areas packed with moist gauze to allow any infection to drain out.

Although the immediate danger of asphyxiation was gone, the disease itself could still be fatal in the preantibiotic era of 1912. Diphtheria was the leading cause of death at that time for children under the age of ten. Diphtheria caused death in two ways: asphyxiation or heart failure. In the first case, the bacteria created a thick whitish mass of tissue called a pseudo membrane in the throat and pharynx that obstructed the windpipe and shut off air to the lungs. The reason for heart failure was that the bacteria secreted a potent toxin that specifically affected the heart. Many children recovering from the throat infection died suddenly from acute inflammation of the heart (acute myocarditis). The second condition was unpredictable and untreatable in that era.

JW stayed with the boy through the night, taking care of the new tracheostomy, giving him sponge baths to reduce his high fever, and administering intramuscular injections of pain medication. He painted the boy's throat with gentian violet, a dye that inhibits bacterial growth. The doctor told the parents that he would not leave until the boy had turned the corner one way or the other. In this situation, the mortality rate was still around 70 percent. He also didn't know, even if the child lived, whether there would be any residual damage to the body or brain from lack of oxygen or damage from the disease itself. He didn't tell this to the boy's mother or father; however, he knew they were well aware of the risks. He needed them to remain positive to take proper care of their critically ill young son.

He looked into the eyes of both parents and with directness and conviction said, "Let's pray." He remembered the Twenty-Third Psalm, which his parents had taught him as a youth, and he had later memorized. He immediately saw that this gave the parents renewed strength and hope. He prayed with them several times during the long, dark night. Through the night, the child was restless and in a semiconscious state.

The next day, the child's fever broke, and his pulse became less rapid. When he finally opened his eyes and seemed alert, he started to cry and held his arms out toward his mother. JW took this as a very good sign. The reduction in the child's pulse was an indicator that the bacterial toxin was not affecting his heart. JW was now optimistic. The parents were profoundly grateful. The boy's mother grasped JW's hands, put her face into them, and cried. The father placed his hand on JW's shoulder. The doctor told them to thank not him but the Lord.

The family had little money to pay for services rendered; however, they would periodically bring JW bushels of corn and vegetables and have their boys perform chores for him. No cash was given to the doctor, nor was it important or expected by him. This seminal event propelled JW into two paths for the rest of his life: medicine and the Christian ministry.

———

In 1988, I was consulted to see an elderly man with abdominal pain in the hospital. The diagnosis was acute diverticulitis. After treatment with intravenous antibiotics, the man's problem resolved without surgery. During my examination, I noted an indented scar in the man's lower neck, characteristic of a past surgical procedure. I asked the old man how he had gotten the scar.

He looked at me and said, "Dr. Graham, are you related to Dr. JW Graham from Highland, Kansas?"

I said, "Well, yes; he was my grandfather."

"Have a seat, Dr. Graham, if you have the time. I'd like to tell you a story about your grandfather, Dr. JW."

I sat down next to his bed, and he told me the story of his childhood critical illness from diphtheria in Highland, Kansas, and how he received the lifesaving procedure. He went on to tell me of his subsequent good life. He became a mechanic and farmer and had four children and several grandchildren. He told me that Dr. JW Graham was revered in the area. The old man said that JW was one of the best people and the most dedicated, intelligent, kind, and hardworking man he had ever known. The old man continued, "Dr. JW not only saved a lot of lives, but he brought a lot of people to the Lord."

In 1978, I was driving to Cameron, Missouri, for a date with my future wife, Barbara, when my car broke down. The car was towed into a small town outside Cameron in northwest Missouri, fairly close to the Kansas border. It was repaired by the local mechanic, who was probably in his eighties. After the repair, I gave the old mechanic my credit card. He looked at it and asked if I was related to Dr. JW Graham, and of course I said he was my grandfather.

The old man pulled his shirt up to show me an old scar on the lower-right quadrant of his abdomen. "Your grandfather saved my life as a kid. He performed an appendectomy right there in our farmhouse. My appendix had burst, and I was close to death. We were a poor farm family, and we never paid Dr. JW. We were always grateful to him and held him in great regard. He sure did have a good reputation around the entire region. There will be no charge on the car repair." I looked at the old man in shock and disbelief. The old mechanic then handed my credit card back. He seemed to greatly enjoy telling me about my grandfather and repaying the old debt, even though it was to JW's grandson nearly a century later. It seemed that the echoes of Dr. JW's life were still present long after he was gone.

JW practiced general medicine and surgery in the small town of Highland for five years. This was the town where he had spent most of his later childhood. In JW's era, doctors in rural areas were responsible for every ailment since specialists were not present in those days. He had a small office just off the main square of the town, about four blocks from the house where he lived with his wife and two young sons. He walked to work daily. During his office hours, he was greeted by lines of patients with all varieties of ailments and injuries.

Because Highland was a small town based on agriculture, JW frequently treated farming accidents. He had a separate room in his office where he performed surgery and other procedures. His nurse assisted him in all the procedures and in giving anesthetics. Bone fractures and dislocated joints were common. He used morphine before manually setting a fracture or reducing a dislocation. Plaster casts were applied when needed. JW was quite adept at fracture manipulation and re-positioning. He didn't have the luxury of x-ray technology to confirm adequate bone alignment. However, his record of adequate repair was excellent because of his clinical experience and expertise.

Obstetrics and gynecology were a large part of his practice. His postpartum infection rate was around 3 percent, nearly today's standard, as opposed to the average 25 to 30 percent average of the day. JW paid careful attention to sterile techniques and made liberal use of alcohol and carbolic acid before any exam or procedure.

One day, a seventeen-year-old girl named Iris came to his office complaining of abdominal pain. During JW's examination, he noted that Iris's abdomen was firm and distended. When he palpated the abdomen, he could detect movement. This was not something he had expected. After further examination, he told the girl that she was seven months pregnant. With that news, she broke down crying. JW knew she was not married and was living with her parents. She was quite small and had been hiding her expanding abdomen by wearing loose-fitting clothes. There was a large element of psychological denial. She had just put the thought of pregnancy out of her mind and gone about her daily business until she could not ignore it any longer. Now she had to face reality head-on. In that era, pregnancy outside marriage was a huge disgrace, carrying with it a perpetual stigma of sin and a life of ill repute.

JW consoled Iris and reassured her that things would eventually work out for the good. He told her to tell her boyfriend and also her parents and that he would care for her. The boyfriend wanted nothing more to do with her despite having said seven months earlier that he loved her and wanted to marry her. Iris's parents were very strict, rigid farm people. JW knew them and knew they had a reputation of being basically good, hardworking but fairly poor people.

When Iris told her parents of her dilemma, they were furious, claiming that she was a disgrace. They were far from understanding as JW had hoped they would. Iris became unwelcome at her parents' house. She returned to see JW, distraught and in tears, and told him of her situation.

JW held her hand and calmly said, "I'll go talk to your parents, I'm sure they will cool down and listen to reason."

JW drove out in his horse and buggy to Iris's parents' house, which was far out in the country. He walked up to the modest farmhouse, which was in moderate disrepair, avoiding some toys that had been left scattered on the walkway. He knocked on the rickety screen door, which was partially torn. Iris's father came to the door in his work overalls. JW noticed that his hands were quite large and dirty from recent manual labor. JW introduced himself. The family already knew him by reputation. He was invited in and sat down at their rough, handmade kitchen table. He quickly noticed that the house was dirty and poorly kept. White stuffing was exuding from an old, torn sofa. Dirty dishes were piled high in the sink. The house had three rooms and five young children. A slight smell of old urine pervaded the house.

JW told Iris's parents that their daughter was a sweet and wonderful girl who had made a mistake. He talked of forgiveness and redemption from sin. He quoted several scriptures from the Bible in Jesus's own words, justifying forgiveness in similar situations. He discussed caring for her at home with his help. JW talked mainly to the father because the mother was busy trying to control crying children while others were running around the house, causing a racket. JW could see that this woman had her hands full.

The father refused to listen to reason, and JW left the house disheartened, not knowing what he would tell Iris. It was possible that the family did not have the money or the space in the house to accommodate a new baby along with Iris. However, JW thought, one can always make do for a loved family member.

Iris was staying in the office with JW's nurse, waiting for his return from her parents' house. As he walked back into his office, JW saw her face, eyes wide with optimistic anticipation. But as soon as she saw JW's expression, she knew what her parents had said to him. She again broke down in tears with her face in her hands. JW and his nurse put their arms around her and attempted to console her. Iris realized that she had no skills and nowhere to go. She had heard of institutions for unwed mothers, but she didn't want to go to an impersonal place like that.

JW said, "You are going to be just fine. If you wish, you can stay at my house with my family, and you can help out here in the office during the day."

"Thank you, Dr. Graham; I would like that very much. Thank you!"

For the next nearly three months, Iris became part of the Graham household. She helped with the housework and caring for JW's two young boys. Every day, she walked to work with JW. Along with his nurse, Wilma, he showed her the skills of nursing and assisting in minor surgical procedures. Wilma told JW that she liked Iris. She said, "Iris is such a sweet girl. She tries to get along with everybody, and she is quite bright." Along with being a nurse's assistant, Iris became a very good receptionist whom all the patients liked. She learned quickly and was not squeamish in serious, bloody situations.

Eventually Iris delivered a healthy baby girl. JW had a long talk with her after the delivery about how she wished to proceed. She elected to give the baby up for adoption. Wilma, JW's nurse, was middle-aged and had never had children, although she had always wanted them. Wilma agreed to adopt the child and raise it as her own.

Iris continued to live at JW's house for nearly a year. During this time, she learned nursing skills and doctor's office management. JW thought she was bright and eager to learn. Iris later applied to nursing school in Kansas City and was accepted with JW's help. After nursing school, she married and raised a family. After her marriage, JW never heard from Iris again. I suspect that she wished to put the entire time in Highland, Kansas, behind her and not look back.

JW became a mentor and father figure to Wilma's adopted daughter, who upon reaching adulthood became a nurse and worked at one of the hospitals where my father, Wallace Graham, worked as a physician. Wallace said she was an outstanding nurse on a medical surgical floor. She had a great sense of humor and was a lovely woman. She married and had a family of her own. Wallace never knew whether she had ever traced her biological parents.

Being a physician in JW's era was not for the faint of heart. Childhood mortality was nearly 30 percent before age five. There were no antibiotics or immunizations for all of the dreaded childhood infections, as there are now. Dysentery, typhoid, measles, polio, diphtheria, and pertussis were all common and potentially fatal. Diphtheria, whooping cough, measles, and scarlet fever each had mortality rates ranging from 5 to 18 percent. Pediatrics was a large part of JW's practice. He was known to be quite good with children, being calm, patient, and understanding.

One of the constant problems of JW's era was infectious disease, whether acute sudden infections or chronic infections such as tuberculosis. Tuberculosis was rampant. It was a scourge of greater proportions than AIDS, influenza, and polio combined. It had run unchecked for centuries, killing hundreds of millions worldwide. The disease was not limited to lung infection but could also be a generalized condition that could produce draining scrofulous abscesses in the lymph glands of the neck, groin, and axilla. These infections frequently needed to be surgically drained. Tuberculosis could also cause bone infections, necessitating amputations. However, all of these procedures were temporizing and palliative in nature since there was no cure. The main way to prevent the spread of the disease was isolation in sanatoriums, thereby breaking up families for long periods, sometimes for many years.

One family on the outskirts of town developed tuberculosis. The two young children developed the disease first. The parents were left with the agonizing decision to either keep the children at home to care for them and risk infection themselves or send the children away to a sanatorium to be isolated with the knowledge that even with this option, there would be no cure. The parents opted for the first option because they didn't wish the children to taken away. The parents subsequently contracted the disease. JW did his best to help the family. He visited the household periodically and did his best to help treat their symptoms and ease their suffering. Over a period of three years, one by one, the entire family of four died of the disease. They all seemed to stoically accept their fate. All developed fevers with coughing blood and debilitating weight loss until their eventual demise.

The emotional and psychological burden that everyday life brought must have been significant. JW felt that it was his duty to heal the physical ailments as best he could but also to tend to people's emotional and spiritual needs to help them get through life's pain. After treatment of a medical problem, if patients still seemed worried or concerned, he would usually ask if they wished to pray with him. This offer was almost always accepted and appreciated.

After several years in Highland, JW moved to Kansas City with his young wife and two sons. His goal was to perform more extensive and complex surgery than he could in the small Kansas town, as well as to teach. To achieve those goals, he needed equipment and the support system of a large metropolitan hospital. By the turn of the twentieth century, hospitals had evolved into establishments vital to public health care and eventually became centers for medical education and innovation. Hospitals also began to provide laboratory and X-ray facilities, which greatly enhanced practitioners' diagnostic capabilities. Because of improved anesthesia techniques, larger and more complicated operations could be performed without fear of operative mortality. JW loved his medical practice in Highland and had difficulty giving it up for a more advanced setting, but he felt that he was being called in a new direction. JW had a saying that "A good surgeon must first be a good overall doctor." Having spent time as one of two doctors caring for an entire rural region gave him a better perspective and experience in how to care for his surgical patients.

After moving to Kansas City, he sold his horse and buggy and bought a Model T Ford. JW and his wife saw that life was rapidly improving. They were amazed by their first radio, which seemed like a human being speaking through a magic box. Cars replaced horses as the main means of transportation. The dirt roads became paved. Streetcars made access to downtown Kansas City inexpensive and easy. Telephones and electric lights became a huge advancement in the quality of life. New improvements in medicine and surgery were on the horizon.

JW was in the midst of the 1918 Spanish influenza epidemic. From the spring of 1918 to the spring of 1919, well over twenty million people died of the disease worldwide. In the United States, 675,000 Americans, including 43,000 servicemen, perished in the epidemic. In New York City, 851 people died in a single day. In Philadelphia, 11,000 people died in one month. Frequently the most severely affected patients were previously healthy young adults and even children. By some accounts, young pregnant women had a higher mortality rate than others. Most people succumbed to secondary pneumonia ten to fourteen days after the onset of the symptoms. However, people occasionally died within two days of exhibiting symptoms in severe or fulminant cases. JW's young daughter was one of the fulminant cases. She died of pneumonia after contracting influenza within three days. No matter what JW tried, nothing worked to turn the rapid downhill course. JW and his young wife Elizabeth were devastated. He stoically accepted God's will and kept performing his duty as a physician.

Kansas City was particularly hard-hit. It came to a point where hospitals were filled to capacity and could not admit any more people. The doctors had to see patients in their homes and do the best they could with the rudimentary treatment of the preantibiotic time.

JW not only treated people in the hospital but also made multiple and extensive house calls. At the time, the main treatment for the Spanish influenza was limited to rest and good nursing care. The viral disease attacked the respiratory system, causing fluid to build up in the lungs. The patient would "drown" in his or her own secretions, or the secretions would become secondarily infected with bacteria and cause a fatal pneumonia.

JW mixed turpentine and camphor oil with a petroleum jelly to place as a plaster on an affected individual's chest. This was the beginning use of the now familiar product, Vicks VapoRub, which became a treatment to improve respiratory symptoms. The concoction is what is now called a "mucolytic," meaning that it has the properties of liquifying and breaking up thick mucus. The mixture was also placed in boiling water with the patient's head over the pot to inhale the vapor. This made it easier to mobilize and cough out the thick secretions that would build up if not expelled. JW gave instructions on the use of percussion and postural drainage at the same time. This entailed placing the patient in a bent-over position while a nurse or educated family member percussed the back, thereby mobilizing the secretions out of the damaged lungs and preventing progression to pneumonia. Patients under JW's care had a significantly lower mortality rate than the average.

Many physicians and nursing staff succumbed to the disease. However, JW was undaunted by this great threat, which took great courage. He never thought of avoiding what he thought of as his responsibility and duty to care for the ailing no matter the risk.

———

JW became a professor at the University of Kansas and taught surgery and anatomy while continuing his practice of medicine. He enjoyed teaching, which was one of his goals in life. His students respected his polite, calm manner. He addressed all of them as "Doctor," even the medical students who had not yet received their MD. If a student gave a wrong answer, he would say, "One could possibly approach it that way. However, my experience has shown me this method is more beneficial," or something similar in order not to humiliate the student. He felt that one learns better in a positive, encouraging environment than in a negative situation or out of fear.

All the residents wanted to perform surgery with JW. Prior to any surgical procedure, he would talk with the resident who was going to assist him and quiz him on the disease they were to operate on. He would then ask his young assistant surgeon about each step in the procedure. He wanted the resident to be prepared. JW always told his students, "You must prepare the night before the surgery. You must go over in your mind each step and the dangers involved in each step." He demanded that the resident be mentally prepared for the surgery so that the student would truly benefit from his surgical teaching expertise. JW methodically walked the resident through the operation, asking him what structures needed to be divided and what were dangerous areas to be avoided. If the resident appeared to be struggling during surgery, he would calmly take over the dissection and then return it to the resident when he reached an easier part of the procedure. At the end of each operation, he had the habit of shaking the resident's hand and thanking the anesthesiologist and the nursing staff for their help. He would later discuss the operation with the resident, giving tips and advice on technique and postoperative care. He was considered highly skilled and the epitome of a gentleman. He was respected by all of his students as a top role model of how to be a physician and surgeon.

JW was always clean and well dressed. He felt that his appearance would help generate confidence and respect from patients, especially if he had not previously met the person. JW would say, "You must play the part to instill confidence and a sense of hope in your patients, plus it shows respect for the patient that you give a professional appearance." JW frequently said that a doctor's appearance was the only thing a patient could see regarding the surgeon's ability. If a surgeon was clean and meticulous in his appearance, the patient could extrapolate that the doctor was likely meticulous and not sloppy in surgery.

A large part of JW's teaching young doctors that unfortunately is lacking in today's medical education is what he called the demeanor of the physician. He lectured his students not just in medicine and surgery but in how they should conduct themselves. He stressed that a physician should not only be proficient in his profession but should be an example to the community in dignity, character, and integrity. JW defined integrity as showing consistency in one's thoughts, words, and actions, in short, saying what you believe and doing what you say. "To be a physician is a great honor which you must live up to. The physician should always strive for courage, moderation, and wisdom. These traits are not inherently present and must be learned and then practiced. One will need these superior characteristics when dealing with stressful, life-threatening situations, which will occur in one's medical career." JW continued, "A physician must always seek the truth in all things, stay calm in critical situations, and give reassurance and hope. This must be done even if the problem appears hopeless. When you have done all you can, and the situation is still in doubt, that is when you turn to the Almighty. Your job as a physician is to bring help and comfort, not only physically but mentally and emotionally. Being a physician should be looked upon as a sacred duty to help your fellow man. You are doing God's solemn work, and hopefully he will work through you; one never knows. Being a good physician is not a regular job; it is a way of life. You are responsible for people's welfare twenty-four hours of the day and seven days a week. This can be difficult on your own family but must be accommodated. Again, it takes great strength and endurance to follow the physician's way of life."

One young surgical resident in training had continued difficulty in one surgical procedure. He became despondent about his lack of improvement in his skills. JW reassured him that the procedure was complex and difficult, and told him that given time, he would master the operation.

When wanting to make a point, JW frequently gave examples and analogies from gardening and agriculture, similar to the use of parables used in the Bible. He said, "No great thing is created suddenly, any more than an apple. If you tell me, you desire an apple, I will answer that there must be time. It first must blossom, then bear fruit, and then ripen. Learning new things takes time." He also said, "Trees, like people, grow at different rates. The redbud tree grows quickly and blooms rapidly, but it is not strong, and its life is short. An oak tree grows slowly but in time becomes the tallest and sturdiest tree in the forest. So it is with people. Some people bloom quickly and later burn out, while others grow slowly but become strong and solid like an oak tree. The same can be said of the mastery of surgery. It takes time and persistence, like many things in life. In the meantime, do not be concerned because better days are ahead for you."

JW went on to say to the young resident, "Becoming a master in surgery takes long years of clinical experience. For instance, I am a better surgeon now than I was ten years ago. You must know your limitations and obtain wise council from experienced physicians if you are unsure about how to proceed with the care of a patient. The philosopher Plato told people to 'Know thyself.' He is basically saying do not get too big for your britches. None of us is perfect. It is a warning to be humble, something high achievers need to hear now and then. You must know your strengths and your weaknesses. Accept the reality of who you are, and don't waste time on what others think of you. There is a famous quote from Sir Walter Scott that has always been a favorite of mine that I have taken heed of over the years: 'All men who have turned out to be worth anything had the chief hand in their own education.' Continued learning and preparation on your own are all a part of the practice of medicine. It is ongoing. I strongly suggest keeping a journal of complex and interesting cases so you will not forget and review how you treated the problems and their outcomes for future reference." That young surgical resident later became a renowned surgeon at the Mayo Clinic and was always grateful to JW for his kindness, advice, and patience.

JW was a deacon in the Baptist church. He was respected for his wise advice and good judgment. He excelled in knowledge of the scriptures and could spontaneously apply known verses to situations in life.

He was frequently asked to make house calls or visits to the hospital, not for medical purposes but to provide spiritual support and guidance. He helped people in emotional turmoil, people who were grieving, and people who were ill. Instead of bringing his medical bag, he brought his Bible.

During World War I in 1917, JW felt that it was his patriotic duty to join the army. He was brought into service at Fort Leavenworth, Kansas, as his father had been years before during the Civil War. JW was placed in the medical corps, where he attended to casualties from the war in France as well as victims of the Spanish influenza. He was stationed in Kansas City, where he met and became good friends with a local farm boy–turned–politician named Harry Truman. JW said that Truman was outgoing, friendly, and a pleasure to be around. He added that Truman was made of tough stuff. JW was well aware of Truman's bravery in World War I, holding his position under direct enemy artillery fire while others were fleeing. Truman had single-handedly halted the retreating men, organized them, and begun to return fire from his battery, subsequently silencing the enemy. JW said Truman was "Honest and concerned about the common man, something rare with most politicians." They remained good friends.

JW became an expert shot with the 1911 government-issued Colt .45-caliber pistol. He had been taught to shoot at an early age by his father, Jack, who was an expert marksman with a pistol and rifle. JW had a steady hand and a sharp eye. He won many tournaments in competition against other services. He received two matching sabers as a trophy for the championship of the entire American Armed Forces.

———

J W visited the Kansas City jail weekly as the doctor on call. There he would treat the prisoners' medical problems and minister to their spiritual needs. He never brought up Christianity, but the prisoners knew whom to come to if they wished to inquire about Christ. One man named Tony came to JW and told of carrying a heavy burden of guilt. He wished to change his life for the better. They talked for hours on numerous occasions.

Tony was a young black man from a single-parent family. He had never known his father well. His mother was employed as a cook at the hospital where JW worked. Tony's mother knew that Dr. JW visited the Jackson County jail frequently and was a good, well-respected man. One day, she saw JW at the hospital, approached him, and pleaded with him to look in on her son Tony.

JW replied, "I've already met your son on several occasions. I think he's a good young man who made a mistake. I'll do all I can for him. I'm a firm believer in forgiveness and redemption. However, there is always a price to be paid for sin."

Tony had been convicted of armed robbery along with two others. He had served two years of a fifteen-year sentence. Until he was eighteen years old, he had been reliable and never in trouble. He was employed and was a good athlete in high school. But Tony fell in with a group of older boys who had a history of trouble. He thought that those guys were cool. He thought they were to be looked up to because people feared them. They smoked, drank, and listened to cool music. They hung out nightly at local "juke joints" and caused trouble. They partied a lot and seemed to be popular with girls. They were always having a good time, and Tony didn't want to miss out. They always seemed happy and without a care. Tony thought that having people fear you showed strength and was how a real man should be. These boys' "Don't give a damn" attitude reinforced his belief that they were cool. Tony didn't have a male role model in his life to show him how a real man should behave. Deep in his heart, he knew this crowd was no good. He wondered how they had so much money to burn, even though they didn't have jobs. He soon found out that they were a criminal gang.

Tony went along on a botched robbery and was arrested. He knew what he was doing was wrong and felt uneasy about it, but he gave in to peer pressure because he didn't want to show fear and wanted to impress the other guys with how tough he was. When the police slapped the handcuffs on his companions, they didn't look very tough or carefree anymore. They even tried to blame Tony for instigating the crime, claiming that they had just been following him. Tony then saw what his "friends" were really like: cowards with no moral values.

JW sat with Tony in his cell many times and had long discussions with him. Tony appeared to absorb the wisdom and guidance JW was providing. JW said, "People get in trouble many times when they join a group or get into a mob because of peer pressure, even when they know something is not right. You cannot be afraid to stick up for something you feel is the truth or is right. If you do this, others may follow, but some may mock and abuse you as well. Someone once said, 'The thicker the skin, the happier the man.' This is a learned attribute that you are rarely born with. It is difficult to be tolerant of abuse and criticism of oneself, but it is something that must be mastered for maturity.

Stand your ground for what you believe in—this is true courage. This is what a real man does!"

"It is important for anyone to have role models in life that exemplify proper living and admirable traits. It is rare for a young man to grow up a respectable man alone and without proper instruction. In an analogous situation, it would be difficult to build a house without a blueprint for its construction. A mentor could be a family member, an older friend, or even someone from history that you read about."

JW continued, "Courage is the rarest of all human virtues but one of the most important. Courage comes in many forms, including physical, emotional, and moral. You are not born with courage. You must identify what it is at an early age and develop it yourself. It is like a muscle—the more you use it, the stronger it becomes. It is a decision that you will be brave because that's the type of man you want to be. It requires independent thought and possibly separating yourself from others. Being courageous at times can be difficult. I have heard it said that 'lonely are the brave.' Yes, it can be lonely at the top of the mountain of truth, but you are closer to God, and you will be rewarded in the end.

"When real men stand their ground in the face of abuse or being ostracized from the group, it is called integrity. Throughout history, great men have been revered for courage because it is a rare attribute. Courage entails standing up not only for yourself but also for others who are unjustly taken advantage of or abused." JW continued, "This is well established in the teachings of the Bible, Exodus 23.2: 'Do not side with the many to do wrong.' This law is a prohibition on people allowing themselves to be led astray by large groups or majority opinion. The most good is achieved by individuals who have the courage to part from the majority when it is morally wrong.

"Jesus and all of the apostles were courageous enough to speak the truth in the face of abuse and even death. Eventually their teachings changed the world for the better. Thank the Lord for their courage."

Tony felt alone, scared, and embittered. He began to hate the police and anyone in authority. He felt guilty for letting his mother down and was ashamed about being in jail.

JW told him, "Bitterness, anger, and hate will consume the vessel that contains them. When anger enters the mind, wisdom departs." He told Tony, "Release your guilt and anger to God, and he will bring peace to your soul. If you do this, you will become a beacon of light and hope to others."

JW told Tony that even King David committed murder and adultery and was forgiven by God. However, he paid a heavy price for redemption. The prophet Joseph was placed in prison for two years owing to false accusations and later became the second most powerful man in Egypt under the pharaoh. Saint Peter denied knowing Jesus three times yet later became the head of the church in Rome. Before his conversion, Saint Paul personally persecuted Christians and was involved with the murder of Saint Stephen. Paul was later imprisoned by the Romans and wrote many chapters and letters of the Bible during his time there. Paul became the key instrument of the Lord to spread Christianity to the Western world. The Roman guards couldn't understand why he was never despondent or depressed while he was imprisoned. What they didn't realize was that Paul was never alone; he had the Holy Spirit with him always. Paul knew that God would look after him, and whatever would come to pass would be God's will. Paul was such a dynamic evangelist and so filled with the Holy Spirit that he converted some of his guards to Christianity. Paul said, "Rejoice always because God is with you no matter what the situation. Maintain a positive attitude even when things look bad. Don't let the light of your soul be extinguished."

JW gave Tony some advice about life: "Be careful about whom you associate with. It is human to imitate the habits of those with whom we interact. We inadvertently adopt their interests, their opinions, their values, and their habit of interpreting events. Though many people mean well, they can just the same have a deleterious influence on you because they are undisciplined about what is worthy and what is not. Be selective about whom you take on as friends. All of these people can affect your destiny."

JW went on, "If you associate with chickens, you will learn to scratch at the ground and squabble over crumbs. If you associate with eagles, you will learn to soar to great heights. Make it your business to draw out the best in others by being an example yourself. Comport yourself as if you are a distinguished person. Hold yourself to a higher standard and avoid acting foolishly without discipline. You will then always be respected."

JW added, "Do not declare yourself to be a wise person or discuss your spiritual aspirations with people who won't appreciate them. Jesus said, 'Do not throw pearls among swine,' to make this point. Show your character and your commitment to personal nobility through your actions.

"It's not what happens to you but how you react to it that matters. If events are not in your control, then the only control you have is within yourself. Worry, anger, and anxiety will serve no purpose except to make you more miserable." He continued, "No man is free who is not the master of himself, which takes discipline. Self-discipline and self-control determine the quality of your life more than anything else. Uncontrolled emotions are frequently associated with destroyed and unsuccessful lives.

"You have come far in developing maturity since I first met you. Remember that growth and comfort rarely coexist, and discomfort is frequently a wise teacher. Just as iron is placed in fire and pounded into shape to create steel, God may make us endure hardship to make us better, wiser, and stronger people. It may be difficult to understand the suffering we are going through at the time, but later it will become more obvious that there was an intended purpose for the pain. It is important to realize that if you are a believer in Jesus Christ, there is a plan for your life and all for the good.

"All human beings have weaknesses that can be tempted by evil and do great harm to their lives. The key is to identify your own weaknesses and prepare your action in your mind before any temptation happens. When in fact you are tempted, you will be prepared mentally and avoid a destructive situation. If you know your weakness is drugs or alcohol, or you have a temper that has caused you difficulty in the past, imagine in your mind what you will do or say when offered these things or if you become angry in the future."

JW continued, "I have great confidence in you. You have some struggles ahead, but in the end, I feel strongly that you will do well. When faced with a decision, many people say they are waiting for God to give them an answer. But in most cases, God is waiting for you! He has given you a healthy mind to gather and sort information and the courage to come to a positive conclusion. Pray and acknowledge the Lord, then act according to your good judgment. The Lord will be with you."

JW gave Tony a Bible, which the young man read extensively. He told Tony, "The Bible should be a guidepost to your life and a shining light in the darkness. It is a beacon of hope and security in the midst of the wilderness and will give you strength when you are alone. Always remember the Lord is constantly beside you. This will become obvious if you look for him in prayer.

"Don't worry about your past from now on; you are a different person than you were two years ago when you first came into jail. I would say you are much wiser and more mature. Adversity has the same effect on a man that rigorous training has on a boxer; it reduces him to his fighting weight. I expect you to be a champion in the fight of life when you are released.

"The most important thing a man can do in life is to be honorable. It doesn't matter what kind of job you have or how much money you accumulate. The key to a happy life is to become a productive member of society and a good provider for your family. Focus your efforts on becoming the best husband and father you can be. The rest is of secondary importance. I remember an old saying by a highly intelligent man, Booker T. Washington. He said, 'Success is to be measured not so much by the position that one has reached in life as by the obstacles which he has overcome.'"

Tony was eventually released early on probation because of good behavior and JW's convincing recommendation. JW had given Tony a new outlook on life and a confident, calm spirit to tackle the world.

JW saw Tony's mother at the hospital after her son's release from jail. She ran to JW, grabbed both of his hands, and began to cry.

"You got my Tony back to me, Dr. JW," she said, wiping the tears from her eyes. "I knew you could do it! You, sir, are a gift from God. I can never repay all the good you have done for us!"

JW's response was similar to what he had said to another grateful mother when her son had been stricken with life-threatening diphtheria in Highland, Kansas, so many years before: "Don't thank me; thank the Lord. I feel very strongly that Tony will do well. He is a strong and resilient young man who has achieved a great amount of maturity in a relatively short time. I am convinced that better days are ahead for him."

After Tony's release, JW helped him through seminary. Tony became a minister and a leader in the black community. Tony later told JW, "One doesn't have to be religious to see the wisdom in the Bible. However, the more I read, the clearer it came to me that the Bible is the true revelation from God to all mankind."

Tony later invited JW to one of his services. The church was packed with people. He told the congregation, "We have a special guest here today. Someone who saved my life, someone who saw the light in me when no one else could. Someone who led me out of darkness." The church members began to sing the old gospel song "Let your little light shine, let it shine, let it shine!"

When the song ended, Tony looked at JW and said, "Dr. JW Graham, would you please stand?" JW stood up. Tony told the congregation, "Dr. JW Graham is my good shepherd who delivered me out of darkness. I would not be here today in front of all of you if not for Dr. JW. Please give him a strong hand of applause."

Everyone in the church stood, looked at JW, and gave the good shepherd a rousing round of applause with numerous amens.

4.

Money Can't
Buy Happiness

John Graham was filled with excitement and anticipation for the future. He was twenty-three years old and finally completely on his own. He felt free, living in an apartment away from his parents. He and two other friends were going on a triple date. The year was 1928, and prohibition was the law of the land. However, for these young men, getting alcohol was no problem. They knew where the right speakeasies were in downtown Kansas City.

John had a Model A Ford with a rumble seat in the back. The car was able to fit six people tightly. The rumble seat was in the far back of the car, where the trunk would otherwise be, and was open to the air with no top. At that time, people thought the Model A Ford was the hottest thing going. John was what some would call a lady's man. He was handsome, well dressed, and quick-witted and had an excellent sense of humor. He was always looking for excitement and a good time. In short, he loved to party and have fun.

John had been expelled from multiple high schools and colleges—usually for practical jokes, skipping school, and cutting up in class. He was never malicious or destructive; he simply had lots of energy and was always looking for things to do. Unfortunately, he frequently found the wrong things to do. His parents tried to encourage participation in sports to burn his energy and give him more focus. However, this never worked out because John lacked the discipline that sports required. He was well liked by his peers because of his outgoing, fun-loving personality. He rarely, if ever, got into fights, but he was known to be a good boxer and wrestler. His father, Dr. JW Graham, repeatedly got John out of trouble and convinced schools to accept him despite his past poor behavior. John did make fairly good grades in school since he was highly intelligent, like both of his parents. He just had a wild side.

A young man in the group who knew the women said that one of them was new in town. John would be paired with her for the evening on a blind date.

The women came out of their apartment to the car, laughing and smiling. None of them were gorgeous, but all were cute and attractive. They were wearing the berets and flapper hats that were fashionable at the time as well as skirts with fringed hems that fluttered around their legs. Belva had recently arrived in Kansas City from a small town in southern Missouri, looking for work and adventure in the big city. She had a round face with dimples that were accentuated when she smiled. John noticed that she had a good figure under her tight-fitting dress. John and Belva both felt an immediate attraction. John beamed his winning smile as he met her. Right away, Belva thought, "I've got the best-looking guy here!"

Everyone had heard of John's reputation as a fun party guy with a bit of an edge. He had connections all over town with people who knew how to have a good time. All of the young people had been anticipating a wild time with John Graham for a week. They were geared up and ready for action. They packed into the Model A Ford like sardines in a tin can. There were legs and arms lying every which way. Nobody seemed to mind the tight quarters because as far as they were concerned, the party had already begun. John put the car in gear and sped away. They were looking for adventure in the big city with John as their captain. As they sped down the street, they laughed and squirmed to adjust their packed-in bodies. They drew the attention of all the pedestrians on the street, eliciting a few laughs and stares at those "crazy kids."

Their first stop was John's favorite speakeasy, hidden away in the back of a large brick business building on Twenty-Third and Baltimore in downtown Kansas City. The group piled out of the car and walked through a dark, gloomy back alley between two tall brick buildings. They had to step around numerous puddles and pass between large dumpsters on both sides of the alley. The alley was much darker than the main street because of the lack of streetlights. The only sounds they could hear were the echoes of their footsteps within the canyon-like walls of the buildings. Everyone thought the dark alley was a creepy-looking place. The women gave each other strange looks. John picked up on their nonverbal communication and said, "Don't worry; you're going to love this place. It's not far."

At the end of the alley, they came to some iron railings by the side of the building, leading downward to some concrete steps that seemed to disappear into a dark, bottomless abyss. They all looked at one another with some suspicion again and then followed John down the steps to a large black steel door with a latched sliding window. John gave a special knock that was known to the proprietors. They waited for some time, standing bunched together on the dark stairs. Everyone became restless except John, who reassured them that the long wait was not unusual.

The small window slat abruptly opened. They saw two eyes and a nose of someone behind the small rectangular window. John identified himself and gave a password. The others thought this was mysterious yet exciting. They heard the unbolting of the locked steel door. They were all curious and a little anxious about what they would see inside.

As the thick steel door slowly opened, they were greeted by a rush of noise, music, talking, and laughter. It felt as though they were entering a different world that was bright and well lit. It was a stark contrast from the dark, damp alley where they had been standing. Cigarette smoke filled the room.

The doorman greeted John: "How are you this evening, Mr. Graham?"

"Just fine, Smitty; we're just getting started. How's the family?"

"Everyone is well, thank you, sir. Please, do come in."

The doorman motioned for the group to enter as he slowly waved his extended arm into the establishment as a formal welcome. The women were excited as they walked down the steps into the club. The establishment was fancier than most, and the room was much larger than they would have expected from the outward appearance of the building. The tables had white tablecloths with candles in red glass containers.

As they looked around, they saw that the bar was well stocked with alcohol. There were more bottles of alcohol of all different types than any of them had ever seen before. A large mirror adorned the back of the bar. The busy bartender and waiters all wore black-and-white tuxedos. This was by far the classiest establishment in town. John waved at the bartender and several of the waiters, and they greeted him loudly and with big smiles. John knew some of the clientele and greeted them as well. He walked to a table to shake hands with some old friends, made some quick small talk, and came back to his group.

A piano player was banging out ragtime and jazz tunes on the keyboards, backed by a drummer and a small horn section. John loved music and was quite knowledgeable about it. He frequently visited jazz clubs and speakeasies where there was live music. He thought, "This band is outstanding." They had a driving hot rhythm. To accentuate their quality, they were just a bit louder than most bands. However, the notes were clear, in tune, and right on the mark with one another. John thought, "Who are these guys? They are on fire." The horn section periodically stood in unison at various times during songs, creating a real show. John had been to this club many times but had never seen this band before. He thought, "These guys are real pros; we're going to have a good time tonight." The band seemed to inject electric energy into the room.

The young women felt a sudden thrilling tingling sensation in their extremities as they walked to the table. They could feel the beat of the bass drum reverberating in their chests. They thought, "What an exciting place!" Their eyes widened as they took in all of the sights of this strange and exciting new world. Belva had never seen anything like it before. She thought, "This sure beats southern Missouri." She immediately reaffirmed her decision to relocate to Kansas City as the right move. She was nineteen years old and quite naive by John's standards.

They all sat down at a table. The waiters jockeyed for position to get to John first since he was known to give generous tips. The drinks came within a matter of minutes. John knew some drinking games that required straight shots if the wrong answer was given. The conversation was lively, and all were having a great time. One of the boys put his hat on backward, crossed his eyes, and started acting silly, which got a big laugh from the whole group. John noted that Belva had a cute giggle. He looked at her out of the corner of his eye when she was not aware. He was covertly inspecting her movements, the way she looked, and the way she interacted with people. She was actively involved in the conversation but a bit more reserved than the other women.

After they had gone through numerous whiskey cocktails and were feeling a little "loose," they all got up and strolled over to the piano player. The young people leaned against the piano, flashing big smiles and moving with the beat of the song. The women put their elbows on the piano, supporting their faces with their hands. The fringed dresses shimmied rhythmically back and forth. Many of the men in the speakeasy, seeing them move, thought, "Wow, those girls are hot!" John and his friends couldn't help but notice as well. Many of the other men's dates told them not to look. The women knew men were looking at them, and they loved it. John thought, "These girls are real teasers!" But that didn't bother him. It just made him more excited.

The piano player loved the attention and began playing the liveliest songs he knew. John took Belva's hand and led her to the nearly empty dance floor. They began to dance the Charleston. The others followed John's lead and surrounded the piano. This group of young people seemed to ignite the entire establishment, and soon the floor was filled with dancing people.

More people got up until the whole room was dancing. The piano player was pounding the keys to bring up the volume and intensity. The horn section was blowing just a little harder, and the drummer was pounding away as hard as he could. The piano player was having a great time with these people dancing around him. He had a broad smile and was shaking his head. He sang loudly and clearly with a real showman's bravado. Everyone thought he was great.

The young women seemed to have lost all inhibitions, raising their arms in the air, shaking their hips, and kicking their legs in coordinated movements. Belva pivoted in a circle, then came face to face with John, giving him a cute flirtatious smile. The women had probably practiced dancing at home, just waiting for a moment like this to let go. The young men followed, dancing with as much energy as they could muster. The entire dance floor was an undulating, energetic mass of humanity. It ran through John's mind that going on this date was the best idea ever. He had been to a lot of dances before, but this outpouring of energy was greater than any other he had experienced.

John took Belva's hand and placed his arm tightly around her waist. She drew closer to him with uninhibited excitement. John was not expecting this level of responsiveness. They circled the floor, spinning like something from a carnival. They seemed to move without effort and with great coordinated speed. Belva had the sensation of being in the passenger seat of a fast race car, speeding around tight curves. She loved it and wanted more. John liked not only the rapid movement of their bodies in unison but the feel of Belva's firm body pressed close to his, responding to each movement of the dance. They were really having a time.

After nearly an hour, the dancing finally died down, and everyone returned to their tables. More drinks were ordered. Belva grabbed John's hand tightly and looked at him in a coy but flirtatious manner. John smiled coolly and confidently. However, he felt like howling at the moon like a starved wolf. The other couples had their arms around one another. John glanced at the group and came to the conclusion that the others were having the same feelings as he and Belva. They were all light-headed and a little tipsy from the drinks. It was after two a.m. when the group got up from the table and started out the door.

John stopped to talk to the piano player before he left. After getting the piano player's name and talking with him for a while, John gave him a large roll of dollar bills for a tip.

The piano player said, "Thank you very much, sir. I'll give some of this to the boys in the band."

John said, "Please do; you guys are fantastic. I'll see you again soon, my friend."

The piano player smiled his broad smile and said, "I hope so. I'll be looking forward to it."

When the group finally left, they brought several bottles of whiskey with them. They drove to a park by the Missouri River, where they told jokes, laughed, and lay on the grass. They polished off another bottle of whiskey as they sat in the park looking at the river. By three a.m., they were exhausted and barely able to walk. They all got back in the car, but John was in no mood to drive clear across town to take everyone home. He crossed the bridge over the Missouri River to

North Kansas City. They all checked into a cabin motel and crashed on the beds and floor. Belva and John were next to one another. Belva was thrilled with John. She had never known anyone like him. He was the most exiting man she had ever known, and she thought that he was very good-looking. She curled up close to him with John's arm around her and went to sleep.

When they woke up, it was late afternoon the next day. They started drinking shots of whiskey to celebrate the new day, followed by eating glazed and jelly doughnuts that they had brought with them. They all wanted the fun to continue. John took everyone home to change and clean up. They were all still half dazed, and their legs were a little wobbly.

That evening, they hurried to get together for round two. John took everyone to the jazz district at Eighteenth and Vine. Duke Ellington and Louis Armstrong, among others, were known to play frequently in the clubs there. They went to several clubs and again had drinks for all from the bottles that they smuggled in, secretly mixing whiskey with their Coca-Colas. They heard some great jazz that night. Everyone enjoyed the club atmosphere. John gave Belva a cigarette, after which she coughed. She momentarily took the cigarette out of her mouth and laughed. John gave everyone cigarettes and then promptly lit them with his lighter. At the time, it was considered a little shocking for women to smoke, but on that evening, no one seemed to care. They were throwing all conventional rules out the window. John knew the people who managed the club had some marijuana, or "reefer," as they called it. He got some for the group. He had never smoked it before but was curious about trying it, since he knew many jazz musicians used it.

After the musicians ended their gig for the night and the club started to close, they all went back to the motel and smoked and drank until they faded out again. The next day, the partying continued. They finished the remaining bottles of whiskey by doing shots again. Some of them complained of upset stomachs, after which they passed around a carton of buttermilk that they had picked up at a local store.

Nobody wanted the party to stop. One of them said, "Why don't we all get married?" They all looked at one another and started laughing.

Belva said, "I'd like that!"

Then the others chimed in: "Okay, let's do it." They found a justice of the peace and were all legally married, even though several of them could barely stand.

John was uneasy and felt a deep sense of dread. However, he was quite attracted to Belva. By this time, he was willing to do anything to spend the night with her alone. Despite his physical attraction, the rest of his body was not doing well. He felt dizzy, and his vision was slightly blurred. He had the unusual sensation that his mind was not in his body. His mouth was so dry and pasty that he could barely open his mouth to talk. His tongue was like a foreign object in his mouth that needed to be pulled out manually. He looked at the other two couples, and they could hardly stand without propping each other up. Two of them had their eyes closed while leaning against another. John thought, "They look worse than me." When he was standing in front of the justice of the peace, he felt his heart drop into his stomach with a sensation of nausea. His legs felt like limp noodles about to give way. He looked at Belva, and she was beaming. She thought John was the catch of the century. He just didn't have the nerve to back out. The alcohol and drugs had altered his judgment, to put it mildly. The force of peer pressure was stronger than John could overcome, even though he knew it was wrong.

Belva moved into John's apartment. He instantly felt as if life was closing in on him. He knew that the marriage had been a terrible mistake. He barely knew her, and the only feeling he had for her was physical attraction. At that time, divorce was greatly stigmatized. The physical aspect of the marriage was addictive, but John knew it could not sustain the relationship for the long term. The longer he waited to get out of the marriage, the more difficult it would be emotionally for both of them. John decided to make the best of the relationship and carry on, even though everything in his soul was telling him to leave.

He soon discovered that Belva was boring, poorly educated, and not very bright. He began spending more time outside the apartment. Belva became jealous of John's friends and tried to keep others away from him. She was not hospitable to guests and made people feel uncomfortable. She cried frequently at minor things and misinterpreted or misunderstood nearly everything John said or did. He tried to be more precise in his speech to help them achieve a mutual understanding, but nothing worked. Belva might as well have spoken another language. When she became upset, which was frequently, she would run crying to the bedroom and loudly slam the door.

Before long, Belva began putting on a lot of weight and stopped taking care of her appearance. She gave up trying to find a job and lay around the apartment all day, listening to soap operas on the radio. She would wear the same dress for several weeks in a row. Her hair was rarely combed and looked as if she had just gotten out of the bed. When John attempted to discuss her appearance, she would cry and again flee to the bedroom, slamming the door. John was never physically or intentionally verbally abusive. He just didn't know how to communicate with Belva.

John returned to the speakeasy several times. Despite the partying and fun atmosphere, everything was different. His old friends at the establishment noticed that John was not his old happy-go-lucky self. The bartender saw what a sorry state John was in and said, "Here you go, John; have a couple of drinks on the house." As the bartender poured two shots of whiskey for John, he said, "Women! Can't live with them and can't live without them. A guy just can't win." The piano player even came up to John on a break, slapped him on the back as a sign of support, and said, "Hang in there, Mr. Graham. It will all blow over in time. Sometimes women can really drive you crazy. Take it from me; it'll get better."

John started to drink heavily but soon found that alcohol made any problem worse. Nothing seemed to help him with Belva. John felt that he had no direction in life, a so-called ship without a rudder—and, for that matter, with no destination.

John decided to complete his degree in business administration at Central Missouri State College in Warrensburg, Missouri. Belva moved in with John's parents. JW, John's father, supported Belva and John during this time. He could tell that John and Belva's relationship was imperiled. He attempted to build up their spirits and instill a more positive view.

JW and John sat down at the sturdy dark walnut dining table where JW frequently discussed life matters and issues of importance with his two sons, and later with me when I was a young boy.

JW told John, "Nothing in this world is perfect, including marriage.

You need to overlook the faults of your spouse and concentrate on the good things about her. You should support her lack of confidence and insecurities with your strength and direction." However, at the time, John had neither of those qualities.

"Be patient and let the seeds of good faith grow. Once you see improvement in the relationship, build on that small success one step at a time until a healthy relationship is achieved." John was skeptical but said he would do his best.

When JW and Belva were alone, they sat down at the dining table, as JW had previously done with John. He held Belva's hands comfortingly and asked her to tell him about her life.

Belva related that she had felt alone and insecure all her life. She had a distant relationship with her father, who was a traveling salesman. He would come home one or two weekends per month and was gone the great majority of the time. Her mother was kind and hardworking but lonely and often depressed. Her younger brother was chronically ill, and her mother spent most of her time caring for him. They didn't have much money, so she had moved to Kansas City to find a job, which had been difficult because she had limited skills.

JW felt great empathy for Belva. He could see that she had little confidence. She appeared to have a dependent personality that was very fragile. JW knew that she was a poor match for John. However, he was determined to improve the relationship between the two.

JW offered Belva a job working for him as a receptionist or medical assistant. He felt that a job would give her life structure and some stability. With his support and guidance, he hoped that work would eventually give her confidence and get her mind off her troubled marriage. Belva declined the offer but thanked him for his concern. She told him that no one had ever been so understanding and kind to her before.

JW could not understand why she did not jump at the chance for employment when she had no other prospects. He was reminded of the parable in the Bible of the sower of the seeds. Some seeds are sown on fertile soil and are productive. However, other seeds fall on rocky, poor soil and never produce. JW was concerned that the seeds of John's marriage had been sown on rocky, unproductive soil.

Belva became pregnant and had a baby girl. John felt trapped and at an impasse in his marriage. He felt terrible and deeply guilty about the situation, but he just couldn't take living with Belva any longer. A divorce ensued, which was quite scandalous for the time, especially with a young child involved. Belva went back to her hometown in southern Missouri with the baby. There was never any further connection with John.

After approximately one year had passed, John began dating a beautiful woman. She was sweet, had an outgoing personality, and was a lot of fun. She had recently graduated from Central Missouri State along with John. Her family was well known and respected in Kansas City. They dated for over a year. She seemed to be the perfect woman for John, and she loved him. John knew that she was probably the best woman he had ever known, but guilt and emotional trauma had left his heart unreceptive to love. Even though he knew this woman was wonderful and loved him in spite of his issues, he wasn't ready to become emotionally involved with her. It takes time for a damaged heart to heal.

He was also unsettled and didn't have a regular job. He felt unsure of the future, as if there was a big question mark over his head. For the first time in his life, he became sullen. He stopped seeing his friends. He had trouble sleeping and lost weight. During this period of his life, John was likely clinically depressed and would have benefited from psychological help.

With the help of his father, John got a job with the Interstate Electric Company in Fort Smith, Arkansas. It was a new company that made large electrical generators for hydroelectric plants.

John left Kansas City for Arkansas and abruptly severed all ties with his friends except for his immediate family. It seemed that he wanted to wipe the slate clean and get a new start in life. He had deemed himself a failure to that point, but now he developed a single-minded determination to change his life and have a good career. This was the first time he had listened to his father. He had always greatly respected JW but had never taken his advice or instruction seriously before. His father had never given up on him and thought of him as the "prodigal son" who would one day return and turn his life around.

JW told John before he left that the most important thing for a young man was to establish a reputation. JW said, "Think of how you wish to be portrayed and then live it. Think of yourself as a product and making a strong brand for yourself that can be trusted and relied upon. Do not leave your reputation to chance or gossip. It is your life's artwork. You must craft it, hone it, and display it with the care of an artist." JW continued, "You will now be living in the South, not Kansas City. They may do things a little differently down there. So as the saying goes, 'When in Rome, do as the Romans do.' In other words, adapt to your new environment and become one of them. Southerners have a tendency to be a little clannish at first, but once they get to know you well, they'll become your trusted friends."

John eventually did become successful. He was a natural businessman and a great salesman. He impressed his superiors with new ideas about how to advance the company. He impressed them even more with his ability to implement the new strategies rapidly and follow up on successes. He ensured that his plans were executed properly by holding weekly short meetings with his project groups. He identified highly motivated, free-thinking individuals in his group and promoted them. John instilled in them a "team spirit" that kept them focused. He kept them close as trusted advisers as he rose through the ranks of the company. He found new ways to cut costs and streamline the work, saving large sums of money. He was energetic and affable. He put in the maximum amount of work plus 20 percent. He hustled and always got things done on time. He became a real "up-and-comer."

John always made good points during meetings. However, he knew when not to talk and how not to offend his boss or other superiors. He tried not to appear too ambitious, although he likely was. He adapted to the business culture and learned how to fit into his environment. He always tried to exceed his superiors' expectations. In short, he tried to become valuable to the corporation but with a happy, good-natured, likable attitude.

When John had free time during office hours, he would walk around the business office and through the factory itself. He would stop to talk with people from the top executives to the janitors. He called this "face time." He presented himself in a very friendly, outgoing, easygoing manner, but he was always well dressed and had the appearance of a top executive. John said, "If you want the position, you must play the part."

Over time, everyone in the corporation came to know John personally and had a favorable impression of him. His "face time" was beneficial to his career. He loved doing it, and it showed. He enjoyed talking to everyone. He knew that his ability in business management was his key to future success. However, if he needed an edge over his competition for advancement in the company, he felt that his likability would be the factor he needed. After several years, it seemed that everyone in the company was pulling for John, hoping that he would do well.

When building my own medical practice, I took a lot of suggestions from my uncle John that served me well. However, he told me, "If the job is not for you, leave on good terms no matter the amount of money. Try to determine this early on before things get too messy. In business, try to avoid burning bridges because you may never know when things may change."

John eventually became the chief executive officer (CEO) of the company through hard work, talent, persistence, and constant improvement. He made some fairly aggressive business decisions early on. He was not interested in preserving the status quo. He was determined to expand the company and bring it into a new era. He hired a new group of engineers to make larger and more powerful generators. He fired the old engineers as well as people who didn't get things done, lazy people, and some people who just didn't fit in with his new corporate environment. He streamlined the company, dramatically removing waste and inefficiency.

John was willing to step out on a limb and take some calculated risks for potential big gains. He bought out some of his smaller competitors and bought the companies that manufactured the copper wire and other components of the hydroelectric generators. This forced his larger competitors to buy the copper wire and other products from him at greatly inflated prices. This initially caused a short-term loss to the company, but the long-term rewards were enormous. He initially received much criticism, but after weathering the storm, he achieved high praise from the board of directors and investors. During the 1930s and 1940s, the government was building large hydroelectric dams throughout the country, and John's company received several huge government contracts. John was in the right place at the right time, and he became a multimillionaire. He was one of the top five wealthiest people in the state of Arkansas. He employed over one thousand people, more than any other business in town. He also employed more people in other cities with his associated companies.

He owned extensive tracts of land in Arkansas and an airplane with his own airstrip. His house was an antebellum-style mansion with large white pillars at the entrance. The driveway to the mansion ran nearly a quarter of a mile, lined by magnolia trees that had large white flowers for much of the year. Around the house was an expansive porch surrounded by red and pink flowering crepe myrtle trees. The porch looked out on a large private lake that was filled with bass and catfish. A floating dock in the middle of the lake was frequently used for swimming. Large overhanging willows and cypress trees surrounded the lake, making it very secluded and almost prehistoric in appearance. There was a large swimming pool behind the house with marble statues in various areas nearby. The pool gave the feeling of an emperor's private sanctuary.

John was respected and well liked in the community. He was generous with his money and gave favors frequently. He was a member of several charitable clubs in town and was a proverbial pillar of the community. He knew and worked with business leaders, politicians, and judges in the local area as well as the entire state.

He relished his new status. He always wore expensive tailored suits with cufflinks and monogrammed shirts. There was always a silk hand-kerchief in the chest pocket of his suit that matched his tie. It was rare for him not to wear a tie and his typical diamond tie tack. He drove a white Cadillac convertible and enjoyed riding around town and wav-ing at people he knew. When I rode with him, I initially thought that this was "over the top." However, everyone responded with smiles and waves in a genuine, positive manner. All seemed to appreciate his greet-ing. It seemed to many that he owned the town of Fort Smith.

If John wished to send something to his family in Kansas City, he simply sent one of his employees to drive eight hours to deliver it and then return to Fort Smith. John took a lot of advice during his career from his uncle Wallace Graham, JW's brother, who owned a large glass factory outside Pittsburgh, Pennsylvania.

Eventually, John married a wealthy local woman named Georgia. Her family was well connected in law, business, and politics. She was tall and had long, jet-black hair. She had a long, sharp nose, thin lips, and light steel-blue eyes. Some people said she had "cold, crazy-looking eyes." She used heavy makeup, with bright red lipstick and dark eye-shadow. She never smiled, and most people described her as cold as ice with a domineering mean streak. She had a definite Southern accent and a thin veneer of politeness that could be easily seen through.

John and Georgia had two children, Barbara and Jimmy. After Jimmy was born, Georgia didn't want much to do with John. They essentially lived in two separate areas of the large mansion. John was always hesitant to bring guests to his house because of Georgia's poor hospitality and bad temper. The time that I was a guest, it seemed as if Georgia tried to avoid me as much as possible.

When John and I entered his marble-floored mansion, the entrance area echoed the sounds of our footsteps. Walking into the hallway ahead of us was like entering a cathedral with a tall domed ceiling and a large crystal chandelier. John called out to Georgia, his voice echoing loudly as if in a cave, but there was no response. We both knew she was there despite the lack of response. We were eventually greeted by the maid. John told her to fix us some sweet tea as we walked to the expansive porch overlooking the lake. While we were sitting in our rocking chairs drinking our sweet tea, Georgia appeared as if out of nowhere, startling me. She was wearing a long, tight-fitting white dress with a pearl necklace and pearl earrings. This contrasted with her bright red lipstick and long black hair. Her movements were slow, deliberate, and somehow elegant.

I stood up, said "Hello," and shook her hand. I noticed the deep red fingernail polish on her long, manicured nails. She gave me her hand with the palm down, almost as if she wished me to kiss the back of her hand. She gave the slightest of smiles.

"So, what brings you down here?"

"Uncle John invited me. I've never been here before, and since I'm now living fairly close in Fayetteville, I thought I'd take him up on his offer."

John said, "I thought I'd show my favorite nephew the business operation here and give him a tour of the town."

With a half-smile, she responded, "I hope you enjoy your stay."

She then turned and walked off in her white stiletto heels and black nylon hose.

Even though I spent two nights there, I only saw her one other time. I noticed her sunbathing by the pool, reading a book in her tight-fitting white bathing suit as she sipped her iced sweet tea. I walked out and approached her.

"How are you today Georgia?" I said.

She lowered her sunglasses and peered at me from below her fashionable white straw hat and above her shades. Although I was standing in front of her and she was reclining, I had the sensation that she was looking down at me from a higher position.

"I'm fine, and how are you young man?" she replied in a subtly sarcastic manner.

"You certainly have a beautiful house."

"It's comfortable."

"I've been impressed with the beauty of the entire state of Arkansas and the friendliness of all the people."

"I'd rather be in New York or Los Angeles."

I smiled and nodded. "Well, that's a far cry from Arkansas."

"Yes, it is."

There was an uncomfortable prolonged silence as she continued to stare at me. I was now at a loss for small talk and excused myself as she placed her sunglasses back over her eyes.

John and I took our meals at restaurants. He said, "The only meal I have at home is the occasional breakfast fixed by our maid."

Everyone said that John was very good and respectful to Georgia. He was faithful to the marriage throughout. He never had a bad thing to say about his wife to me. Despite this, Georgia was cold and spiteful to John. There was clearly some dynamic between them that I didn't know about. However, it seemed to me that Georgia was just naturally mean and arrogant. She frequently criticized John in front of the children and friends. It was never clear why he had married Georgia. Possibly it was primarily a business decision to gain connections and power through her family. It was well known that he was a deeply unhappy man despite his wealth, power, and outward appearances.

Uncle John was very proud of my success as a wrestler when I was a young man. He would send me a gold Bulova watch every time I won a major tournament. At the end of my senior year in high school, I had a whole box of expensive watches. I liked Uncle John very much because he was engaging and funny. He always had a big smile and told a lot of jokes. I was always happy to see him.

After graduating from the University of Missouri, I enrolled in graduate school at the University of Arkansas with a major in cell biology and the intent of applying to medical school again after my initial attempt was rejected. Uncle John called me to tell me how excited he was that I was in Arkansas. He said that he was so thrilled that he had bought me a Cadillac, and all I needed to do was go down to the dealer and pick out the color. I thanked him greatly, but I could not accept the gift, although I appreciated his thoughtfulness.

When John invited me to Fort Smith, we had a wonderful time. We ate dinner at the best place in town. He had a reserved table where he dined nearly every night. Two waiters were dedicated only to us. I know he tipped extravagantly. The owner of the restaurant would stop by the table and talk with us, and the chef would come out and offer to fix something special off the menu. I know that John used this elegant restaurant for meetings in a back room and entertaining special clients.

Later, he gave me a tour of the factory. I could tell he had a hands-on approach with his employees. He stopped to introduce me to many of his workers. He would ask how their families were doing and make small talk with genuine interest in the people he employed. I could tell his employees liked and respected him. I heard "Good morning, Mr. Graham" and "How are you doing, Mr. Graham" as we walked through the factory. He paid his employees quite well, far above the national average for the work they were doing. He was also generous with bonuses for work that was well done or for holidays. All of his employees had good health insurance coverage from the company, which was unique among companies at that time.

Uncle John told me, "Everything you achieve in life is going to be with the help, support, or cooperation of other people. My goal is to help other people in business so they will help me back. It's a key point in business success to be genuinely interested in people. You can make more friends in two months by becoming interested in other people than you can in two years by trying to get other people interested in you. Ask people how they spend their time, what their interests are, where they grew up, and about their families. Give people the joy of talking about their lives and interests." He continued, "Always give praise to people that have earned it. We are all starving for appreciation; it's part of being human. In this way, you'll gain their respect and confidence."

After the tour of the factory and business building, we walked back to his office, where I sat down in front of his enormous desk. His personal office was spacious and immaculate. It had beautiful carpeting and artwork on the walls, mainly paintings of old Western scenes. He said it reminded him of his grandfather and namesake, John Graham (Happy Jack), and the stories his grandfather had told him as a child. I thought the name was a misnomer since the two were so different except for their sense of humor and affability. The office was on the top floor of the building with large picture windows overlooking the factory and the city beyond. It was a stunning and impressive view. I noticed that there were framed photos of his father, JW; his brother, Wallace; and his children. There was no picture of his wife.

He leaned over the large desk, looked directly into my eyes, and said, "Bruce, I really think you have what it takes. I'd like you to take over the business as head of the company when I retire in the next two years. I could teach you all the things you need to know to run this operation. Jimmy and Barbara want nothing to do with the company, and I would like to keep it in the family." John stood up from behind his desk and motioned me to come over to the large picture window. As we looked out over the factory and business buildings, he said, "All of this can be yours."

I realized that if I accepted, it would mean becoming a multimillionaire. Even if I accepted just to sell the company and do something else with my life, it would mean millions. However, this would be betraying my uncle, which would be dishonorable and unacceptable. I told him I was honored and flattered, but I wanted to be a doctor more than anything in the world, and if given a chance I knew I could become really good at it. Naturally, I declined the offer. Sometimes I regret not taking Uncle John's offer, but that feeling doesn't last very long after I reflect on my greatly meaningful and successful career in medicine.

When they are younger, many people may lack the wisdom and caution usually associated with older adults. Frequently people will do things in the presence of their friends that they wouldn't think of doing alone. The powerful force of peer pressure has involved many young people in terrible situations that they have regretted later. The decisions you make in your late teens and early twenties can follow you for the rest of your life. Unfortunately, at that age, one lacks experience but often has a great amount of energy and unrealistic idealism that can cause trouble and lead one astray.

At that early age, many feel that others are having more fun than they are, and they don't want to miss out on the action. This is rarely true. Most of the time, everyone is thinking the same thing. Even the people who seem happy and popular and are going to a lot of parties are more often than not trying to impress others with how much fun they are having when they are actually self-conscious and insecure.

When John married Belva, he should have listened to his inner feelings that were screaming at him to run. His father, JW, was one of the wisest men that I have known, but John refused to listen to him. John loved and respected his father but just couldn't stay away from what he thought was the "action." It is unfortunate that many people make serious mistakes at an early age that follow them for the rest of their lives. John not only damaged himself, with probable permanent effects, but also inadvertently damaged other people. It is said that you should be careful sowing your wild oats when young, for you may reap the whirlwind.

Some wounds never truly heal, including emotional wounds, scarring the heart. No matter how much time has passed or whether you begin a new relationship or find yourself in a different environment, the pain and guilt can still be present. There is an old saying: "Guard your heart." While in a love relationship, you must make sure it is very good before becoming emotionally and physically involved. Otherwise, leave before it becomes too painful and too complicated.

John thought that becoming a business success would bring him happiness. I believe that happiness and success are independent of each other and must be pursued separately. Then you can achieve both.

I can't help but think that somehow his first marriage affected the trajectory of John's life. He seemed to love his job and was a great success in business but hated his life. John finally focused on a career after his first marriage but never achieved a successful personal life. I think there was residual permanent damage. I could see that without a loving family, your life is hollow no matter how much power or money you have.

I have frequently wondered how things might have been different if he had not gone on that wild weekend with his friends so long ago.

I concluded that fame, money, and power cannot buy happiness.

5.

Quality and
Hard Work

One thing Stanley and Hadden Hill knew was quality construction. The brothers built the reputation of their new plastering company on high-quality work that proved to last as long as the buildings they constructed. The Hill brothers realized that the end product and workmanship, not the profit margin, would be the key to their long-term success.

Stanley and Hadden Hill were brothers on the verge of making a very large business success of their company. Their success depended on completing two large projects for the city: the Municipal Auditorium and the Power and Light Building.

This was the 1930s, when Kansas City was undergoing a huge building expansion of downtown with large skyscrapers made of concrete, steel, and plaster. All of the iconic buildings of the city—City Hall, the Federal Building, the Municipal Auditorium, and the Power and Light

Building, among many others—were built in this era. It was the perfect time for a contracting business to succeed. The Hills used the best-quality materials and the most expert workmanship. They always finished the job on time, which set them apart from competing companies.

In order to get the original bid from the city government, they needed to commit to completing the job on a tight schedule to avoid the risk of the job being granted to a competitor. The brothers knew it would be necessary to contract some of the plastering to subcontractors whom they felt they could depend on. They were willing to take a chance on the subcontracted plastering to gain two large projects at once, which would guarantee a huge and immediate expansion of their company.

The men who worked for Stanley and Hadden were dedicated to the brothers because they were treated well and with respect. They also had higher salaries than the standard pay in the area. In return, they were expected to work hard and perform to a high standard. The men knew the Hill brothers had started out where they were now and had worked their way up from common laborers to running an up-and-coming plastering business. Their employees felt a type of camaraderie with the two brothers. They wanted to please their employers and were willing to go the extra mile for a job well done. The men also knew that if they didn't perform to the Hills' required level of craftsmanship, they would be out of a job. Any person who was disruptive, late to work, or lazy was immediately fired. The Hills were tough but fair. It was the Depression, and money and jobs were hard to find.

To secure the meeting of their timeline, the brothers hired a subcontractor who had gained their trust with his past good performance on smaller jobs for them. They used the subcontracting firm for the Power and Light Building project in downtown Kansas City while their own crew was tied up on the new Kansas City Municipal Auditorium, a very high-profile structure for the city.

They had agreed with the city that both jobs would be done in fourteen months. They were now in the twelfth month, with only two months left before the deadline. The Hills completed the Municipal Auditorium far ahead of schedule to great fanfare and publicity from the city.

Now it was time for the Hills to inspect the progress on the Power and Light Building that they had subcontracted out. They had been reassured by the subcontractor that the building was nearly complete and that things had gone well.

The Hills showed up to the construction site unannounced in an optimistic and nearly gleeful spirit because of their recent great success with the auditorium. They were expecting a real one-two punch that would project them into huge success as the preeminent plastering company in the city, if not the entire bistate area.

They walked up the concrete steps and began a tour of the building. They stopped in the entrance of the skyscraper and looked at the plaster walls, inspecting them closely. They both felt their hearts sink into their guts with slight nausea. They didn't say a word to each other but kept walking from floor to floor. Each knew what the other was thinking. Stanley scratched the surface of a plaster wall with a pocket knife, which resulted in nearly the entire wall of plaster falling to the ground. They looked at each other in silence. Stanley knelt down and picked up some of the fallen plaster. It crumbled easily to near powder in his hand at the slightest touch. Stanley stood up and threw the powdered plaster to the floor. He clenched his teeth and furrowed his brow. He made a fist and punched his other palm with a slapping sound. Hadden was silent and didn't show any outward signs of emotion. Their initial sensation of illness now turned to anger, if not rage.

Much to the Hill brothers' dismay, their inspection of their subcontractor's work revealed that the plaster had been mixed improperly. Poor materials and substandard workmanship had been used in the construction. The subcontractor had used only half the amount of the ingredient in the plaster mix needed to make a durable, long-lasting product. Kansas City was plagued by contractors who used cheap, substandard materials that usually fell apart within five years. The subcontractor hadn't realized that the Hill brothers would know the difference. They learned later that the subcontractor had sold the rest of the plaster material for a large personal profit.

They immediately fired the subcontractor and his entire crew. Their excellent reputation was now at risk. The Hills were moderately more expensive than their competitors, but their construction was worth more because the higher quality they were known for meant the project would last over the long run without need of future revisions or repairs.

Stanley and Hadden had a long discussion about what to do next with nearly a year's work wasted on substandard plastering and the deadline two months away. Should they just let it go, knowing that the material would fall apart within five years? Should they renegotiate with the city for more time and bring to light the subcontractor's substandard work, or should they redo the plaster in the entire building within two months—which seemed impossible?

The first option was out of the question. They had worked too hard for too many years to build a reputation for high-quality work to allow their business to be tarnished by this bad job. They planned to be in Kansas City for a long time to come, and they could not afford to have their reputation darkened by poor work on such a high-profile project. All the success they had just begun to realize hinged on their reputation for high-quality workmanship.

The second option would be embarrassing and would potentially lose them city contracts in the future. The city already had tenants scheduled for the building and reimbursing the new renters could cost the city a significant amount of money.

The Hill brothers chose the last option, the seemingly impossible. With hard work, determination, ingenuity, and luck, it could be done. The Hill brothers were confident that they had the best and most highly motivated craftsmen in the city.

Stanley and Hadden had a meeting with around fifty of their workmen and outlined their plan of action, which would entail twenty-four-hour, around-the-clock work in alternating twelve-hour shifts. Large floodlights would be placed in the work areas at night. The men would receive double pay. The Hills were willing to utilize any payment they received from the job to pay the workmen in order to maintain their reputation. The Hills told the men that if they succeeded, this would be a job they would tell their children and grandchildren about. The Hills gave the workers a real pep talk, as if they were going into some sporting competition. It seemed that the men were excited about the challenge facing them—and, of course, the increased pay.

The work began that day. Either Stanley or Hadden was on the job every hour of the day and night, providing expert guidance to their crews. The job was progressing amazingly well after four weeks. Everyone was tired but still highly motivated and doing an excellent job. A glimmer of hope that the impossible could be accomplished began to emerge.

While on the job, without warning, the Hill brothers learned that their material delivery trucks were being blocked by a group of big, rough-looking men, thereby halting further progress on the building. Stanley rushed out of the building and onto the street to assess the situation. He found several men stopping the trucks and intimidating the drivers. These large men blocking the trucks had reportedly been hired by a competing larger company that had heard of the Hills' recent difficulty. They were hoping the city would fire the Hill brothers and give the job to their company. The truck drivers were beginning to turn around and head out. They didn't want anything to do with these loud, dangerous-appearing thugs threatening anyone who didn't do what they said. If it hadn't been for Stanley Hill, the thugs would have gotten their way.

Stanley was short, stocky, and muscular. He was handsome, with an almost round baby face. He was five feet, four inches tall, but it would be hard to find a more fearless and courageous man. As a young man, he had played baseball for a semiprofessional team as catcher. He had played with Casey Stengel, who went on to play major league baseball and became the famous manager of the New York Yankees in their heyday in the 1950s and '60s. Stanley was an expert at throwing the ball to second base when a player was stealing from first base. He had a tremendously powerful throwing arm which was lightning-fast and accurate.

Stanley knew that the police were frequently bribed by corrupt companies to stay away in these situations. Even if the police came, the issue would likely take days to sort out, thereby halting construction for a period of time that they didn't have to spare. Stanley attempted to talk to the thugs. He even tried to bribe them with cash, but to no avail. They cursed and threatened him. He was smart enough not to take on several larger men at one time with his fists alone, but he also knew from past experience that if he was in the right and his adversaries knew it, they would be less likely to put up a determined fight.

He realized that his greatest weapon was something he had learned from baseball long ago. He remembered the Bible story of David and Goliath, where the giant Goliath was brought down by a young boy with a sling and a rock, saving the nation of Israel.

Stanley picked up several hand-sized round rocks from the ground. With tremendous power and accuracy, he began throwing the rocks at the thugs. One was struck in the head and fell to the ground, unconscious. Another was hit in the face, fracturing a facial bone and damaging one eye. The thug fell down screaming and holding his face, blood streaming through his fingers from his wounds. The others ran off, unable to escape the blows from Stanley's sure-shot stones pounding them in the back and neck as they ran. An ambulance was called to take away the two badly injured thugs. The Hills never had a problem with harassment again.

On the given deadline, the job was finished. They had done the impossible. All the workmen were proud of what they had accomplished. The city was satisfied and had a ribbon-cutting ceremony at the opening of the building. Stanley and Hadden were simply relieved.

From then on, the Hill brothers had an even stronger reputation in the city for integrity, high-quality workmanship, hard work, and honesty. Their business grew rapidly. They became the largest plastering company in the city. Later, they expanded the business into sales of building materials. Financially, they did well in the midst of the Depression. One lesson they did learn well from their experience was to never use a subcontractor again. Quality was of paramount importance to the two brothers.

The Hill brothers came from modest beginnings. They grew up in Slater, Missouri, and migrated to Kansas City as adolescents with their parents. Their father, who was originally from Virginia, was named Lee Jackson Hill after the two famous Confederate generals. Lee Jackson's father had fought for the South with the Army of Northern Virginia in the Civil War. After the Civil War, the Hills moved to Missouri.

Stanley and Hadden started working as laborers for various construction companies. Although they knew all aspects of building and construction, they grew into the specialty of plastering. They found a niche in the new building market and became respected by their employers for their expertise. They worked mostly with Mr. Norris of Norris Construction Company. The two brothers were more than willing to work overtime and to clean up the work site at the end of the day. They began doing extra work for Mr. Norris, free of charge. Mr. Norris noticed their extra effort, which added value for their employer in excess of their compensation. In short, they hustled above and beyond their job description. Because of their intelligence and unshakable work ethic, the two brothers became assistants and foremen for Mr. Norris. Eventually he taught the two young men the business end of the company. The Hill brothers were eager to learn and spent extra time and effort to improve the company, all on their foremen's salaries.

After nearly ten years of dedicated service from the Hill brothers,

Mr. Norris retired and handed the company over to the capable hands of Stanley and Hadden Hill for a fair price. Even so, it took all of their savings, along with a generous bank loan, to buy the company. Although the company was fairly small, it was profitable. The Hill brothers had big dreams. They saw a large building boom on the horizon. The city had plans to build skyscrapers in the downtown area. The brothers were going to do their best to take advantage of the upcoming growth of Kansas City.

Hadden was outgoing, personable, and highly intelligent. He solicited new clients and handled public relations and advertising. Hadden always had a big smile on his face. He was a born salesman. He used to call me "Captain," his nickname for his young grandnephew. He was nice, and I liked him very much.

Stanley was hard-driven and tougher than nails. He knew how to get a job done with efficiency and quality. He was excellent in the day-to-day management of the construction projects. The brothers' wives, Lena and Edna, kept the books and did the office work. Both wives were lovely, engaging people who were just as dedicated to their roles in the business as their husbands. When children came to both families, the office work was given over to Grover Hill, the third but oldest brother. Stanley and Hadden seemed to be the perfect team, each having qualities that the other lacked.

Stanley and Hadden found a niche in a profession, an area of expertise, where they could create superior results and with better productivity than anyone else in the city. Through persistence and by continually looking for opportunities, they achieved tremendous success and respect from the entire city. Considering their humble beginnings as common laborers, this was a significant accomplishment. Their success continued due to their pride in their work, their ability to adapt, and cooperation with each other as trusted business partners.

Hard work is important, but it alone is not enough to achieve success. One must have goals and continue to find new markets to expand into, even though the new areas of growth may not have been part of the initial plan. I don't think either brother would have guessed that expertise in the use of plaster would eventually make them successful when they first started out as workmen.

Stanley and his wife, Edna, were very social people. They hosted large gatherings of people from the neighborhood or church in a local park or on their farm in Lees Summit, Missouri. It is impressive to look at old photos of the Hills along with nearly one hundred people at a massive picnic. There was a sense of local community in that bygone era that is rarely seen today. Edna, along with the other women, was expert in the art of cooking for large groups. Stanley had one dish that he always prepared: boiled turnips with a lot of salt, pepper, and hot sauce. Although there were only a few select people who liked the dish, Stanley sure did.

Stanley would frequently help people out with his expertise in building and mechanical things. He had an extensive workshop in his basement. All of his tools and devices were neatly arranged in perfect order. People thought nothing of asking Stanley Hill to fix something in their house that needed repair. He was happy to help, without strings or payment.

Edna too was often called upon to help others with sewing projects or cooking needs. Edna's sewing machine and knitting equipment were on the other side of the basement across from Stanley's workshop. The basement seemed like a small multiuse factory. Both areas were used a great deal. She was an amazing seamstress. I frequently had my clothes altered to fit better by my grandmother Edna (Nenna). Many people would give her clothes to be mended, and like Stanley, she did so without charge. Both Stanley and Edna used their skills and expertise for the benefit of others. They seemed to me like throwbacks to the pioneers. They just loved to work and help others at the same time.

Stanley and Edna were quite active in the Baptist church. Stanley had an excellent voice and sang in the choir. I remember him singing hymns while driving his car with me as a passenger. In the 1960s, all of the Baptist churches in the Kansas City area gathered money and material to build a hospital in South Kansas City. This was an ambitious project taken on by the church community.

The Hills donated their workmanship and money to build the new hospital. When it was completed, Stanley and Edna were extremely proud of the new hospital that they had helped build. They frequently took me to dinner in the hospital cafeteria with great pride. They would show me around the lobby and take me into the gift shop, where they would usually buy me a treat.

Edna worked as a volunteer at the hospital for over twenty years, longer than anyone else. She loved the cheery cherry-red dress that the volunteer ladies wore. The volunteer women were called the "cherry ladies" because of their dress color. Edna worked at the hospital until she was ninety-two years old, still with great mental acuity and in excellent health.

I was fortunate to become a member of the hospital medical and surgical staff when my grandmother was still working as a volunteer. I loved seeing her occasionally in the hallways and waving at her. There was a great amount of nostalgia when I went to Baptist Hospital to see patients and perform surgery. It was especially poignant when visiting the cafeteria or the gift shop, which I had visited frequently with my grandparents as a child.

Edna and Stanley Hill showed charity and goodwill to other people. Like most Baptists, they believed in a clear and straight moral code, yet they were never overbearing. They were just good, hardworking Christian Midwestern people. One might say their principles were the foundation of America. They lived their lives with humility and compassion for others. I respected and loved my grandparents deeply.

After I finished eighth grade, I was compelled to work with Stanley (Boppa), my grandfather, for the summer. I complained because I wanted to just hang around, have fun, and do whatever would suit me each day. My father demanded that I either work or go to school, and that was that! Whining and complaining were futile. I had learned long ago that you did not negotiate with "The General" (my father). I was not living in a democracy but in a benign dictatorship. I had no choice in the matter.

During my first week, I was assigned to pick up sacks of plaster and concrete mix weighing between fifty and one hundred pounds from a train boxcar and then place them in trucks for transportation to construction sites.

This process continued all day for nine hours, eight a.m. to five p.m., with thirty minutes for lunch. At the time, I weighed around 105 pounds. It was the most physically demanding, mind-numbing work I had done in my life. I was totally unprepared for such challenging physical labor. The summer heat and the thick humidity were oppressive. It was even worse in the poorly ventilated boxcars, where it felt as if I were slaving away in a dark, dust-filled oven. Nowadays, we would probably be required to wear face masks because of the thick plaster dust that permeated the air. The tasks we were performing are likely now automated by some machine—but not then. After emptying the boxcar of the plaster-filled sacks, I felt great relief, thinking the job was done. We jumped out of the boxcar. I noted that the other laborers were going to an adjacent boxcar and opening its broad sliding door. The car was filled with more heavy plaster and cement mix sacks. My heart sank when I saw hundreds of boxcars lined up along the rail line, all filled with the same materials.

After the first day, my whole body ached. I was weak and slightly trembling. I felt as though I could barely walk, but I refused to show my misery. I couldn't imagine how I was going to continue with this killer labor that I was so unaccustomed to. However, if you worked for Stanley Hill, you completed the job and didn't complain. I never said a word but just showed up every day and worked until the end of the day. I saw no end in sight. I recalled an ancient Greek myth of Sisyphus being punished in Hades by having to roll a huge, heavy boulder up a steep incline, and when he finally reached the top, the boulder would roll down to the bottom just to start the process all over again. I felt like Sisyphus.

I was a child working among adult laborers. These were hard-core, tough men who knew I was suffering.

They would say, "You gonna be okay, kid?"

Although I didn't think I could survive, I would always say, "I'm fine."

They would chuckle and say, "Hang in there, kid."

After work, I went home, and my mom gave me dinner. She would always ask, "How did work go today?" in her usual cheery, upbeat manner. I would always say, "Fine," and nothing else, barely looking up from my dinner plate. She had no idea of my misery. It wouldn't have done me any good to tell her how much I was suffering and how unfit I was for the job that her father had me doing. I just had to suck it up. However, I wasn't quite sure how. After dinner, I just went to bed every night and became unconscious until I was rudely awakened from a dead sleep the next day to start the misery all over again.

After about three weeks, when the boxcar job was done, I worked with Stanley on his farm cutting acres upon acres of tall grass and weeds with a large scythe and sickle in the hot summer sun. This was still grueling work but much better than being in the "boxcar prison." Amazingly, I started getting used to the work. My mother noticed a big change in my attitude at dinner as well. My diminutive muscles seemed to be adapting to the point that there was little if any soreness or pain. At the end of the day, the weakness that I had previously felt was now gone.

I considered the possibility that the boxcar job might have been a test of will and endurance that had been set for his grandson by Stanley. I thought of the old saying about "Throwing the child into the deep end of the swimming pool to see if he could swim." I was faced with the hard-core reality of sink or swim. I had no way of knowing whether it was planned or not, but I wasn't going to ask.

At the farm, Stanley was part of the work crew. Stanley, I, and two other men cut down vast areas of tall, overgrown weeds and shrubs. We did this all day.

After the first day, my hands were sore and blistered from using the scythe. That evening, I bandaged my blistered hands with Band-Aids and gauze wrap. I bought some thick leather gloves that were of great benefit and made all the difference. I grew to love those gloves as a symbol of a transition from someone who was totally inactive to someone working with his hands. I grew to appreciate certain tools used in labor and how the tools made my life so much easier. I had certain favorite tools and came to appreciate high-quality workmanship in their manufacture as opposed to a cheaper variety. It definitely makes a difference and is usually worthwhile to pay a higher price for a better-quality tool, especially if you will use it for the rest of your life, or at least for many years.

By this time in his life, Stanley was retired from business in his late sixties. That old man could still outwork me by far. The thirty-minute lunch break was like heaven. I would sit under a tree out of the sun and relish doing nothing. I would drink gallons of water and wolf down a sandwich. I remember closing my eyes, resting my head against a tree trunk, and trying to regain my strength for the next round. The next thing I knew, it was back to work until the end of the day. We stacked bales of hay in a barn, painted farm buildings, dug postholes for fences, and performed many other chores.

At the end of the workday, it was a Stanley Hill rule to clean the work site and pick up and clean our tools. He used to say, "The tools will take care of you if you take care of them." I learned that it is easier to start the next day's work when you don't have to clean the area first to get started on the job.

I slowly began to appreciate some simpler things in life that I had previously taken for granted. Things like cold water after hard hours of work. A good sandwich for lunch. Thick leather work gloves and well-made tools. Last, but certainly not least, a respect for the working-man who uses his hands every day, day in and day out, to bring home a paycheck to support a family.

For weeks, it seemed as if I were in a torture house. As the days went on, the work seemed less painful but just as strenuous. I got accustomed to the heat, which I had never thought would happen, and developed a deep suntan. A lot of the improvement was mental. As Stanley would say, "Get your head into the job." I found that things were made easier if I looked at the job as a challenge and avoided the thought "I'd rather be doing something else." I simply resigned myself to the situation.

Over time, I actually began enjoying the work. It seemed like a challenge every day to see what kind of work we could attack and then conquer. My "head got into it." It seemed that not only my body but also my mind and attitude had transformed. It was odd, but I seemed to feel stronger and to have more energy both physically and mentally.

Stanley seemed to relish hard work—the harder the better. He loved the satisfaction of building something along with the comradeship of hardworking men working toward a common goal as a team. At the end of the day, he frequently viewed what had been done and said, "Isn't that something, what we did today." I thought, "That really is something." That sort of pride in a job well done was an infectious attitude. It encouraged good work and loyalty. Some would call this "leadership by example." At the end of the summer, Stanley gave me the biggest compliment he could give. He told my parents, "Bruce is a good worker." This was very simply put, but coming from Stanley Hill, it was a huge compliment.

That summer of work had a big impact on me for the rest of my life. I realized that through hard work and perseverance, big things can be accomplished that initially seem out of reach and painful. I found that these life lessons could be applied to any endeavor, not only sports but learning algebra or chemistry as well as difficult medical or surgical situations. One of the key components was, as Stanley Hill would say, "Get your head into it": focus, and don't complain or quit just because a task is difficult. Above all complete the work with quality.

I also realized that quality control can be adapted to life for success. Virtues such as being generous, courteous, kind, obedient, hardworking, cheerful, thrifty, brave, loyal, and trustworthy are all examples of quality of a person's character. These examples that I had memorized as a Boy Scout became clear while I was working for Stanley Hill. The Hills were perfect examples of quality, character, and virtue.

After the summer ended, I came away with a great sense of accomplishment. Having been paid for hard work was new to me. It felt good to have my own money, and it gave me an appreciation for its judicious use. I didn't have to beg my parents for money to buy things, and I actually opened a bank account. I was grateful that my parents had forced me into the job against my will. At the time, I hated my parents for subjugating me to what I deemed a torture camp, but after about a month, my attitude changed completely. I realized that I had worked in the adult world and held my own. I knew that I had gained a great sense of maturity that I had subconsciously been striving for and that could have been accomplished only by hard work, pain, and suffering. I had the sense that somehow, I had proven myself as a young man and passed the test.

When I went back to school in the ninth grade, I tried out for wrestling and, to my great surprise, I made the varsity squad. I was able to defeat upperclassmen who had been in the sport longer than I had. I was able to do so in part because of the strength and endurance I had built up over the summer and the learned ability to persevere through pain and difficulty. The confidence it engendered in me was essential to my success, especially in a sport like wrestling.

When I was a young man, riding in the car with my grandfather Stanley Hill, he would point out with pride certain buildings along the Kansas City downtown skyline that he had helped build. He told stories about each building. With great pride, he would say, "I helped build Kansas City."

He not only helped build Kansas City, but he helped build his grandson into a responsible man.

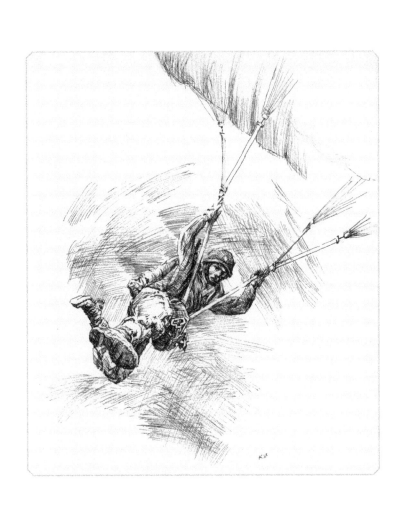

6.

Braveheart

A feeling of great anticipation gripped the group of airborne soldiers as they lined up on the airport runway to board the transport plane. Most of the men were making last-minute adjustments to their gear. There were thirty-five planes lined up in a row stretching down the runway, with lines of soldiers next to each plane. Many other planes carrying four divisions of airborne troops at other airfields were designated to rendezvous in the air over eastern France before entering enemy territory.

The September autumn air was cool and crisp. The hours before the dawn were dark with no moon. Wallace Graham, climbed into the C-47 transport airplane with his combat parachute and medical gear, joining other members of the 101st Airborne Division. He was an experienced field surgeon who had been ushered into World War II in June 1944 during the invasion of Normandy. During his duty in Normandy, he had suffered a leg wound from flying shrapnel, but he had recovered without taking any leave and felt well prepared for this new operation. His leg was still sore with mild pain, but he didn't let the discomfort slow him down. It was now the fall of 1944, and Operation Market Garden defined his division's objective: to take control of several key bridges in the Netherlands so that British forces could secure a gateway to drive armored and infantry divisions into Rotterdam and then into Germany. This was the largest airborne operation in the war since the Normandy invasion. It involved two American and two British airborne divisions. Wallace was confident while filing into position to board the plane. However, many of the paratroopers were mildly concerned about being placed under overall British command. Wallace had already been through D-Day, the battle for Carentan, and seen extensive combat throughout France.

Wallace's aircraft roared down the runway, and then abruptly lifted into the air. Within minutes, the other thirty-five planes of the first group had climbed into the pitch-black sky. After a short while, Wallace looked out the window and saw an armada of other planes coming together at the rendezvous point like an enormous flock of geese covering miles of air space. There were airborne troop-carrying transport planes as far as he could see. There were 1,438 planes carrying over 35,000 paratroopers. This sight gave him a thrill to see so much military might in one place directed for a single objective. He suddenly felt a sense of power and confidence at the awesome site. Wallace was grateful that the German air force, (Luftwaffe) had been relatively suppressed by this time in the war. However, he knew that the German antiaircraft guns were well intact and notoriously accurate.

Inside the plane it was quiet, out of the ordinary for the usual talkative and at times boisterous G.I.s. Nothing could be heard except for the steady drone of the plane's engines. So far, the flight had been smooth. Wallace took a sheet of paper from his pocket and reviewed his orders and objectives to set up a small field hospital after a strategic bridge was taken. He performed a last-minute check of his equipment. Over the steady pitch of the engines, the troopers began to hear the muffled crumps of exploding antiaircraft shells in the distance getting closer. After approximately forty minutes, the plane began to take heavy antiaircraft fire. Wallace thought they had now clearly crossed into enemy territory. Nearby explosions rocked the plane, and metal fragments pelted its thin hull. Wallace felt as if he were in a large tin can with gravel being thrown against it. The plane pitched in all directions, from side to side and then up and down. The concussions of the explosions jarred the aircraft and buffeted the men inside. Wallace looked around at the other paratroopers, some had their eyes closed as if they were asleep, but Wallace knew they weren't, while others stared stoically forward. All were silent. The antiaircraft flak they were taking was not that much different than what they had experienced during the Normandy jump at D-day

All of the soldiers knew that the Germans were excellent at all things military however, one thing they were particularly good at was their artillery. The most notorious of which was the German 88 mm cannon. This was initially designed as an antitank weapon. It could destroy any allied tank long before the tank could come into range. It was the most accurate of all cannons in WWII. Because of its range and accuracy, the Germans adapted it for an antiaircraft weapon. All allied soldiers were well aware of the "88's" capabilities and now they knew they were being shot at by this fearsome weapon.

The soldier next to Wallace had a rosery in his hand clutching it tightly. He saw another man give the sign of the cross over his chest. Suddenly Wallace felt the sensation of fear. He had experienced fear many times before as he knew every soldier in the plane had. He knew that experience and training was critical to control fear. He knew these soldiers were physically and mentally disciplined and would be able to manage it. Wallace realized everyone is afraid during combat and everyone deals with fear in their own way. In Wallace's point of view, it was "Mind over matter." He was just going to put it out of his mind, because he knew that if fear is unchecked it would destroy his ability to function and think properly. He also knew that to show fear is contagious to others, like a deadly virus. He took a deep breath and tried to relax. He focused his thoughts on the objectives of the mission. All of the soldiers in the plane had seen many of their friends die in combat. Wallace knew that many of the soldiers felt that they were not going to make it out of the war alive. He realized that with this attitude they could perform combat with more courage. However even with this fatalistic attitude the overriding feeling was that tomorrow I may be killed, but not today! Today is the enemy's day to die! They turned fear into aggression.

Looking around, Wallace could barely recognize his fellow soldiers because of the darkness and their facial camouflage paint. These men were the 101st and the 82nd airborne divisions. At this point in the war, they were experienced combat soldiers and were considered hardened veterans who had undergone intense nonstop battle for months. They were the elite of all allied combat soldiers. They were the tip of the spear to be thrown into the most difficult life and death situations. Wallace felt proud to be associated with such brave men. Being a surgeon, he was on average much older than most of the soldiers. Many were just out of their teenage years, but by now their maturity was far beyond their age. Wallace tried to keep his mind focused on the impending parachute drop and what he would have to do after hitting the ground.

Suddenly the plane was violently thrown to one side, flinging the occupants in all directions with some scrambling on the floor. He heard a loud screeching sound like metal being torn apart. Cold air gushed into the plane like a pressure tornado in your face at nearly two hundred miles per hour. Flurries of paper and debris were flying around the plane. Wallace looked down the inside of the plane and saw a large, ragged hole in the fuselage. The noise of the air rushing into the plane was deafening. There were already casualties. Several men lay on the floor of the airplane. Peering out the window, he noticed that one of the engines was on fire.

Little did Wallace know that from this day forward, he would have to use everything he had learned in his life to stay alive. The aircraft was losing altitude and began veering from left to right. The crippled plane broke formation with the other planes in the armada of hundreds. The jumpmaster signaled the men to hook onto their static line for the pending parachute jump as the red light turned on indicating prepare to jump. The men lined up next to the open side door as the wind from the gaping hole in the fuselage of the plane rushed in. They were all anxious and wanted out quickly. Wallace knew it was much too early for their objective, but he surmised correctly that they were about to crash. The men were being ushered out before the catastrophe. The green "jump" light came on, and the men quickly filed out the open door of the stricken plane, plunging into the darkness.

Just as Wallace jumped out, the plane tipped onto its side. One of the wings turned toward the ground and the other upward to the sky. This caused him to fall head over heels, out of control. He barely missed hitting one of the wings, avoiding certain instant death by inches. The cold wind hit his face like a hard slap as he flew through the air at over a hundred miles per hour. Wallace pulled his parachute ripcord but kept falling at an excessively rapid pace. Combat parachutes had a much faster rate of fall than regular civilian parachutes in order to get the soldier on the ground as quickly as possible; however, he felt that he was falling much too rapidly. Since he was still plummeting so swiftly, he thought his parachute had not opened. He looked skyward and found that the large green combat parachute was fully deployed. As he continued to hurtle downward, Wallace realized that he had packed too much gear, mainly surgical equipment, making his pack far too heavy. Urgently, he started to jettison gear to reduce his rate of descent while rapidly falling to the ground.

His heart quickened as he heard gunfire and saw red tracer bullets coming through the dark at him. The bright red tracers filled the air, coming from the ground in all directions. He knew that one out of every five shots was a tracer, which meant that a tremendous amount of fire was being leveled at the descending paratroops. He knew this meant German forces pervaded the area. He had the dread thought that he might land in the midst of deadly and determined enemy forces, which would probably result in his death or capture—most likely the former.

Suddenly his head was violently knocked backward, and blood flowed down his face. He quickly did a neurological check. He still knew his name, the date, and where he was. He could still move all his extremities. A bullet had grazed his nose and forehead and put a small hole in the front edge of his helmet.

Wallace temporarily felt lucky, but the earth was still approaching much too rapidly. Within a few seconds, he was going to hit the ground faster and harder than he had ever hit before. He tried to dispel any apprehension and to focus on properly completing the jump and his mission. He remembered his airborne training to slightly bend his knees to give his legs flexibility and then roll with the momentum. He braced himself for a hard landing.

With an abrupt jolt, he hit the ground hard, hearing an audible crack. At once, he felt excruciating low-back pain. He tumbled forward, becoming tangled in his parachute lines. He finally came to rest faceup, staring at the moonless, star-filled sky. No other parachutes or combat groups were in sight. He was alone and couldn't move his legs. There was movement and sensation to his arms, but any other movement caused intense back pain. Wallace realized that the fall may have resulted in a spinal cord injury with concurrent paralysis of his legs. He momentarily wondered where the other paratroops were, hoping they might be able to help. Had they all been killed or captured? He realized that many must have gone down with the plane. That thought quickly faded with the resumption of the severe back pain. He again attempted to move his legs, but to no avail.

He lay there and waited for dawn. He was afraid to yell for help for fear of Germans in the area. He was flat on his back in an open field of tall grass. The sky was dark and filled with stars. It reminded him of the pastures where he had grown up as a boy in Highland, Kansas. He thought of his wife, Velma, and two young children at home in Kansas City. Everything was silent, with no gunfire to be heard, which he thought was unusual. He remembered the Twenty-Third Psalm, which his father, JW, had taught him. He truly felt that he was in the valley of death. He prayed deeply in a soft voice to God for help.

After several hours, he began to regain sensation in his legs and some movement. His first sensation was tingling in his feet, as if someone were poking him with tiny needles. He thought he had broken his back and had undergone spinal trauma without severing the spinal cord. Otherwise, he would have remained paralyzed. He now became more optimistic because he was gaining better sensation and more movement in his legs. He carefully started to roll over in the grass and eventually got to all fours. He stayed in this position for some time until he got his bearings. Despite the significant back pain, he slowly made it to a standing position. He put his hands on his knees and stayed in this bent position for a while to steady himself. He slowly reached to untangled and unhook himself from his parachute with a great amount of effort and pain. He slung his rifle over his shoulder and discarded the rest of his gear. He thought, "I won't need any surgical equipment now." The sun had just risen over the horizon. He scanned the area and saw none of his comrades from the plane and no sign of the enemy. The landscape seemed to be idyllic, almost beautiful, flowered grass pastureland intermixed with tall, treed forests. It was strangely silent except for the occasional muffled artillery fire in the far distance. He took his map and compass out to determine his location. He knew he was behind enemy lines, so he started heading south toward the Allied area of control.

Each step brought excruciating back pain radiating down his legs. He walked with small steps to minimize the discomfort. He walked slowly, bent over to lessen the discomfort. He stopped periodically, taking a few deep breaths and then proceeding. He knew how to push himself through pain from his extensive athletic experiences in boxing and track as a young man. He knew he had to keep going to avoid the Germans. His body was screaming at him to stop and lie down. However, he refused to allow himself this luxury. He tried to avoid open fields and edged his way along forested areas to avoid detection. He stopped to brace himself against a tree to lessen the pain. He pushed his forehead hard against the trunk, nearly breaking the skin on his forehead to redirect the back pain and focus it to another area of the body. He pulled off a piece of bark and bit down hard on it in order to turn his thinking away from his injured back. Sweat poured down his face. He took a deep breath and vowed that he would use "mind over matter." He simply would not think about the pain. He decided against injecting himself with morphine, as it would impair his judgment and reduce his mobility. He would suck it up and keep moving one foot, then the next. He remembered a famous recent quotation from Winston Churchill: "If you are going through hell, keep going!"

He was determined to do just that, to keep going. He struggled with each step causing pain radiating down both legs. After each several hundred yards he would stop, rest, and reward himself with a swig of water from his canteen. He didn't dare sit down for fear of not being able to get up again. It was as if his mind was tricking his body into doing things it was refusing to do. This same start and stop trek went on for nearly half of the day. He had been walking for many hours, and it was now midafternoon.

During one of his rest stops, while leaning against a tree, he heard the faint sounds of muffled screams in the distance coming from a large barn. He put his canteen away and stealthily walked closer with rifle in hand. Wallace was now on high alert as he walked closer to the barn hearing the frantic screams of men, women, and children loader as he drew close. He noted wires extending from the barn out of sight toward enemy lines. He didn't know quite what to make of this, but he knew it wasn't good. Wallace pulled out his combat knife and cut the wires. He then lay in wait for the enemy to investigate. He hid behind a rock wall with large bushes on either side of him in a perfect ambush position. He knelt down, steadied his M1 rifle on the wall, and waited patiently. Several yards away from the barn, he sighted two German soldiers coming into view, walking toward one side of the barn. All the while hearing screaming people from the barn. He could tell by their insignias that they were from the Waffen-SS. These were the elite of the German army, known for their total loyalty to the Nazi Party and their fanatical bravery in combat. Wallace knew he could be in for a real fight. He silently took aim with his rifle, ready to fire as soon as the Germans moved to repair the wires. He took a deep breath and slowly exhaled. He focused his aim on the man nearest the barn. The gunsight of the rifle was pointed directly at the German's chest. His plan was to fire on one man, then quickly aim for the other, then look for any more who might come. His finger was gently touching the trigger of his rifle. He was single-minded in his thought. Everything in his life came down to this moment, and he was going to be ready.

The German soldiers walked around the barn looking toward the ground at the cut wires, oblivious to the screaming people. They stood and talked for a while, then turned and walked away. Wallace breathed a silent sigh of relief. He remained vigilant, keeping his rifle pointed in the same direction. He didn't know how many other Germans were out of sight or when or if any might return. With the impending combat, his adrenaline was high, and he nearly forgot about his pain. Wallace waited for nearly one hour with no obvious enemy activity. He then cautiously came out from behind the rock wall. In a crouched position with his rifle at the ready, he crept toward the barn. Again, his ears were assaulted by the panicked screams and sounds of people inside the barn pounding on the walls. As he came closer to the barn, he saw explosive charges deployed around the entire structure, ready to be triggered before the Germans left. Wallace found the door locked and barricaded from the outside. When he opened barricaded door, he found nearly one hundred French and Belgian citizens packed tightly inside. Many of the people inside had torn off their fingernails and cut their hands by frantically trying to tear down the wooden walls and door to escape death.

It was not clear why the two German soldiers had left. Possibly they were in a hurry to leave because of some other more important duty, or they had decided it was not worth their time and effort to repair the wires. They may have felt remorse at having to kill innocent civilians. Either way, it worked out well for Wallace and the people imprisoned in the barn. The civilians took care of Wallace, gave him food and shelter, and eventually took him back to the Allied lines.

Operation Market Garden was a large defeat for the allies. The paratroopers were dropped in the middle of and surrounded by two highly mechanized elite German armor divisions, as well as several other infantry divisions. The allies lost over 17,000 men killed or captured.

Wallace received the Croix de Guerre from France as well as a high-level medal from Belgium for valor. He also received the American Bronze Star and his second Purple Heart for having been wounded in combat. Later in his life, I asked him why he had risked his life with this act of rescue. Why hadn't he just bypassed the situation and moved on?

Why not avoid being drawn into high-risk combat, especially since he was outnumbered, wounded, alone, and in pain? He had so much to lose. He was married and had two children. He simply said in his usual straightforward manner, "It was my duty."

Wallace recovered from his injury fairly rapidly despite a compression and articular fractures of his back. He resumed his position with his unit. He was not to be deterred. However, his lower back was a continued problem for the rest of his life, eventually requiring surgery.

Wallace's first combat experience was at D-Day, the third day after the Normandy landing. The Twenty-Fourth Evacuation Medical Unit set up field treatment and surgical areas in a long hospital tent several miles off Omaha Beach, close to the front lines. He operated on critically injured soldiers for three straight days and nights without rest. The mobile hospital was built to handle five hundred patients. During this time, there were over two thousand patients. The least injured soldiers were placed just outside the tent because of lack of space. Wallace along with the other physicians slept in fox holes dug in the ground adjacent to the hospital tent. They were under constant artillery barrage as well as intermittent sniper fire making sleep difficult if not impossible. There were over ten physicians killed as well as several nurses in Wallace's medical unit during the war.

Wallace would triage patients prior to any surgery. He determined which soldiers were stable and could wait for treatment and which needed emergency lifesaving surgery. Some severely injured soldiers who were too badly injured for treatment to preserve life were moved to a different area and kept comfortable with morphine. All American casualties were assessed and treated first. Wallace then addressed the medical needs of German prisoners of war. Germans were kept in a separate area from Americans. After patient's surgical needs were met and their conditions stabilized, they were transported to England for follow-up care away from the combat zone.

Wallace had to muster all of his surgical knowledge to that point for his patients. He not only dealt with major abdominal surgeries but also performed cardiac and lung trauma surgical procedures. He carried out repairs to extensive bone fractures as well as any vascular repair. When a limb could not be saved, he performed amputation. Wallace had to deal with all surgical specialties in critical situations under fairly poor battlefield conditions. It is hard to fathom what he had to go through, attending to surgical needs day and night for days on end with little or no sleep. In my experience as a physician, it is exhausting to perform a complicated surgery for eight hours. His determination, focus, strength, and stamina were surely extraordinary. His previous mental and physical preparation must have carried him through.

At one point, a German artillery shell fell close to the hospital which resulted in a tremendous explosion. Everyone felt the violent concussion of the blast throughout the large canvas tent. Some of the medical staff lost their footing and fell. Some of the patients were knocked out of their beds. Intravenous poles fell breaking the glass bottles holding the contained fluid and plasma. Shrapnel came flying through the tent. One doctor was killed, and a nurse was severely wounded. Wallace was in the middle of a large abdominal surgery when felt a hard hit and searing pain to his upper thigh. He suddenly rocked forward with the concussion nearly falling into the patients open abdominal cavity. He caught himself from falling and called to the orderly to check the extent of his leg injury. The orderly came over and knelt down next to Wallace's bloody leg to investigate. Wallace could feel fluid running down his leg filling his shoes which he realized was probably blood.

"Sir, you have a hole in your leg, and there's a lot of bleeding." Wallace told the corpsman "Put a compression dressing on and tape it tightly so I can finish this operation!". The corpsman took Wallace's pants off and applied the dressing while Wallace continued with the surgery. The corpsman did an excellent job of dressing the wound, and the bleeding stopped. After closing the patient's wound, Wallace attended to his own injury. The shrapnel was removed from Wallace's leg under a local anesthetic by another surgeon. However, the anesthetic didn't work as well as hoped because of the size of the wound. After cleaning and bandaging the wound Wallace went back to work within the hour. Despite significant discomfort, he never took pain medication. He continued performing surgery and attending to his patients. He felt that there was no critical structural injury to his leg, and the only limiting factors were pain and discomfort. He knew he could get through the pain with mental discipline and focusing on the task he had at hand. He would commonly say, "Mind over matter." He never took off for recuperation since his skill and medical expertise were sorely needed. He received the first of his two Purple Heart medals for this combat injury.

Several days later, a seriously injured eighteen-year-old soldier was admitted. The young soldier first saw an army nurse named Betty. When she opened his shirt, her heart dropped, and she felt slightly nauseated by what she saw. She knew immediately that the injury was fatal. The soldier asked her, "Am I going to be all right?" Betty gently smiled, looked into his eyes and said, "You're going to be just fine." She stroked his hair and kissed him on the forehead, as he smiled at her. Betty's hands seemed to be a gift from God calming the injured young man. They then talked for a while as she held his hand. The soldier thanked Betty for her kindness. He was from a farm outside Appleton, Wisconsin. Betty was from Milwaukee, not far from the young soldier's home. The soldier spoke of his home, family, and places that they were both familiar with. His voice gradually became slower and softer. He then closed his eyes. Fifteen minutes later, he died. Betty pulled the cotton sheet over his head and began sobbing. Despite having seen death before, she felt a connection with the young soldier and was overwhelmed. She had known it was a fatal injury the moment she had seen his wound, but she had temporarily put it out of her mind. The best she could do for the young man was to give him as much comfort as she could.

Wallace saw Betty crying with her face in her hands as she sat beside the young soldier's body, which was hidden from view by the cotton sheet. He walked over and gently put his arm around her. They slowly walked outside. Betty's head was down, and she was still sobbing. He tried to console her. He told her what an excellent nurse she was and how good a job she was doing. He told her that her work in the hospital was essential to the entire combat medical team. He calmly and with great empathy told her that he felt the same way. "However," he said, "We must give these soldiers hope, no matter what their condition. We can never cry in front of these young men. This would be bad for morale and would diminish their confidence in us. We can cry later, but for now, we have a lot of work to do. We must do our duty." Betty agreed and thanked Wallace for his understanding. They slowly walked back into the combat hospital and resumed work.

Death was everywhere, previous healthy young men with bright futures were stacked up like a wood pile in long lines just beyond the landing point at Omaha beach. Some were buried in quickly constructed cemeteries there, while others were shipped home. Americans, British, Canadiens, Germans, Civilians, including women and children all with life stories and families who loved them, now gone. Dead farm animals were everywhere. The stench of death and decay pervaded the area for miles. The scene of the Normandy landing was pure horror. Wallace quickly discovered you didn't want to look at the dead very long. It would send your thoughts questioning who this handsome young man was, what was he like, the anguish and grief his family must endure. If left unchecked ultimately these thoughts devolved into questions, "Why are we doing this? Why must there be war? Has the world gone mad?" Wallace realized that he had to control his thoughts. If one let this continue, depression and deep despair would follow. Just like fear, depression is contagious and could destroy the morale of everyone resulting in a state of hopelessness and the inability to perform what their job required. Soldiers and medical staff were vulnerable because of the constant stress, and lack of sleep. Just as control of fear is necessary, these thoughts had to be suppressed which required discipline of one's mind. As a commanding officer and chief surgeon, he knew he had to be an example of courage and positive thinking even though surrounded by death, and destruction. He knew everyone there was in the same boat having the same thoughts he was. He was impressed with the mental fortitude of his staff as well as the soldiers. However, he didn't think any less of soldiers suffering from "battle fatigue," "shell shock," or what is now called post-traumatic stress syndrome, (PTSD).

Wallace always amazed me with the breadth of his knowledge across all surgical specialties. He had gained this expertise and experience by necessity as a combat surgeon under dire circumstances. The emotional and mental burden of his duties in combat must have been enormous. Wallace had dealt with trauma during his training, but war was different. The numbers of complicated, severe cases were staggering, day in and day out, with no respite.

Wallace was born in Highland, Kansas, the second son of JW and Elizabeth Graham. The family later moved to Kansas City, where they lived in a house at Fifty-Fifth Street and Troost Avenue. Wallace had a fairly typical boyhood. He loved Boy Scouts and went on to become an Eagle Scout. He enjoyed camping and excelled in earning merit badges. He developed a keen interest in nature, including horticulture and all kinds of animals. As a Boy Scout, he helped hold line ropes for crowd control at the opening dedication of the World War I Liberty Memorial in Kansas City in 1926.

Wallace recalled seeing Jack Dempsey fight in an exhibition match in Kansas City when he was a boy. This sparked his interest in the sport. He joined a local boxing club at a young age and received good and fortunately intelligent coaching. The coach of the team was an old ex-boxer whom everyone called "Pappy." The name came from the father of the cartoon character Popeye. The old coach was thick and muscular with a scarred face and displaced nose. He was kind and considerate with his young fighters but knew when to be tough and push them to their limit. Pappy knew how to grow a young boxer's confidence and skill by not putting the novice in the ring with a more experienced fighter until he was ready. Pappy instructed the young men on his team to be polite and to be gentlemen outside the ring. He told his young men to always address an adult or someone in authority as "sir" or "ma'am" to show respect.

Wallace showed a unique ability for boxing and advanced rapidly. His parents were neutral regarding his new sport and told him to be careful. His mother never witnessed any of his fights, and his father, JW, went to matches only later in Wallace's career. Under Pappy's guidance, Wallace began boxing against young men of his own size and ability, but he gradually improved until he was able to beat young men who were much more experienced and larger than he without difficulty. Wallace enjoyed the competition of fighting men from other boxing clubs and the camaraderie of his teammates. He felt that he was with a band of brothers that was unique among others. Pappy became a role model for young Wallace, showing him the basics of leadership and the development of young men.

Pappy said that he had never seen anyone train harder than Wallace Graham, who trained longer and harder than any of the other fighters. Wallace became an inspiration for his teammates to perform better than they normally would have. The team as a whole began winning championships because of the leadership not only from the coach but from their team captain, Wallace. It amazed many people that Wallace could be such a "savage" in the ring when he was a perfect gentleman and nice guy out of the ring.

After training in the boxing ring, he would run two to three miles and then finish up at the gym. Every morning after waking up, he would perform calisthenics, go for a quick run, and then lift weights. He did this before weight training was later popularized. He tried to develop every part of his body, upper and lower. He always said he didn't want any weak links in the chain that could cause an unexpected defeat. He performed this rigorous routine daily throughout his early life, from junior high school through college.

Wallace would say that he always wanted to "finish strong." His goal was to always be in better condition than any of his opponents. His philosophy was to come out fast, put on continuous pressure, and then turn up the intensity in the last round, when even the most accomplished boxers were weakening. Wallace would say there is nothing so demoralizing as to fight an opponent who comes at you nonstop with the same energy or more than at the beginning of the fight.

Wallace had enormous amounts of energy. I think he realized at an early age that unbounded energy, if not channeled in the correct direction, can lead to trouble in life. He witnessed the results of this in his older brother, John, who also had tremendous amounts of energy but was undisciplined and consequently repeatedly got into trouble.

Wallace was known for his excellent left jab, which he was able to use as a knockout punch even though he was right-handed. This technique was uncommon but very effective. He became the Golden Gloves champion of Kansas City several times. While at the University of Missouri, he became the Big 8 champion. He missed being on the U.S. Olympic team on a split-decision loss in a bout at Madison Square Garden in New York City.

In high school, Wallace got into a fight with a very tough guy named Mibbs Golding. Mibbs was much bigger than Wallace and a star on the football team. Wallace thought he was an arrogant bully. He had seen Mibbs push people around who were smaller than he and laugh at their reluctance or inability to do anything about it. Wallace's experience with bullies was that they were usually cowards beneath their bravado and tough exterior. When confronted and called out, the bully would usually shrink away. But this was not the case with Mibbs. Mibbs rushed Wallace in an attempt to tackle him. Wallace pivoted, sidestepped, hit him with a right hook that broke Mibbs's nose, and then followed with a left and a second right to the bloody face, nearly knocking down this bull of a man. Most people would have been on the ground and out with the combination of hits to the head. Wallace was surprised that Mibbs was still on his feet. He knew then that he was in for a real fight. Then a big right-hand swing seemingly from nowhere hit Wallace, bloodying his nose and mouth. This unseen hit left Wallace slightly dazed and temporarily "seeing stars." He peppered his opponent's head with punches but felt as if he were punching a rock. The fight drew a large crowd, which surrounded the two fighters. The cheering and yelling were nearly deafening. Wallace hit Mibbs's head ten times more often than Mibbs hit him; however, just one hit from this brute was so hard that it caused significant pain and rattled Wallace's brain. The fight seemed as if it would never end, and both were tired and bloody but refused to give in. The altercation slowly wound down to the point that the two fighters were facing one another with their fists up.

During a short lull, Mibbs cracked a smile and said, "Graham, you're all right." Both young men put their hands down. Afterward, they became the best of friends and remained close through their lives. Mibbs's personality seemed to change after the fight to that of a well-behaved, nice guy. Wallace always thought the fight had done him good.

Later in life, when Wallace was in medical school, his roommate Ken Fujii came in bruised and disheveled from a date with his girlfriend. He told Wallace that three men had harassed and beaten him and his girlfriend because of his Asian appearance. Ken Fujii was an American with Japanese parents who had grown up in Hawaii. Wallace looked at his good friend and was furious but silent. He asked Ken if he could find them now. Ken said he thought he could. Wallace got up and said, "Let's go find them."

As they walked down the street, two old Bible verses came to Wallace that his father occasionally quoted, one from the New and one from the Old Testament: "Blessed is the man who bears his brother's burdens for righteousness' sake." "I will execute terrible vengeance upon them with wrathful rebukes for what they have done. Then they will know that I am the Lord when I lay my vengeance upon them." Wallace felt that he was being used by the Holy Spirit as an instrument of God's judgment.

JW may have taken exception to this interpretation; however, he had always told Wallace to stick up for his friends and do the right thing because the rest didn't matter. Wallace knew from extensive past experience that he should never become angry or emotional going into a fight. He always kept his cool, and tonight was no exception. He was well aware that anger expends too much energy, leading to bad mistakes. One of his old strategies in boxing was to make his opponent angry and let him flail away and expend his energy. Then Wallace would go in for the kill.

After walking several blocks, Ken and Wallace stopped in front of an all-night diner. Ken pointed to three men sitting at a table. "There they are. That's them."

Wallace analyzed the situation quickly. He had never fought three men at once before; however, from what they had done to his friend, he knew they must be cowards. He would also have the element of surprise in his favor. At twenty-four years old, Wallace was six feet tall, weighed 195 pounds, and was in the prime of his physical condition. He realized he would have to take one of the three out of the equation immediately and seriously damage a second; then he could easily dispatch the third.

Wallace told Ken, "Wait here." He calmly strolled into the diner and up to the three thugs. He positioned himself perfectly—at a little less than arm's distance—for an impending strike. He nonchalantly placed one foot in front of the other so that he could deliver a punch with his entire body or easily step back in defense. With a calm half smile, he asked the three why they had abused Ken and his girlfriend earlier that evening. Wallace didn't like their response, and with a tremendously powerful, lightning-fast left jab, he hit one man in the jaw. He felt the jaw fracture and immediately deform from the blow. The other two began to rise, but Wallace turned quickly and delivered a devastating right to the nose of one, causing blood to spurt and immediately sending the man crumpling to the floor. Just as planned, Wallace grabbed the third and last man by the neck and shoulder and dragged him outside. He proceeded to beat the man to the ground, leaving him in a fetal position, groaning in pain.

Ken Fujii's mouth was open in shock. He couldn't believe what he had just witnessed. He knew Wallace as a very friendly person who was a dedicated medical student like him. He knew Wallace had been a boxer but had no idea what his roommate was capable of. They casually walked back to their apartment, picking up some jelly doughnuts on the way.

Wallace was a highly skilled, strong, and confident fighter. He would fight outside the ring only when justified or in dire circumstances. He viewed this ability as a tool to be used only in extreme situations. He never let his physical powers define him and never bragged about his abilities. However, he was definitely not one to trifle with.

In the 1930s, fistfights were much more common than they are in the present time. They were viewed as a fair way for men to settle things. Unfortunately, guns are frequently present nowadays, and fighting can lead to deadly consequences.

Ken and Wallace remained lifelong friends and kept in close touch. Years later, when Ken's son attended Creighton University, instead of flying back to Hawaii, he and several friends from Hawaii would stay at our house in Kansas City during school breaks. For many years, Wallace received boxes of orchids and other Hawaiian flowers every Christmas. Ken's children and their friends from Hawaii remain close family friends.

After high school, Wallace went to the University of Missouri for a year and focused mainly on sports. He later transferred to Central Missouri State (CMS) University after becoming more serious about his future. CMS was a smaller school with smaller class sizes, and Wallace thought he might receive more individual attention from his professors there. After his transfer, as he was pre-med, his goal became academic excellence. He shifted all his effort and energy from boxing to making top grades in school. He realized that this was a difficult road, and admission to medical school would be a great challenge. He studied long and hard. When he felt that he was struggling in a class, he obtained a tutor with the help of his father so that he could get an A. One key component to his success was that he always tried to develop a personal relationship with his professors. This was something he could do better at CMS with the smaller number of students in each class. He frequently spoke with his professors, telling them of his goals. It was hard not to like Wallace. He had an outgoing, self-assured personality. He was polite and gave great respect to authority, even though at times it might seem unjustified. Like many of his family members, he had a sunny and optimistic disposition and an easy, confident smile. He had a broad-shouldered athletic build. He seemed to have a magnetic presence when entering a room. Wallace made a point of remembering names and inquiring about other people's lives and families. He truly liked to be with people, and most people liked to be around him. His senior year at CMS, he was voted most popular man for the school yearbook.

Wallace was accepted to Creighton University Medical School in Omaha, Nebraska. During this time, he maintained a long-term relationship with Velma Hill, whom he had known since grade school. She was working as a surgical nurse in Kansas City while Wallace was in medical school. After he completed medical school, Wallace and Velma got married.

Wallace did an internship and surgical residency at General Hospital in Kansas City. In true form, he wanted to be the best surgeon possible and maximally prepared prior to entering private practice. He discussed this with his father, JW, and they agreed that Wallace would travel to Europe for further postgraduate training. At the time, Europe was the worldwide pinnacle of medical knowledge, especially in surgical technique. This was during the Great Depression, and money was tight. However, JW agreed to pay for Wallace and Velma to spend two years in Europe so Wallace could receive advanced instruction. This placed a great financial strain on JW, but it was well worth it to help his son. JW had to extend his office hours into the night, sometimes to ten or eleven p.m., to pay for Wallace's expenses.

Wallace and Velma spent time in Vienna, Austria; Budapest, Hungary; Germany; and Edinburgh, Scotland. This was a very special time for the couple, newly married and living in various foreign countries. Wallace especially loved Austria and Germany. He became fluent in German and was so adept in the language that he was even able to detect the accents of German dialects from different areas of the country.

Years prior to World War II, Wallace had joined the army after being a member of the ROTC in college. Before his deployment to Europe, he trained to be in the best possible physical condition. He began preparing himself as if going into the fight of his life. He lifted weights, ran, and even sparred with local boxers. He trained with different types of handguns and rifles so that he would know how to fire them proficiently if needed. JW was an expert marksman, especially with a pistol, and Wallace worked extensively with his father with this weapon. Wallace learned to fly and to drive any type of vehicle so that if he were captured and escaped, he would be prepared. He brushed up on all surgical procedures, especially trauma of all kinds. By the time he returned to Europe, he was mentally, physically, and emotionally prepared for war. From June 1944 until the end of the war in May 1945, Wallace was in nearly every major battle in Northern Europe—Normandy, Market

Garden, Battle of the Bulge, and Bastogne, among many others. He saw action in France, Belgium, Holland, and Germany.

Wallace's unit was entering a town in eastern France that they thought had been evacuated by the Germans except for a few scattered snipers. Wallace and his team were looking for a building where they could set up a frontline hospital. Wallace's sergeant, Sergeant Gorsky, was ordered to clear the building of any Germans prior to setting up the combat hospital. Gorsky was from Cicero, Illinois, outside Chicago. He was loyal and an excellent combat soldier. Wallace said he was one of the toughest men he ever knew, and coming from Wallace, that was saying a lot. Gorsky took his platoon into the building, after which Wallace heard extensive gunfire and then an explosion from a grenade. He could tell that it was an American grenade from the sound. Then all was silent. Gorsky and his men came out of the building and told Wallace that three German SS troopers on the third floor had been "taken care of." The SS was a fanatical branch of the Nazi military that frequently fought to the death. They showed little mercy and took few prisoners.

When Wallace looked around the building, he saw broken glass and shattered cement everywhere. Spent bullet shells casings were scattered on the floor from previous firefights. Wallace climbed the stairs to the third floor, where he found the three German soldiers on the floor, presumably dead. He slowly walked around the room. While looking out the nearby window, he heard movement behind him. Wallace quickly turned and saw one of the German soldiers lunging at him with a large knife. With a rapid and powerful reflex learned long ago during his boxing days, Wallace landed a hard-left jab to the German soldier's jaw. The German immediately crumpled to the floor. The action happened so quickly that Wallace was unable to grab his pistol. Wallace placed him in an arm bar wrestling hold and put him to the floor. He told him in German to surrender and he would attend to any injury he had. All the while the German was struggling to get away. The German said he would never surrender and cussed at Wallace in German. As Wallace and the German were scuffling on the floor, Sergeant Gorsky walked in, grabbed the German, and threw him out the nearby window. Gorsky looked out the window and saw the lifeless body of the German three stories below in the street. Two American soldiers were there, pointing their guns and staring at the now dead SS officer. Gorsky turned around and addressed his commanding officer: "Major, you have no business fighting this German and trying to talk sense into him. The situation is too dangerous, and anything can happen in hand-to-hand combat!" Wallace knew Gorsky was right and thanked him for his help.

By March 1945, the Allies had crossed the Rhine River into Germany. The Russians were pushing in from the east, and the Allies had nearly taken Italy from the south. The German army continued to fight valiantly. Wallace and three others, including Sergeant Gorsky, were riding in a jeep in Cologne, Germany, when they were suddenly hit by a German 88 cannon shell that cut the jeep in two, flinging the occupants in all directions. Luckily the explosive charge of the shell was a "dud," and it did not explode. However, they knew that the charge sometimes detonated later in such cases. They all got to their feet and ran in all directions as fast as they could.

Wallace sprinted nearly half a mile, something he had been accustomed to in his school days on the track team. He eventually slowed to a walk to regain his breath. He turned a corner around a building where he came face-to-face with a pistol to his head. Holding the gun was a German officer, who told him in German not to move. Wallace immediately raised his hands and with a small, courteous smile said, "Good morning," in perfect German. This took the German officer completely off guard. Wallace could tell that the officer had a Bavarian accent. Wallace began to speak calmly and confidently, saying that he had been to Bavaria many times and loved the people and the area. The German let him continue talking, becoming somewhat less alarmed because of Wallace's relaxed attitude, easy smile, and perfect command of the German language. Wallace went on to say that he admired and respected the courage of the German soldiers, that they were the best soldiers in the world, and he knew they were good people. He related that he was part German on his mother's side. He told the officer that the war was nearly over, and it was useless to shed more blood of such brave soldiers needlessly. Wallace said that the German officer and his troops would be given respect, food, shelter, and returned to their homes, after the war if he and his soldiers would surrender to him.

Wallace told the officer, "If you are captured by the Russians, they will kill all of you. As an officer myself, I will ensure the safety of you and your men."

Wallace presented this proposition calmly, matter-of-factly, and convincingly. He showed great respect to the German, as one officer to another. Wallace felt that he could make a connection with this veteran soldier, who had seen years of deadly combat. In a strange way, he felt as if he actually liked the man. Wallace could tell that the tension in the officer's face had dramatically decreased. Wallace knew that the German officer could have and probably should have killed him. So he knew that the German officer was thinking about Wallace's proposition.

The German officer stared intently into Wallace's eyes for a long time while in deep thought, all the while pointing his pistol at Wallace's head. He then abruptly turned the gun around by its barrel and handed it to Wallace. It must have been quite a sight to see Major Wallace Graham with the pistol behind eighty-five German soldiers marching in unison back into the American camp. There they were disarmed, given food, and processed as prisoners of war.

The German officer asked permission to address his men before being taken away, and it was granted. He stepped up onto a wooden box in front of his battle-hardened veterans, who had seen heavy combat for over five years. His men came to attention.

The officer said, "It's been a long war, and you have fought bravely and proudly for your country. You are a special group. We have formed a bond with one another that exists only in combat among brothers. We have seen dire moments. I am proud to have served with each and every one of you. You all deserve long and happy lives with peace." With just these few words, the soldiers were all emotionally moved, and some cried. Wallace had the feeling that those words could be applied to his own comrades in his unit. What Wallace and his military unit had been through in the war and the emotional bonds they had formed were similar to what the German officer had expressed. He felt a unique and surprising connection to the German officer. Afterward, Wallace shook hands with him and talked more about Bavaria. Then they both came to attention and saluted each other before Wallace wished the German good luck.

Later that month, Wallace's unit was involved in liberating Bergen-Belsen, a German concentration camp. He described huge mounds of starved corpses. The smell of burning flesh was present for miles because of the continual use of the crematoriums there. Many of the prisoners died after eating too much food too quickly given to them by the GIs. The Twenty-Fourth Evacuation Unit set up a hospital tent and attended to the starved and debilitated victims just outside the concentration camp. Many were given intravenous fluids and small amounts of liquid food gradually. The German people in the surrounding towns were transported to the death camp to view what their government had done under Nazi rule. They were all shocked and appalled as they were escorted through the horror-filled camp. Wallace knew that the Germans were inherently good people. However, they had been taken over by a small minority of extremists. Through control of the press and propaganda, the entire nation had become deluded.

Wallace and most of the GIs knew there was a great difference between the Wehrmacht, or regular German army, and the SS, who managed the death camps and committed most of the atrocities. The SS were fanatical Nazis, while the German army was made up of patriotic German men with no political convictions related to the Nazi Party.

Toward the end of the war, the German army was running out of fighting men, so in desperation, it enlisted young boys and older men into service. A fifteen-year-old German boy named Claus was brought into the hospital with an American bayonet in his chest. The initial assessment was that the boy did not have long to live, and he was put quietly aside so that the surgeons could address other men who could be saved. After all of the injured patients had been taken care of, they looked over at the young German, who amazingly was still alive. When Claus's position had been overrun, he had been stabbed in the chest by a GI. The GI had not been able to get the bayonet out since it was stuck in Claus's sternum (chest bone), so the GI had simply unclipped the bayonet and moved on. Wallace walked toward the boy and noted that he was trembling with fear and had tears in his eyes. Wallace was again shocked that his vital signs were normal. Wallace placed a blanket around him and spoke softly to him in German, reassuring him that he was going to be just fine and would be well cared for. The boy felt better after talking to Wallace and being shown some compassion. Claus was taken to surgery; however, little needed to be done. The bayonet had missed the heart by a few inches and gone between the ascending aorta and the vena cava, missing all vital structures. The bayonet was removed, and Claus recovered quickly.

Wallace took Claus under his wing and trained him to be his personal orderly. The boy seemed to revel in this new job. Wallace taught him how to take vital signs, perform dressing changes, and clean infected wounds. Claus was able to free up the nursing staff and corpsmen for other, more pressing duties. He was especially beneficial in helping care for wounded German prisoners of war. Wallace could see that Claus had real talent and was impressed with his intelligence and care for his work. Wallace began teaching him English, which he picked up quickly.

Eventually Claus was sent to a prisoner-of-war camp in the state of Maine. He actually liked the camp since the food was far better than what he had gotten in the previous four years of war. The scenery was beautiful, and the Americans treated Claus well. He liked the Americans' open, easy manner, so different from the cold, rigid demeanor that he had been accustomed to in Nazi Germany. Wallace kept in contact with him. After the war, Claus stayed in the United States since all of his family back in Germany had been killed. Wallace brought him to Washington, D.C., where Velma taught him how to drive a car. With Wallace's help, he went to school and did extremely well. He eventually went to medical school and became an orthopedic surgeon in Maine. He married an American and had two sons. Dr. Claus Koch and Wallace stayed in contact over the years.

At the end of the war, Wallace received orders to go to Potsdam, Germany, for a new assignment. He had no idea what this would entail. He thought he might be transferred to Japan for further combat surgery. He had recently been promoted from major to colonel. He was accompanied by several high-ranking staff officers, which he thought unusual, but he didn't ask questions since he would know soon enough.

After arriving in Potsdam, a suburb of Berlin, he was brought to a nondescript concrete building. Two soldiers guarding the entrance of the building came to attention, saluted, and then opened the door. They accompanied Wallace down a long concrete hallway to a room with a single desk and a wooden armchair in front of it. There was an American flag and a general officer's flag on each side behind the desk. The room was stark and otherwise bare, although it had a window on each side. The room seemed to echo as Wallace walked toward the desk. Behind it sat General Harry Vaughn, a two-star general who was the military attaché to the president of the United States. Wallace came to attention and saluted. Vaughn told him to be at ease and to have a seat. After a few informal questions, Vaughn leaned forward and said, "Colonel Graham, how would you like to be the personal physician to the president of the United States?"

Wallace was shocked. After regaining his composure, he told Vaughn that he was flattered and honored, but he would have to decline. He said that he did not wish to take care of just one person, and he wanted to return to Kansas City to practice medicine with his father. It had been a long war, and he wished to go home. On that note, he thanked Vaughn, got up from his chair, saluted, walked back down the long concrete hallway, and returned to his quarters.

Early the next morning, he was again summoned to General Vaughn's office. He walked in and sat down in the same chair. Vaughn leaned over in a serious, no-nonsense manner, looked straight into Wallace's eyes, and said, "Colonel Graham, I don't think you realize that you are in the United States Army, and you will do what you are told! You will follow the orders of the president! However, if you wish to treat more people besides the president, we can arrange this. You will also be chief of the surgical staff at Walter Reed Army Medical Center. You can pick whomever you wish to assist you. You will see the president daily and any White House staff members that may need your assistance."

Wallace said, "That will be fine, sir. Thank you, sir." He stood up, saluted, and walked out of the room.

He first met Harry Truman during the Potsdam Conference. The president shook his hand and with a big smile said, "I know your father well; he is a fine man and a good doctor."

Wallace had excellent medical training and was a highly decorated war hero. His reputation in the military and in medicine was excellent. He and the president hit it off right away. Two days later, he had dinner with Truman, Vaughn, and Winston Churchill. This was the first of several meetings that the four men would have.

The purpose of the Potsdam Conference was to decide how the Allies would manage postwar Germany and Japan. It was at this conference that Truman told Stalin of America's new devastating weapon (the atomic bomb) that would probably lead to Japan's surrender after its use. Wallace saw Stalin at the conference and was shocked at how small in stature he was. Wallace talked to Stalin's medical team about the use of a new drug, penicillin, to fight infection. They were eager to obtain shipments of the drug to the Soviet Union.

During the two-week conference, Wallace and Sergeant Gorsky drove into Berlin. The city was completely devastated by war. Most buildings were in ruins, and fires still smoldered. The Russian army was still roaming the city and looting. Germany had officially surrendered less than two months before. What dramatically caught their attention as they drove in was seeing many dead German men hanging by their necks from streetlights. A few wore German army uniforms; however, most did not. All of the victims showed clear evidence of extreme torture. It was not known why the hanged men had been killed long after the surrender. Possibly they had died while attempting to protect their families or to prevent looting of their homes by the Russians, or possibly they had taken the brunt of Russian revenge for the atrocities inflicted on Russia by Germany.

During a lull in the conference, Sergeant Gorsky and Wallace again drove into Berlin to visit the famed Berlin Museum of Art, which held many world-famous works of art. Many had been taken from France and Holland, among other countries, by the Nazis. They witnessed Russian soldiers throwing priceless works of art out the windows. Some paintings were torn by bayonets and destroyed. Gorsky and Wallace tried to stop the destruction but were scoffed at and brushed aside. They found the ranking officer of the Russian soldiers, but he didn't seem to care. The Russian officer and Gorsky both knew rudimentary Polish and thus were able to communicate.

Then Wallace offered the Russian officer a deal. Wallace would trade a German Luger pistol for the Russian's Red Army officer pistol on the condition that he would stop his troops from further looting the museum. This offer was gladly accepted because German Luger pistols were highly valued and felt to be the best sidearms in the world. The Russian lived up to his side of the bargain and cleared his men out of the building. The soldiers were likely uneducated peasants who couldn't appreciate the art and didn't comprehend its value. Wallace couldn't help noticing that many of the Russian soldiers appeared to be Mongols from eastern Siberia and Central Asia.

As Wallace and Gorsky walked down the street by the museum, they noted several paintings still in their frames, half buried in rubble. Wallace removed the broken bricks and cement lying over the paintings. He took the paintings carefully out of their frames, gently dusted them off, and put them all in the jeep. The paintings were later identified as works of art by Rembrandt and other famous artists. They were all sent intact to the United States and are now on display at several locations in America.

Wallace and Sergeant Gorsky then drove over to the bunker where Hitler had spent his last days. They took their time and investigated the entire underground structure. The place was in a shambles. It was an extensive underground complex. Obviously, the Russians had been there several times before, but they probably had no idea what to look for. Papers, files, and books were scattered everywhere. All of the furniture was overturned and broken. There were several floors to the underground installation and many tunnels extending to endless rooms. The two Americans gathered what appeared to be interesting and important items and placed them in the jeep along with the artwork. One of the large black hardcover folders that they retrieved turned out to be the last will and testament of Adolf Hitler. Wallace gave the book to his superior officer, General Vaughn, who subsequently gave it to the president. The book is now in the Library of Congress.

Wallace developed a unique relationship with Truman, not just as the president's doctor but as his trusted confidant and adviser. Wallace's office was in the west wing of the White House, quite close to the oval office of the president. Wallace went along on diplomatic missions to other countries when Truman wished to get his take on international situations along with the opinions of envoys from the military and Department of State. The president trusted Wallace's commonsense judgment and valued his opinion as a non–career Washington diplomat.

After World War II, most industrialized nations were in shambles, while the Third World was far behind in medical advancements. The United States was fairly unaffected by the devastation inflicted on the rest of the world by the war. Wallace was sent to many countries to treat and operate on ailing heads of state. While in the White House, he was promoted to a two-star general, or major general.

Saudi Arabia had recently become united under one ruler, King Ibn Saud, after extensive warfare, eventually uniting all of the different tribal fiefdoms of the Arabian Peninsula. It was known to have vast oil fields that were not yet developed. The Arabian kingdom was very suspicious of outsiders, especially non-Muslims. The United States had made overtures to the king for diplomatic relations, only to be rebuffed.

Quite suddenly, the kingdom sent word to the U.S. State Department that King Ibn Saud, ruler and namesake of the country, was ill and would entertain any medical help the United States could send. Truman knew exactly whom to call. Wallace's mission was to treat the king and attempt to establish diplomatic and business relations with Arabia.

An entire military hospital was built by the U.S. Army Corps of Engineers and Medical Corps and set up with all specialties and advanced equipment available. This was an enormous accomplishment. The industrial capability and military might of the United States were unleashed to the maximum extent to establish a state-of-the-art hospital in a fairly backward and primitive setting within three weeks.

Shortly after arriving, Wallace, who was the head of the medical mission, was invited to a state dinner with the king and the royal family. This was a rare and great honor. The dinner was held in a huge tent with numerous oriental and Persian rugs on the ground. Everyone sat on the ground around a large, low table. They were served all of the delicacies of the country, including lamb and camel heart. Large platters with metal handles on each side were brought out, carried by two servants, one on each side. A small mountain of food was heaped on each large bronze platter.

Wallace was given the most treasured delicacy, a large bowl of soup. He noted something round floating in the soup. He touched the floating object with his spoon. It rolled around and appeared to be an eyeball with a blue iris. He had the feeling that his intended meal was looking at him. He asked politely what type of soup this was. His hosts said it was the most special part of the meal. In Saudi culture, it was an insult to your host if you did not eat all that was given to you. Wallace knew this, so he calmly placed the sheep's eye in his mouth. It popped, and Wallace swallowed it with a smile. He could discern the very salty, thick, gelatin-like vitreous humor of the eyeball. His hosts were watching, and all smiled with approval.

Wallace performed an initial physical examination on the king. The king proudly pointed out each of his scars from bullet and knife wounds. He told the story of each old wound and how he had eventually vanquished his adversary, with descriptions of his enemy's demise. The king was obviously old, but his body was made of hard, sinewy muscle from a long life of strenuous hardship and warfare. Wallace realized that Saudi culture was very traditional, almost medieval in certain ways, with little Western contact. He knew he had to be respectful and diplomatic yet confident with his royal hosts.

The king was found to have a diseased gallbladder, vocal cord polyps, and severe arthritis and was scheduled for surgery. Prior to entering the operating room, Wallace was pulled aside by one of the royal princes and two heavily armed guards. He was told that if anything untoward happened to the king, Wallacwe would be beheaded. Wallace took this in stride and calmly reassured the Saudis that the king would do well. The king was rolled into the operating room, where the prince and two large bodyguards with swords were present to witness the operation. This did not faze Wallace, and he proceeded with the surgery.

The operation for both the gall bladder and the polyps was a success, and the king's arthritis was also greatly improved with medication. To the king and the entire Saudi royal family, it seemed that Wallace had performed a miracle or magic. They were unfamiliar with Western medicine and amazed at how it could benefit people so much. The king and the royal family were tremendously grateful.

As he often did, Wallace seemed to make a unique connection with the king and several members of the royal family. He actually became the most popular new person in the king's royal court. Many of the princes and various ministers invited him to events and private dinners. When they spoke of Wallace, they used the preface "El," doctor, as a sign of great respect. They sensed his easy confidence but lack of pretense or arrogance. As Bedouin warriors, they seemed to admire his courage in the face of a serious threat.

Wallace was given the sword that he would have been executed with had he failed. He was also given rugs and many other items. He even received several gazelles when it became known that he loved animals. The gazelles were transferred to Wallace's house in Washington, D.C., and then to the Washington Zoo. In Saudi culture, it was considered bad manners to refuse a gift, especially from the king. Hospitality to guests is considered sacred in their holy book, the Quran.

After the king had recovered, Wallace had long discussions with him about opening the country for development by the oil industry. Wallace proposed a win-win scenario in which Saudi culture would be respected and left intact, while Arabia's oil reserves could be developed to make the country extraordinarily wealthy. No Westerners or Western development would be allowed in the holy city of Mecca. The king trusted Wallace, and the relationship between the United States and Saudi Arabia was initiated—a relationship that remains intact to this day.

Wallace was sent on other diplomatic missions around the world. He operated on and helped care for many heads of state. He was occasionally used for nonmedical diplomatic missions associated with the State Department as well. Wallace went everywhere that the president went, whether during political campaign events or occasional vacations when Truman took the entire White House staff to Key West, Florida. Key West was called Truman's second White House.

Shortly after World War II ended, it became increasingly obvious that the Soviet Union was behaving no longer as an ally but as an enemy aiming for world domination. Winston Churchill had been voted out of office halfway through the Potsdam Conference. Despite feeling devastated, Churchill felt that he had unfished business. He needed to warn the world of the steadily increasing Soviet threat to freedom for the world. He had realized this long before the war ended because of his dealings with Stalin. Now his suspicions were coming true with the

Soviet takeover of Eastern Europe. He felt that the previous special relationship between the United States and Britain must be renewed and strengthened to combat the impending Soviet threat. Churchill realized correctly that Western civilization was at a crossroads, facing a threat in communism equal to or greater than the threat of the Nazis. He also realized that the only country strong enough to combat this threat was the United States. Churchill felt that the current British prime minister, Clement Attlee, was not up to the task of warning and mustering the free world against the communist threat. He called Atlee "a sheep in sheep's clothing. "Churchill had delt with weak leaders in the past with Neville Chamberlin's appeasement of Hitler prior to World War two, with catastrophic results.

Churchill received an unlikely letter from the president of Westminster College in Fulton, Missouri, requesting that he give a speech and receive an honorary degree. As a footnote to the letter, Harry Truman wrote, "Hope you can come to my home state. I would love to introduce you," and signed it with his name. It was in this nondescript venue that Churchill gave his now famous "Iron Curtain" speech that delivered the first declaration of the Cold War.

Churchill, Truman, and Wallace took the long train ride from Washington, D.C., to Fulton, Missouri. Their mode of travel was chosen partly to give the two world leaders time to better know each other, since their only previous meeting had been at the Potsdam Conference. During the train ride, Wallace became well acquainted with Churchill. Churchill was a highly gregarious who loved human contact and continuous conversation. Wallace said that Churchill slept very little, taking only periodic naps throughout the day when the activity subsided. He would stay up most of the night reading if there was no one to talk to.

There were many poker games among Wallace, Churchill, Truman, and Vaughn. Churchill claimed to be a novice to the game; however, he nearly always won and took away all of the poker chips. Wallace and the other Americans wondered later whether Churchill was just playing dumb as a ploy. Churchill thought it amusing when "jokers were wild" in one game. He retorted, "Of course, jokers are always wild." Everyone chuckled at his comment.

Wallace greatly enjoyed his individual time with Churchill. They both had a great love of gardening and agriculture. They talked about growing roses and the benefit to farmers in America of planting winter wheat. Wallace told Churchill of his fondness for English gardens and commented on how large boxwood and yew bushes grew in England. Wallace was impressed with Churchill's broad scope of general knowledge. Churchill discussed the newer advances in medicine with Wallace and wished to know more. The two enjoyed each other's company greatly during the long train trip to Fulton.

Churchill treated the train trip as one big party. He frequently had a glass of bourbon in his hand during his many conversations walking from car to car, engaging all of the people he met on his way. He would say to Wallace, "You know, my dear doctor, that this drink I imbibe is purely medicinal. It dilates my vascular system, keeping the blood flowing to my brain and allowing me to think properly." Wallace smiled and replied, "Yes, Mr. Prime Minister, it definitely causes vasodilation, and we certainly want sufficient blood flowing to your brain." They then had a good laugh. Churchill went on, "What in the world would we do without your good state of Kentucky, where so much of this medicinal drink is made?" as he took another sip of "medicine." By the end of the train trip to Fulton, Churchill had become the most popular man in the entire entourage. He and Truman had become good friends who had great admiration and respect for one another.

After the speech and Churchill's return to Britain, several letters passed between Wallace and the former prime minister. The two seemed to have made a mutual friendship. Churchill sent Wallace an autographed photo of himself. Wallace was greatly impressed with Churchill's quick wit, humor, and great intelligence. Not one to give up easily, Churchill was reelected as prime minister of Britain in the next election.

After serving as president for over three years after the death of Franklin Roosevelt, Truman was up for election again. The press was uniformly against him, and he was dramatically down in the prelection polls. He traveled by train throughout the United States, stopping at American towns large and small. This tour was called the Whistle Stop Campaign, and Wallace accompanied the president throughout his travels. Truman's opponent, Thomas Dewey, hardly campaigned at all because he was so high in the polls, and he was supported by the press. Truman campaigned hard, never taking a day off. The Whistle Stop Campaign ended at Excelsior Springs, Missouri, where Truman and Wallace stayed at the Elms Hotel on election night.

Truman said to Wallace, "Well, Dr. Graham, do you think we're going to win?"

"Yes, sir, I do, I don't care what the polls say. I could see huge crowds everywhere we went. You told people the truth in language they could understand and identify with. Yes, sir, I think you are going to win."

"Well, Doctor, I think I'm going to win as well. We sure gave old Tom Dewey hell, didn't we?"

"Yes, sir, you certainly did. You told the truth, and that's what the people want to hear."

Both Truman and Wallace went to bed early that night, confident of victory despite the polls and the press predictions of a victory by Thomas Dewey.

The next day, Truman won despite the predictions and naysayers.

In October 1950, the United States was involved in the Korean War. General Douglas MacArthur had just orchestrated the Inchon landing, and the North Korean communist army was in full retreat. MacArthur was considered a war hero and was wildly popular with the American public. However, on numerous occasions, he had defied and openly insulted President Truman. MacArthur frequently publicly challenged the administration's policies. While still in uniform, he courted a presidential bid. He later threatened to use nuclear weapons against China. The Soviet Union under Stalin also had nuclear weapons, and Truman was concerned about countermoves by the Soviets in Europe and the Middle East. The Soviet Union had just blockaded Berlin from contact with the Western democracies. China was threatening to invade Taiwan. Greece and Turkey were undergoing communist insurgencies. The Arab states surrounding the new state of Israel were threatening invasion. Truman had great concerns about the potential of the Korean War to expand into another world war, which the United States could ill afford at the time.

When Truman insisted on a face-to-face meeting, MacArthur agreed to fly only a half day away from his headquarters in Tokyo. Thus, Truman was forced to fly fourteen thousand miles to meet with the general at Wake Island in the central Pacific. The president brought with him all of his key advisers: Charles Ross, the press secretary; Admiral Arthur Radford, commander of the Pacific Fleet; Frank Pace, secretary of the army; General Omar Bradley, chairman of the Joint Chiefs of Staff; and Wallace Graham, personal physician and adviser to the president.

MacArthur's plane arrived at Wake Island just before Truman's, but the general's plane was circling the island, waiting for the president's plane to land first. This was so the president would be seen waiting for the general to walk out of his plane, giving Truman a more subservient appearance. MacArthur had brought along a crew of photographers and journalists to show the general in a more favorable light than the president. MacArthur was known for staging flamboyant events and photo ops to heighten his prestige and reputation. Truman was fully aware of the general's intention and caustically called MacArthur "God's right-hand man." Wallace and the others chuckled.

Truman was furious at the breach of military and political protocol and ordered MacArthur's plane by radio to land immediately. Wallace knew that the president was slow to anger, but when he was seriously provoked, "all hell could break loose." He was truly a man after Wallace's own heart.

The president's plane landed after the general's, and the general was there to greet the president as he walked out of the plane. After a ceremony on the tarmac in which Truman bestowed the Distinguished Service Medal on MacArthur, the White House entourage and the general went to a bunker on the side of the runway to discuss military and foreign policy. Things seemed to go well, and everyone appeared to be on the same page regarding strategy. However, Truman knew actions are often different than spoken words. In the past, MacArthur and Truman had often been in similar situations, only to be at odds again later. It seemed to Truman that the general had trouble following orders from the commander in chief. Truman wanted to set things straight once and for all despite the political fallout from MacArthur's great popularity.

After the meeting ended, Truman asked MacArthur to take a walk with him down the tarmac toward the beach. The president waved to Wallace to come along but to stay a few yards back while the two men walked in front.

When the two were well away from the main group, Truman turned to the general, looked him straight in the eyes, and said, "Look! I don't give a damn what you think about me, but I do give a damn about what you think and how you behave to the president of the United States. I am the commander in chief, and you will follow orders, or I will remove you. Is that understood?"

"Yes, sir, it is understood."

Wallace said that MacArthur looked white as a sheet and timid as a lamb. He looked like a child that had been spanked. He probably had never been talked to like that before. He was in shock. He had always surrounded himself with sycophants and yes-men because of his huge ego. Now he was spoken to as if he were a private being dressed down by an officer. Truman had been in the military, and both were well aware of the military chain of command. The Constitution clearly states that the president of the United States is commander in chief of all armed forces, and all generals and admirals are subservient to the president.

They walked back together, smiling for the reporters and photographers as if nothing had happened. After some concluding ceremonies, the general and the president boarded their planes and flew off.

While on the plane, President Truman looked at Wallace and said, "Well, what do you think, Dr. Graham?"

"I think I am very proud of the president of the United States, sir."

"I know you would always give it to me straight. You know that if it ever comes to the point where I have to fire that prima donna, all hell is going to break loose, and I might even lose my job over it."

"I know that sir; that's why I'm proud of you. I don't know many who would have had the guts to say what you said. It showed courage."

It is not clear why the president wanted Wallace around during his talk on the tarmac. Possibly he wanted some feedback from a trusted confidant, as opposed to partisan White House staff or professional military personnel, or proof of what had been said. At that time, physicians were considered to be nonpolitical and respected men of integrity.

Later that year, China invaded Korea and came into direct conflict with the United States. MacArthur had left the army isolated, overextended, and totally unprepared for the devastating Chinese counterattack. He had disregarded reports of a Chinese military buildup and an impending attack.

MacArthur went to the press and blamed any and all military setbacks on the Truman administration, a charge that was accepted as the truth by the media, the majority of Congress, and the public. The general also threatened the use of nuclear weapons. Truman then relieved him of his command. MacArthur came back to the United States and was given a New York ticker-tape parade, which was considered the highest of honors at the time. He addressed a joint session of Congress. He also made an unsuccessful attempt for the presidency. Truman's popularity polls plummeted to below 30 percent, and he never again ran for public office after his term ended.

At the end of the Truman administration, Wallace returned to Kansas City with his family and continued to monitor Harry and Bess Truman's health. He visited the Truman's home every Sunday. He recommended that the president walk one mile every day, which the president became noted for. My father would occasionally take me to the Truman home on his weekly visits. I remember the first time I went to the Truman residence. My dad and I were walking up to the house when we noticed a lady on her knees digging in a garden putting in flower bulbs. The lady turned around and it was Bess Truman, the former first lady, performing a menial task that any common person does. She stood up with a big smile and greeting "Good afternoon, Dr. Graham, I see you brought some good help with you today." She took us into the house via the back door. The old wooden house was painted white with long vertical widows. It had a Victorian appearance and was Bess Truman's house when she was growing up. The house was in a standard Independence, Missouri neighborhood with sidewalks and streetlights close to the house. Certainly nothing out of the ordinary, especially for an ex-president of the United States. We entered the relatively small but tidy kitchen and sat down at a small table.

"Doctor, would you like some coffee? I have some already brewed. I think the president might want some too."

"Yes mam, I would like that." My dad said.

"Cream or sugar?"

"Black would be fine."

"I'll bet your young assistant may want some cookies and milk while you and the President visit."

"That would be great Mrs. Truman," I said.

I enjoyed the Orio cookies and milk with the former first lady at her kitchen table as she asked me about my school and the subjects I was studying. I was impressed by her friendly, down to earth manner. Bess Truman had the reputation as a taciturn lady with a drab personality. I did not find this to be the case. It was well known that she hated politics and all of the hypocrisy of Washington D.C. I believe her disdain for this became obvious to the press and her supposed unfriendliness was overblown.

Later I met President Truman and we became friends. He acknowledged my interest in history as a young man and encouraged my further study in it. President Truman was well read and knew American and world history exceptionally well. This was especially remarkable for someone who never went to college. He told me knowing what happened in the past can influence an important decision in the present, whether it be American policy or a personal situation in your own life. He told me by knowing the life histories and challenges of famous individuals in the past, you can pattern their success into your own future. You could also learn of their mistakes and the pitfalls they experienced and apply the lessons to your own life. The President told me that human nature doesn't change and if we did not know history, we were doomed to repeat the same mistakes that were made in the past.

The President said, "Study history, not just in school but for the rest of your life. So many Americans know little of our country's past, of the struggles and sacrifices that so many endured to build this wonderful land in which we live. Immerse yourself in history, the story of our nation, of western civilization, and of other countries. We are the sum of all those men and women who have gone before us. When we remain ignorant of their failures and accomplishments, we live as children rather than adults."

The President told me that when he had to make a big decision, he would obtain wise council with people who had expertise in the field and from people he knew had good judgement. He would then do research from his library about what past presidents or past historical figures had done in similar situations and evaluate the outcomes. He would then sleep on it and make the decision the next day. If of course, he had time.

Mr. Truman always said leaders are readers and gave me a list of books to read which later we would discuss. This of course, my parents much encouraged. The President was highly intelligent and had an open and practical mind. He seemed to me to be a good and kind man interested in young people. We would talk extensively on topics such as Julius Caesar, Alexander the Great, Robert E. Lee, Abraham Lincoln, Andrew Jackson, and many others.

Outside of history, he gave me some advice on life. He said "Life is like a table. It is based on four main factors, like legs on a table. If any of the four legs is missing, or not strong enough, it leads to insta bility.

1. *Intelligence and mental activity.* A young person should try to develop his intellect and education as much as possible in all areas. This should be ongoing in life. One should never stop learning. If your aptitude in a particu-

lar subject is lacking, attempt to overcome this deficiency with harder application to its study.

2. *Physical activity.* One should attempt to be in the best physical condition possible. Playing sports not only helps your body but develops character. Good physical condition also helps the mind become more active and clear.

3. *Community.* Human beings are social animals. We need others for our own development and well -being. One should develop social skills to the best of one's ability. Try to make friends with accomplished people with good character whom you respect. A person will be much happier by surrounding himself with the right people.

4. *Spirituality.* A belief in a creator who is just and merciful is essential to one's moral development and code of conduct. This belief will give a person's life meaning and strength in dire circumstances. Whether one is religious or not, the Bible is an excellent source for wisdom and a blueprint to conduct your life. Adherence to the ten commandments will lead to a good and stable life.

Wallace was admired and respected by all. He was not pretentious and never bragged about his past accomplishments. He never drank alcohol or used profane language. He always told me, "Be on the right side of things, and you will have the power of the Holy Spirit behind you, no matter what the odds are against you." He said to always stand up for what I believed in if I was in the right. In short, he taught me and others courage.

In many ways, he lived vicariously through me, always reveling in my successes. He convinced me that I was good, that I was smart, and that I could do anything I set my mind to do. At an early age, I had his great reputation to live up to, and I never wanted to let him down. Amazingly, I can remember only a few times that he became angry with me. Although I deserved far worse, I definitely did not want to mess with him. He was my lifelong advocate and primary source of motivation.

I once asked my father, "What would you wish to be if you were not in medicine?" He answered, of course, "A doctor, then career military or a Christian minister." He excelled at the two former endeavors. I was interested in what they all had in common that would attract him. I concluded that all three of these pursuits demanded complete and total dedication. Each carried great responsibility for other people and demanded a profound sense of duty and loyalty, which was key to his existence. Wallace never really strove for money or power, but he had a sense of single-minded purpose which all of these professions demanded.

At eighty-six years of age, this giant of a man died after a truly amazing life. I was honored to give the concluding part of his eulogy. It was one of the hardest things I have ever done, but I was told by many that it was a remarkable tribute. I was later told by one of his colleagues at the funeral, "The best thing your father left you was a good reputation." I thought that quite true but amusing because I recalled that someone had told Wallace the same thing when his father, JW, died. It is my hope that someone will say the same thing to my children and grandchildren when I leave this earth.

Wallace was known for his infectious positive attitude, courage, and boundless energy. There was no harder worker than Wallace Graham. Even his father, JW, said, "That Wallace is something else."

He was a truly gifted and unique individual. He was brave as a lion and had a kind heart. He truly was Braveheart.

7

Forever Young
at Heart

Velma Hill paced the floor, periodically glancing out her fourth-floor nursing student dorm window at St. Mary's. The Catholic nursing school at St. Mary's Hospital was run by nuns who were also nurses. It was 1936, and the students were held to a strict curfew and were not allowed to be out past 7:00 p.m. The consequences for breaking the rules could be severe. Velma was a good student and followed the rules, but not this time; nothing was going to keep her from seeing Wallace. Upon arrival, Wallace was to honk the horn outside, and Velma would descend the fire escape. Her nursing student friends had agreed to listen for her signal and lower the fire escape to let her back into the dorm when she returned.

Velma anxiously looked over at her roommate Janey, "Where do think Wallace is? He was supposed to be here long ago."

"He probably just got out of class late. He'll be here. It really hasn't been all that long. It just seems that way because you're so anxious."

Velma crossed her arms and continued to pace back and forth in front of the window.

"The weather isn't that great; it's probably raining or snowing north of here where he's coming from, making him drive slower and more cautiously. So being late is really a good thing for safety," Janey said, giving Velma more reassurance.

Velma looked out the window and took a deep breath. "I guess you're right; it's much too early to be worried. I just want to see him so badly. I miss him so much."

"Relax; everything is going to work out fine, outside of him being a little late. Don't worry!"

Velma knew that Janey was right. She tried to calm herself down but continued to look out the window.

Wallace Graham couldn't wait to see his girlfriend, Velma. As soon as he got out of class, he hopped into his Model A Ford and headed to Kansas City from Creighton University Medical School in Omaha, Nebraska. Velma was expecting him no later than 11 p.m. With attention to the road, the four-hour drive was usually uneventful, but November weather could easily turn the roads into a hazardous nightmare. This night brought heavy mist to the dark, cold trip.

He gripped the steering wheel tightly with both hands and kept his eyes fixed ahead, concentrating on the road. He tried to keep himself from thinking of Velma, but it was difficult since they hadn't seen each other in two excruciating months. The road was poor, with many hills and sharp turns, making it difficult to manage even at the speed limit in good conditions. Wallace was driving as fast as he could in the heavy fog and mist.

He was halfway to Kansas City when he saw something large with feathers fly in front of him and felt a heavy thud against the front of the car. Wallace pulled over to investigate. Embedded in the grill of his car was a very large wild turkey. He pulled it off the grill and threw it into the back seat. This somehow seemed to be destiny since Thanksgiving was only two days away.

Velma and Wallace had been sweethearts since third grade. Wallace had sat behind Velma in their classroom. Always a prankster, he had dipped her long blonde braids into his inkwell as a joke. He was very impressed with her after she refused to divulge the guilty party who had inked her hair, even though she knew it was Wallace. Velma's family always called her "Honey" as a nickname because she was always sweet and had a perpetual smile.

Velma and Wallace had broken up for a short time when they were seniors in high school because Wallace had thought there were greener pastures elsewhere. He came to realize that no one could compare to Velma. However, after having a broken heart for a while, Velma had moved on emotionally. Now it was Wallace who was distraught. He couldn't bear the thought of Velma dating other people. When Wallace had issues with life, he always sought advice from his father, who was the wisest and most understanding man he knew. JW, Wallace's father, told him that it would be hard to find someone who suited Wallace better than Velma. Over the years, JW had gotten to know Velma and her family well, in part because they lived only about a half mile away.

JW said to Wallace, "I know you're a long way from getting ready for marriage, but quality women like Velma are hard to find. I suggest being very gracious and slowly persistent to get back with Velma. Keep the relationship going and tell her about how she will play a big role in the future for you. Women usually respond well when you express heartfelt honesty and sincerity. As long as you hold up your end of the bargain, Velma should stick with you through thick or thin." Wallace knew his father was a good judge of character, so this advice made him feel even worse about the breakup. He was remorseful about his decision to break it off. It took nearly six months of constant courting to win Velma's heart back. Wallace had learned a hard lesson that sometimes the pastures are not greener over the hill.

Velma and Wallace's relationship had had its ups and downs over the years, but in the last two years, a serious change had occurred. Both felt that they could not be apart, and each goodbye was more difficult than the last. They wrote letters once or twice a week. Neither could wait for the mailman to arrive. It seemed that their letters actually made their love for one another increase dramatically.

I t was past midnight when Velma finally heard the honk of the horn in the darkness. She had become worried, knowing how treacherous the roads could become between Omaha and Kansas City. When she heard the horn, she thought her heart might pound out of her chest with relief. She climbed out the window and nearly flew down the wrought-iron fire escape. In the cold drizzle, she thought of going back to get her coat, but she couldn't wait to see Wallace. Wallace saw her scampering down the fire escape. She descended so fast that he thought she looked like a little monkey. He began to chuckle. He watched as Velma sprinted to his car. She quickly opened the door and jumped into the warm vehicle, and they fell into each other's arms. Both of their hearts were pounding as they kissed. They jumped into the back seat. Velma felt something unusual on the seat and asked Wallace what it was, but he told her not to worry; it was just an old pillow. After a while, they began to talk. Marriage came up. It seemed that the more they talked about it, the harder it was to do without it.

After about an hour, Velma's friends in the dorm heard Wallace's horn, the signal to let the fire escape down. Velma hurried up the steps. The iron railings were damp, slippery, and cold. At the top, she crouched down and came through the window. Janey gave a gasp and asked, "What happened to you?" Velma looked down and saw blood and feathers covering her dress, courtesy of the turkey.

Velma invited Wallace to Thanksgiving dinner at the Hills' house, and of course he accepted. Wallace plucked and dressed the errant turkey from his drive to Kansas City and gave it to Edna, Velma's mother, to fix along with the regular turkey. Edna was an amazing cook, and she put out quite a spread. Fixing a big dinner for a large number of people was an easy task for her, as she was used to fixing big meals for farmhands and workmen with large appetites. The menu included hand-mashed potatoes, green beans, giblet gravy, cranberry sauce, and, of course, the turkey. Pumpkin and pecan pies with ice cream were dessert. Anytime you went to Edna and Stanley's house, coffee was brewing. I remember that the smell of coffee was always present in their kitchen.

The entire Hill clan was there. Wallace's turkey was cut up first and passed around. The meat was difficult to cut through, requiring unusual force. Velma's father, Stanley, thought he had a dull knife. The bird looked appetizing but appeared different from the regular turkey. Everyone began chewing. The turkey was tough as leather, but no one wanted to say anything because it was Wallace's gift. Finally, Stanley scowled, spit the bird out of his mouth onto the plate, and said, "This is terrible. It's like eating an old shoe!" Wallace, Velma, and the rest broke out laughing. The turkey was put out in the trash, but the laughter and humor lasted the whole day.

V elma graduated from nursing school and became an operating-room nurse. She was first assistant to the surgeon in all types of major surgery. She was highly regarded because of her technical skill, intelligence, and perky, positive attitude. Later, she became the head surgical nurse of the hospital. She ran the department well. She was fair and professional and backed any staff member that she felt was unfairly treated despite potential adverse consequences. Needless to say, she was highly respected and liked by all. While she was head of the operating room, it ran as a cohesive, orderly unit.

Dr. Vander was one of the busiest surgeons in the hospital where Velma worked. He was notorious for being abusive to his assistants and other staff. He was slightly above average as a technical surgeon but difficult to work with. One day, one of the surgical nurses came into Velma's office, anxious and tearful. She sat down in front of Velma's desk and told Velma that she had inadvertently handed Dr. Vander the wrong instrument. This was hardly a serious offense from an otherwise excellent nurse. Dr. Vander had thrown the instrument across the operating room, breaking a glass cabinet. He had screamed at her and told her to get out. Velma had some difficulty finding another available nurse to assist Dr. Vander because they were all helping other surgeons. Velma scrubbed in to take the previous nurse's place and contacted a cleaning crew to clean up the broken glass. Velma had worked with Dr. Vander before and had never had any problems with him aside from some minor verbal abuse that she had simply shrugged off.

Velma began assisting in the surgery, gaining exposure for Dr. Vander in an abdominal operation. Dr. Vander was already in a bad mood and was just looking for trouble. He became very abusive to Velma. Velma replied, "Dr. Vander, I can't read your mind. Instead of yelling at me, just give me your instructions, and I will do it."

Dr. Vander said, "You know nothing! Have you somehow lost all of your ability to properly assist in surgery?"

"No, I have not. Just tell me what you want me to do." Velma then placed her hand to retract the bowel away from the gallbladder, which the doctor was trying to remove. Dr. Vander slapped her hand with the blunt end of an instrument, causing a stinging pain on the back of her hand.

Velma immediately removed her hand from the operating field, glared at Dr. Vander, and said, "Dr. Vander, you can yell and scream at me all you want. It doesn't bother me like it does the rest of the nursing staff. But when you hit me, that is something I will not tolerate. I will report you to the administrators of the hospital [not that this would have done any good in the 1930s]. Not only that, but I will also tell my boyfriend, Wallace Graham, who is a boxer, and I am sure he is not going to like what you have done to me." Almost everyone in the city knew who Wallace was, as he was a hometown boxing champion. Dr. Vander hadn't known that Velma was associated with Wallace. Little did he and others at the hospital know that Velma and Wallace were secretly already married.

Velma continued as she stared into the surgeon's eyes, "Dr. Vander, you're wasting your energy and taking your focus away from the patient and the problem at hand, thereby endangering your patient. You need to control your temper for the patient's sake and the success of this operation. You can yell and scream all you want after the surgery is completed."

Velma then gave him a lesson on proper behavior: "A physician and surgeon should be a gentleman at all times. You will get more respect and efficiency from others if you act properly. Since you are in an elevated position, your behavior needs to be an example to others. However, you have damaged your reputation with everyone here by acting like a child!"

Everyone in the operating room—the nurse circulator, the anesthesiologist, and the cleanup crew for the broken glass—was aghast and transfixed, some with their mouths open under their surgical masks. They could barely believe what they were hearing. Velma was saying what everyone in the surgery department had wanted to say to Dr. Vander but was afraid to. In the 1930s, if a surgeon wanted anyone fired, it was usually done whether the other person was right or not. The people in the operating room all thought that today was going to be their friend Velma's last day.

Dr. Vander stared at Velma in silent shock. No one had ever talked to him this way. It seemed as if the air came out of his sails. He said calmly, "Well, all right, then." He then completed the operation with

Velma assisting and no further word from either of them. Afterward, Dr. Vander's behavior changed, especially around Velma.

Dr. Vander was a bully. When confronted, he backed down and became a better-behaved person from then on. It was unheard-of for a nurse to challenge a doctor at that time. However, Velma got away with it and became a hero among the entire surgical staff. Velma was not afraid to risk losing her job for a principle and her honor, which took great courage. She knew she had done the right thing despite expecting to lose her job. Over the following week, she continually expected a notice of termination to come to her, but it never did.

When some of the other surgeons heard about Velma's run-in with Dr. Vander, most laughed. They had never seen that side of Miss Hill's personality. Most agreed that Dr. Vander needed to be taken down a notch. When Velma told Wallace of the situation with Dr. Vander, he laughed and said, "He should have known not to tangle with a girl with as much spunk as you! He might as well have gotten in a fight with a wildcat."

When Wallace had graduated from medical school, he and Velma had married, and Wallace had begun working as an intern and resident at General Hospital in Kansas City. At that time, nurses were not allowed to be married. When the hospital administration found out that Velma was recently married and had broken the rules, she was called into the administrative office to discuss the situation. Velma stood her ground and simply told them, "You can take me or leave me." They certainly didn't want to lose their efficient department of surgery director, especially such a popular and well-respected nurse as Velma. Velma became the first married nurse in Kansas City.

———

The next several years were difficult because Wallace was working long hours as a resident at Kansas City General Hospital. He was on call at the hospital every third night. Velma's schedule was demanding as well. They felt like two ships passing in the night. She longed for the old days, when they could be more free-spirited. In the past she and Wallace had enjoyed frequent evenings out dancing. They had even won dance contests on several occasions. She particularly loved the Charleston. She loved wearing her dance gowns with fringe at the hem, the standard party dresses of the 1930s. The girls were sometimes called flappers. The dresses were relatively long and usually loose-fitting with sequins. She remembered how much fun they used to have. Now it seemed that both her life and Wallace's were consumed with nothing but work. When they were together, both were usually tired from a long, stressful day of dealing with serious situations. Wallace frequently had to study to prepare for the next day's surgery despite being profoundly fatigued. When he was on call, he was frequently up all night. They both would have liked to at least go out with friends, but even this was usually out of the question because of their demanding schedules. Neither of them complained; they just hoped for better days in the future. They both realized that a job that you love and is tremendously rewarding cannot come close to bringing as much happiness as a close personal relationship and love.

After Wallace completed his residency, he had the opportunity to further his surgical education in Europe. Initially Velma was horrified at the thought of Wallace leaving her for two years until JW reassured her that he would pay for them both. Velma was thrilled; she had never been to a foreign country before, and this seemed to be a promising adventure. They would live in various countries for two years. Wallace would be working in surgery with some of the finest and most renowned surgeons in the world at that time. Velma was always up for anything new and exciting. She was very adventurous and always had an open mind, like her husband. She definitely was no "stick in the mud." This would be something that would be good for them and their marriage. Velma was looking forward to breaking the heavy burden of the daily routine that they had become used to.

Over a two-year period, they lived in Munich, Germany, then Vienna, Austria, then Hungary, and then Edinburgh, Scotland. In each country, Velma dressed the way the natives dressed and tried to learn the language. Wallace spent his days at the hospital in training, and Velma shopped for dinner and prepared meals of the local cuisine. She was basically on her own all day, creating a home for the couple. She explored the city she was in and made friends with local people. This was a magnificent adventure for Velma. She felt more free and alive than ever before. She and Wallace were having the time of their lives. Wallace was excited about the new surgical techniques he was learning and detailed to Velma his thrill in the new surgical advances he was experiencing. On weekends, they would choose a destination and make an expedition to the surrounding area, whether hiking in the Bavarian mountains, skiing in the Alps, or taking long bicycle rides with picnics in the Hungarian countryside.

In Vienna, they met a couple who lived in an apartment down the hall. The couple invited them to a "get-together" with food and drink at a meeting/dining hall. They joined the couple at the venue and were met with greetings of "Hail, comrades." They listened to a speaker extolling the virtues of Marx and Lennon. These people were communists! Velma and Wallace felt very out of place. They realized that their new friends had gotten the wrong impression of them and quickly left.

The year was 1938. Europe was very unsettled, and disturbing events were taking place before Velma and Wallace's eyes. Adolf Hitler had just annexed Austria. Overnight, they witnessed battalions of goose-stepping, helmeted German soldiers marching through the streets of Vienna. The Nazi brigades had torchlight marches at night, singing German patriotic songs. The whole city seemed electrified. They went to a Nazi rally at the city center the day after the German troops entered Vienna. They were curious about this new leader from Germany who was stepping onto the world stage. At the rally, they were among thousands of people who were there to see and hear Hitler speak. Velma described his speech as beginning slowly and then increasing in pitch and intensity until finally, while working the crowd up to an emotional high, he raised his right arm and yelled, "Sieg!" and the crowd responded, "Heil!"

The next day people greeted others by saying, "Heil, Hitler!" instead of "Guten tag," or "Good morning." Velma and Wallace were quite impressed with the emotion delivered in the speech, but they knew this was an ominous turn in world history and definitely not good for America. Later that week, they noted signs being placed on Jewish-owned businesses that read, "Juden," or "Jew." The windows of the businesses were broken by the Hitler brownshirts, or Sturmabteilung. This came to be known as Kristallnacht because of the broken glass on the street, which sparkled like crystals in the night. Their communist acquaintances were arrested, and the Jewish people they knew were being harassed. It was a frequent occurrence where they saw uniformed brown shirt thugs of the Nazi party harassing private citizens for any-thing they thought as against the state. At checkpoints, Velma was ques-tioned about being Jewish since her middle name was Ruth, which they considered a Jewish name and therefore suspect.

They had two young friends about their age who were Jewish. Glenda and David Frankel lived across the street in another apartment build-ing. David was newly a lawyer, and Glenda worked as a secretary. The Frankels invited the two young Americans to a beer hall, where they spent a very enjoyable evening eating bratwurst, sausages, and sauer-kraut and drinking beer in the characteristic large German mugs. They sang German songs while toasting with their beer mugs. The Frankels were highly educated and fluent in English. They had relatives who had emigrated to America. The two couples occasionally had coffee together in outdoor cafés and enjoyed each other's company.

Wallace and Velma had dinner with the Frankels in their apartment and celebrated Passover with them. They were introduced to pickled herring, lox, bagels, and cream cheese, things they enjoyed for the rest of their lives. Glenda took Velma shopping, and Velma bought an Aus-trian Tyrolean outfit. Glenda took a photo of Velma in her new out-fit, and Velma was thrilled. Glenda and Velma became good friends. The Vienna public transit system was excellent. The two young women toured the city by the local street cars. They routinely shopped for gro-ceries together at the nearest markets. Velma was instructed on the preparation of typical Austrian food, much to the enjoyment of Wal-lace. Glenda took Velma on a tour of Vienna showing her the historical sights. The two had great fun together and became good friends.

Glenda and David were fans of the symphony and went often. Both couples went to the famous Vienna Symphony, where Mozart,

Beethoven, Brahms, Bach, and others had performed in the past. The auditorium was enormous, with giant crystal chandeliers, brightly gilded domed ceilings, and a huge red carpet leading into the venue. There were marble statues of past great composers who had performed there. The performance was electrifying. They had never seen anything like it. The couple from Kansas City were very impressed.

On their way back from the symphony, as the two couples were walking along the cobblestone streets of old Vienna in the late evening, they were stopped by two Nazi brownshirts. The brownshirts were a paramilitary group of local street thugs and criminals hired by the Nazi Party to terrorize anyone who wasn't a Nazi. They were given uniforms but no formal training and had broad leeway regarding whom they harassed. Even regular German citizens and the police were afraid of them because they were backed by the Nazi government and military.

The two brownshirts asked to see the two couple's identification papers. They quickly saw that the Frankels were Jewish and told them to come with them. Wallace firmly told the Nazis that they weren't going anywhere. He quickly stepped between the Frankels and the two brownshirts, having noticed that the men were not carrying firearms. Wallace stared at the two Nazis with a half-cocked smile that Velma knew was the prelude to serious action. The Nazis immediately felt an overwhelming sense of dread, as if they were prey facing a predator. Wallace was like a tightly coiled, powerful spring ready to be triggered, and the Nazis felt this viscerally. After a long pause, the brownshirts told the couples to be on their way, especially the crazy American. Velma and Wallace tried to get the Frankels to come to America while it was still possible, but to no avail. Glenda told Velma that Jews had always been looked down upon to some degree. This was just a bad time that would eventually pass. She didn't think things would get any worse. Later, Velma found out that the Frankels had been arrested, sent to a concentration camp, and killed.

After Munich and Vienna, Wallace and Velma went to Hungary. They loved it; however, it seemed much more foreign than Germany or Austria. The people were friendly, and although they did not speak the language, they could usually get their point across. They rented a room from a spry elderly lady in a house close to the medical center where Wallace was doing his residency. Their landlady was short, round, and had rosy cheeks. She wore a colorful headscarf, as older Hungarian women frequently did. She took care of the young American couple as if they were family. She talked to them as though they knew the Hungarian language. Velma and Wallace became adept at using sign language to communicate. It seemed like a continual game of charades. The landlady was quite patient with them and even began learning many words in English. The language barrier didn't seem to be much of a problem. When people wish to communicate, it usually can be done. The landlady always had a smile and a cheerful greeting when they returned to the house. She brought people from her family over to meet the young Americans. Everyone was curious about America. Wallace and Velma got many questions about cowboys and Indians, gangsters in Chicago, and movie stars from Hollywood. The young Americans enjoyed their interactions with these people and gladly tried to describe America. The landlady turned out to be an excellent cook, fixing all types of Hungarian dishes that were unfamiliar to the young couple. The landlady had a special name in Hungarian for the couple, and they later found out that the phrase translated as "My little dumplings." She made the Grahams feel at home in their rented room. The American couple and their always cheerful landlady became quite attached to one another despite the language barrier. During the day Velma would go out on her usual exploration of the city with instructions of the landlady where to go and visit. The landlady's niece accompanied Velma several times and was invited over to her house. The niece's family lived in the countryside and onetime took Wallace and Velma horseback riding on their family farm.

Hungarian society was still old European, with a very distinct and rigid social class structure. There was a wide gap between upper-class aristocrats and lower-class peasants. Since the peasants were of little consequence to the majority of the upper-level medical staff, Wallace was given near total care of his patients with little supervision. As a young surgeon, he was now able to apply what he had been learning. He did an outstanding job of caring for his patients. His operative outcomes were excellent, much better than usual. He was complimented by his superiors and given even more responsibility.

It was the custom in Budapest to take walks on a promenade in the main park of the city. Upper-class aristocrats walked on certain days, and the common people walked on the other days. The young Americans were politely told that it was most appropriate for them to walk on the promenade on the upper-class days. Velma and Wallace paid no attention to these rules and walked on either day; it made no difference to them. They were just thought of as the odd American couple who didn't know better. While on their walks, they were occasionally given long looks, and they heard occasional subdued snickering. Their landlady finally told Velma that the only women who wore lipstick in Hungary were prostitutes. Velma had always worn lipstick; however, that changed quickly.

One weekend, Velma and Wallace took a long bicycle ride in the country and accidentally crossed the border into Yugoslavia. Soon they were surrounded by soldiers pointing guns at them. They were taken to military headquarters and charged with espionage. It took many phone calls and explaining before they were released.

After Hungary, they lived in Edinburgh. The boat trip to England was a harrowing three-day adventure that should have taken one day. They experienced one of the worst storms in the North Sea for many years. Many ships were lost during that storm. They felt lucky to reach dry land, and it took them nearly a week to recover from seasickness.

Wallace and Velma's apartment was close to the Edinburgh Castle, which was still used as a military facility. The famed Black Watch Unit, renowned for valor, was stationed there. The soldiers still wore their kilts of green, blue, and black plaid. The unit periodically paraded through the streets, accompanied by bagpipes and drums. Velma and Wallace were always stirred by the sight. They loved to hear the piper on the castle turret play every evening.

Velma found the people of Scotland cordial, and it was nice to speak the same language, but she thought the food was not good. It was quite bland, partly because pepper and spices were hard to come by. Neither Velma nor Wallace was fond of mutton, and it was the most common meat available. They also found that organ meat, such as kidney, liver, lung, and spleen, was common fare. Oats in all forms, along with potatoes, rounded out the menu. Cabbage, carrots, and onions were the only so-called vegetables.

The sun rarely shone in Scotland, The days always seemed to be damp, grey and cloudy, especially since it was winter. The one sight both Velma and Wallace loved to see was the purplish-pink flowering heather that blanketed the hillsides. It was a beautiful and majestic sight. When they eventually had a daughter, they named her Heather for the beautiful Scottish flower.

At this point, Velma and Wallace were getting a bit homesick. Velma was not feeling well since she was in her first trimester of pregnancy. After two eventful years in Europe, they returned to America on the Queen Elizabeth ocean liner. They were very happy to be back to "Home sweet home." Velma said she always felt very fortunate to be an American and felt like kissing the ground after arriving back in the United States. After leaving Europe, Velma had a strong foreboding about the future based on all they had witnessed. She would soon be proven right. After they returned to the United States, the couple's first child, Wally, was delivered in Kansas City. The second child, Heather, was born a year later.

America was in preparation for war, and Wallace was soon brought up to active duty in the army. Velma and their two young children followed him to various areas of the United States for training and maneuvers. She found it difficult at times to obtain goods and services in the American South, since the people there thought she was a Yankee and because of her association with the military, which they did not trust. Drawing on her sharp wit, Velma quickly found that when she spoke with a Southern accent and adopted the mannerisms and local phrases she heard, things became much easier. Velma was pretty much on her own with her two small children in strange areas since Wallace was usually gone with the military on training and maneuvers.

One day, Wallace was on a furlough, riding in a car with Velma and the children. They heard a news bulletin on the radio that Pearl Harbor had been attacked by the Japanese. Velma and Wallace silently looked at one another. They both knew what this meant.

For the next three years, Wallace was overseas in Europe during World War II, while Velma stayed in Kansas City with the two children. She had great help from her parents, the Hills, and her in-laws, the Grahams, especially JW. Wally, her oldest child, once became seriously ill. JW spent day and night alongside Velma for over a week with the young child until he was well.

Velma wrote to Wallace at least once a week, and Wallace wrote when he could. Velma kept the letters she received in a box. I recently discovered these letters and read them. They were the most touching, heartfelt letters of love and affection I have ever encountered. These letters showed a side of Wallace that I didn't know existed. I am sure that Velma's letters to Wallace boosted his morale immensely. Wallace knew that his children were in good hands with Velma. He always had great admiration and respect for his independent, capable, and very loving wife. Velma kept a map of Europe handy and showed the children with colored pins where their father was and where he had been. She spoke about him daily as if he were just down the street. She always reassured the children that their father would be all right and would come home to his family. It was sometimes hard to maintain an optimistic attitude, as she knew that Wallace was frequently in the thick of battle. She occasionally would not hear from him for weeks at a time. Velma was especially concerned about the two times that Wallace was wounded in action. She prayed that these were not the prelude to something more drastic.

After the war, Velma and the children moved to Washington, D.C., and the family lived on the military post at Walter Reed Army Medical Center. Wallace was President Truman's personal physician as well as chief of surgery at the medical center. Velma was thrust into the limelight of Washington, which she could not have cared less about. She really wanted to be in Kansas City. However, like Wallace, she was willing to do her duty and make the best of it.

Wallace worked long and hard hours leaving Velma alone frequently with the children. This didn't bother Velma. She made the best of the situation as well as she could. True to her independent, adventurous, and lively spirit, she and the children took extended vacations to New York, Florida, and even one time to Cuba, before it was communist. It was not uncommon for Velma to take hikes with the children in Rock Creek Park in Washington D.C. Velma was frequently required to attend state dinners at the White house. Although she met many famous people there, she didn't really enjoy the formality and would have rather been somewhere else.

Velma and the president got along famously. She admired his lack of pretense and up-front honesty. Velma, like Bess Truman, wanted nothing to do with politics. The president was always suspicious of social climbers and people who wanted power and prestige. He called it "Potomac fever." He saw in Velma a good woman like his wife, with no agenda but to be a good wife and mother. He allowed Velma's children, Heather and Wally, to play in the White House. They had parties in the Rose Garden and swam in the White House swimming pool. They frequently went to the president's mountain retreat, Camp David.

After Truman's term ended, Velma, Wallace, and the family returned to Kansas City. A few years later, when I was eight years old, my mother was in the hospital for a minor surgical procedure. I was in the room when I heard a knock on the door. President Truman walked in with a broad grin and flowers. He said, "Hi, Velma, how are you doing?" He walked across the room, jumped up on the radiator to use it as a seat, and started small talk. This small event of the former president of the United States sitting on a radiator, revealed to me his lack of pretentiousness. He truly was the president of the common man. He of course acknowledged my presence and shook my hand. I was mesmerized.

Before I left for college, Velma told me a few things about life. "From here on out, you are going to be exposed to many different ideas and lifestyles. Some will be good and others bad. There are certain things in life that are non-negotiable, some things you must never change and should stand by no matter what. These things are the pillars of your character that must stay the same, or what some people call your core values. You must always stand by and support your family. Have the courage to stand up for yourself and what you believe in if you are in the right, despite the consequences. Stay away from dangerous or illegal situations. Always treat women with respect. Chivalry is never dead. Be kind to the disabled and the less fortunate. Be proud of who you are and where you came from. Avoid the bad influences of evil people because they are everywhere." At the time, I took this advice for granted. However, life has a tendency to test one's basic convictions.

———

After my father died, Velma became lonely living by herself. I offered to have her live with my family or to get a condo in an assisted living place that had activities and dining. She was adamant that she didn't want to live with a "bunch of old people." Velma moved into my house with my family. True to form, she fit right in and became closely involved with all the children's activities. The children never thought of her as old because she was so energetic and had an open and active mind. She accompanied us on all our family vacations, and she loved every minute. This may have reminded her of past trips with Wallace. It seemed to satisfy her sense of adventure.

Her kindness and understanding were instrumental in raising my children. When my children were younger, they had difficulty saying "Grandmother," so they just called her "Mar." The name stuck, and she seemed to like it. Mar's most important duty was helping with Andy, my youngest son, who has Downs syndrome and significant medical problems. They slept in the same room, and she attended to any need he had. She frequently held him and sang to him as she had to me as a young boy. She would read books to him for long hours at a time, as she had with me. She was completely devoted to him, as she had been to me. She gave us both unconditional love until the day she died. I have never loved anyone as deeply as my mother, and I can safely say that her two other children would say the same.

All three of Velma's children, including me, were extremely different in all ways, but we all got along well and loved each other, which I attribute to the cohesive influence of unconditional love with no favoritism given by Velma.

Even when Velma became older, she never seemed old to me or to others. She always had a smile and a spring in her step. She could be described as perky. She was active in conversation and could usually find common ground with anyone. She always kept an open mind and never discounted someone's opinion if they were able to back it up with reason and fact.

Her appearance was very important to her. She would never think of letting anyone see her without her makeup and lipstick. She was fashionable in her dress but never "fancy." She always tried to be appropriate. She carried herself well and always with a smile. She loved to go on outings on the spur of the moment. In fact, she liked it better that way. She loved being spontaneous. She played a part in a high school film production with my oldest son, Douglas, and his friends when she was in her late eighties.

When she was in her nineties, she sang the cutest duet with my wife, Barbara's, brother Mike, a Richard Rodgers song made popular by Frank Sinatra, "The Lady Is a Tramp." This was performed at a Christmas party in front of friends and family. Both singers received much applause and many bravos.

Velma was active and energetic and had an open mind, true to her adventurous and independent nature, until the end at age ninety-nine. She never seemed to age because, as her favorite song by Frank Sinatra went, she was always so very young at heart!

8.

The Bohemian

In 1967, Wally Graham, his wife, Charlene, and their young son, Brandon, were driving through New Mexico in their VW minivan, coming back from a long and extended vacation through Mexico. So far, it had been a wonderful and much-needed break from Wally's grueling work schedule as a professional jazz guitarist in Philadelphia. He did gigs and session work in New York and various other cities on the East Coast, and when he wasn't working, he was practicing in the basement with his guitar. He was driven to perfection and been obsessed with his guitar for the past several years. His whole psyche seemed to revolve around his guitar. Charlene barely saw him during this time. While in Mexico, they had camped on the beach and eaten the local food. They loved mangos and avocados, which were uncommon in the United States at the time. They also relished the spicy red and green chili peppers. They loved walking through the markets and buying local goods, such as blankets and pottery. Many of the small towns they visited still had cobblestone streets. They had great fun interacting with the local people, who were friendly and at that time liked Americans. Charlene spoke fluent Spanish and was a Spanish teacher in Philadelphia.

The high chaparral topography around Santa Fe, New Mexico, was captivating. They could smell the aroma of the piñon pine and juniper trees that were characteristic of the area. The sky was vivid blue, and they were surrounded by pine- and aspen-covered mountains in the distance. This was a far cry from Philadelphia and the East Coast. Wally felt that art and music were his calling. However, he felt entrapped and burdened by his current situation. Several years earlier, when Charlene and Wally were first married, he had attended several art schools in Europe while being financially supported by his father. His focus at the time was mainly sculpting and painting. Wally was taught various methods unique to each specific country. They traveled through Europe on a motorcycle and had many exciting and wonderful experiences. They had the same feeling of freedom and excitement now, traveling through New Mexico, as they had in Europe. Santa Fe had an old-world charm to it, with old Spanish architecture built in the 1700s. As they walked through the town, they noticed that it was a thriving, exuberant center for the arts. Wally was thrilled. He had never seen anything quite like Santa Fe.

After two days there, they decided to quit their jobs and relocate. This was despite his job as a promising jazz guitarist on the verge of success and a promising career that he had diligently worked at for several years. Although they had limited financial resources, they were not concerned.

They bought some land outside Santa Fe on the side of a mountain overlooking the Santa Fe Basin. It was an amazing vista. At night, one could see the lights of the small city flickering in the valley. The Sangre de Cristo Mountains were in the distance beyond the city. The sunsets from this vantage point were breathtaking. The mountains seemed to turn purple with a red, pink, and orange sky at sunset.

They began building their house by hand while living in a tent for nearly a year. Charlene became proficient in plumbing and electricity, while Wally built the main structure of the house. He had some previous experience with cement, plaster, and house building from working for Stanley Hill, his grandfather, who was an expert builder.

Houses in the Santa Fe area were mainly built in adobe style with mud bricks, straw, plaster, and supporting beams of pine logs called vegas. That style of house is perfect for the dry environment of the American Southwest, as it is warm in the winter and cool in the summer. A fireplace was built in the main room with a built-in seat around it. The burning piñon pine had a smell like fragrant incense. The house faced south, with large picture windows looking out over the valley. Pots of flowering vivid red geraniums along with various cacti were placed next to the windows. The back of the house was built into the mountainside to shelter it from the north wind. Several round pieces of thick colored glass were placed on the west wall of the house. In the afternoon, beams of colored light shone through into the main room, giving it a rainbow effect. Large tanks on the roof stored rainwater for subsequent use in the house. The floors were made of beautiful Mexican tile. The base of the steps to the upstairs were made of ceramic painted tile. Below the tile floors were pipes that were buried vertically in the ground, keeping the tiles warm in winter and cool in summer. Skylights were placed overhead so that there was never a need for electric light during the day. Wally and Char mainly used candles and the fireplace at night for light. A greenhouse was placed on the side of the house connected to the kitchen. Citrus trees, bananas, and beautiful flowers were grown there. Wally sculpted various things, such as a whale and dolphins in the bathroom, a motif of ancient Indian cliff dwellings in the hallway, and a blue heron in one of the bedrooms. He colored them with natural pigments mixed in with the adobe plaster obtained from different soil strata from the surrounding hills. It was a truly environmentally efficient house that was unique, artistic, and beautiful. The adobe house was nestled amongst the pine and juniper trees, which made it look like part of the natural environment.

Wally and Char built several other houses and obtained some revenue from the rent, which was quite high in Santa Fe. Wally made most of his money by sculpting frescoes on the adobe walls of usually high-end client houses. He worked for several Hollywood actors and some famous rock stars. Money was never a concern for him, though. He had what I would describe as a hunter-gatherer lifestyle. When he needed money, he would find a job, and when he got paid, he would go fishing, skiing, or whatever suited his fancy. Charlene worked for the state and had good benefits from her job. She also taught Spanish. Charlene was mainly responsible for the practicalities of their life taking care of the paperwork. Wally periodically gave guitar lessons. Looking back, I think these days were the happiest days of Wally and Char's life.

When Wally was younger, he was fiercely independent and somewhat of a loner. However, when he was with people, he was very outgoing, funny, and charismatic. He despised dishonesty, arrogance, and hypocrisy. Most people recognize these issues with people and deal with them. Wally would not tolerate them, which led to not infrequent conflict with others. He was a rebel from the start who mistrusted authority. However, the rougher edges to his personality seemed to disappear after he moved to Santa Fe. He became a nearly transformed spiritual person seeking beauty and truth in life.

In high school, he had been the Golden Gloves champion of Kansas City. All his fights were won by knockouts. He was very athletic, quick as lightning, explosive, and tremendously powerful for such a small-framed but muscular man. In high school, he had a fearsome reputation. He was known to take on boys much larger than he as well as several boys at a time and winde up the victor. Boxing was probably an outlet for his frustrations from the routine, regimented family life of the 1950s. Wally went to numerous colleges but quickly left for one reason or another—William Jewell, Beloit, Tulane, University of Missouri–Kansas City, and University of Illinois, to name a few. While in New Orleans at Tulane, he signed a contract to fight professionally. After one year, he had to leave suddenly because his contract was owned by members of the mafia who wanted him to throw fights for an extra cut of the money.

While at the University of Illinois at Urbana-Champaign, he bought an Austin-Healey roadster sports car. These were well-made fast cars from England with tremendous maneuverability and large, powerful engines. He had a good friend, Allen, who was an excellent mechanic specializing in sports cars who helped him keep the car in top racing condition. Wally loved driving at high speeds, turning on a dime and then rapidly accelerating. He entered numerous small local sports car races and always did well. He practiced daily, racing in his car at an old, abandoned airport as well as at a racetrack when it was not in use. Allen frequently accompanied him, making adjustments to the engine after practice runs. Allen seemed to be emotionally invested in the performance of the car, like a parent with a child. Allen and Wally got to know the car's strengths and limitations like part of their own bodies. On a few practice runs Wally took Allen as a passenger in the car running it at top speeds and then quickly downshifting, then taking sharp turns on a dime. Allen knew these rides were important to properly adjusting the car's motor however, for him it was a was a hellish experience, going at such high speeds. Each time he drove with Wally he felt as if he was going to die. He grasped the door handle tightly as he gritted his teeth. He closed his eyes around turns and held his breath. Allen just sucked it up and suffered through the engine diagnostic rides.

Wally and Allen had heard about an advertised sportscar race with a substantial prize for place winners. It was a national event to be held within their area. When they heard about the event, they both looked at each other smiled and said in unison "Let's do this!"

After a few minor adjustments to the carburetor Allen felt that the car was in as good a condition that they could get it. They were ready. Wally was one of the best drivers Allen had ever seen, especially since Wally had no formal training or previous experience, which Allen had a hard time believing. It was all-natural ability of quickness, coordination, tenacity, and fearlessness.

The day prior to the race Allen and Wally drove out to the racecourse to evaluate it and formulate a racing strategy. There were other drivers there inspecting the track doing the same thing Allen and Wally were doing. The track had many tight turns as well as one long straightaway. It mainly favored maneuverability as well as quick acceleration and then rapid downshifting for the tight turns. There were cars from all over the country which had entered this event.

Wally dropped Allen off after which he went over to visit his girlfriend. He was planning to stay just a moment, so he left the keys in the car. He spent a little more time than expected in her house. He happened to look out the window and saw someone driving his car away. Wally bolted out the door and sprinted down the street after the thief and his stolen car. The thief was having difficulty getting the car in proper gear. He obviously didn't know how to drive a stick shift with a clutch well. Wally caught up to the slow-moving car which was jerking intermittently down the street. The top was down, and Wally pulled the thief out of the car and drug him onto the street. The car slowly came to a stop. The thief then tried to stand at which time Wally clenched his fist and landed a powerful right-hand punch to the jaw rendering the thief temporarily unconscious. Wally heard an audible crack and felt an instantaneous horrific burning pain in his right hand. He looked at his right hand and noticed a deformity in his fourth and fifth knuckles. He then hopped in the car and drove himself with great difficulty to the nearest hospital leaving the thief laying in the street.

An x-ray of Wally's hand revealed he had fractured two bones in his hand. The orthopedic surgeon placed a plaster cast on the hand and gave Wally a prescription for some narcotics. He drove himself home again with great difficulty. He placed ice on the hand and took some Tylenol and ibuprofen. He was going to reassess things in the morning regarding the race. When dawn finally came after a sleepless night, he was still in a significant amount of throbbing pain. He took a handful of ibuprofen and said to himself "The hell with it, I'm driving!" No one ever doubted Wally's courage.

He drove to the racetrack where he met Allen. "What happened to you!" Allen said.

"It's a long story, take a look under the hood and make sure everything is still alright."

Allen looked under the hood at the motor while Wally revved the engine. Allen then checked all of the fluids and the tires.

"It's all good to go," said Allen

On the drive over to the track Wally had to make some adjustments in the way he shifted the gear shift. He placed the trunk of the shifter between his first and second fingers. Down shifting was more difficult and caused extreme discomfort. Shifting gears wasn't as firm as grasping the top of the stick with your entire hand, but it would have to do. His hand was still killing him with throbbing pain, but he wasn't going to think about it. Wally said to himself "I don't care anymore; I'm going to win this race whatever it takes!"

The cars lined up, and the checked flag came down, indicating the start of the race. Initially Wally was at the back of the pack, but he slowly worked his way up until he was behind the three front-runners. Wally stayed close behind the top three cars for nearly the entire race so that he could use the front cars as a wind drag. His hand was still painful. It seemed that his body was punishing him every time he needed to downshift. His adrenaline was flowing, and he just chose to ignore the discomfort. In the last two laps, he noticed that the front three cars were trying to outdistance each other by dramatically increasing their speed on the straightaway. The front three cars were oblivious to Wally lurking just behind them. Wally noted that when the front cars increased their speed, they took the upcoming turn a little too wide. This left a small space to pass the lead cars on the inside.

Just before going into the turn, he downshifted before the others shifted. This gave him more power and the ability to make a tighter turn around the corner, passing the front cars on the inside. After he made the sharp turn, barely edging ahead of the other three cars coming out of the turn, he floored the gas pedal and accelerated rapidly, creating distance between his car and the others. Wally used tremendous driving skill and some risk to pass the leading cars on the inside and won the race. Allen was at the finish line, jumping up and down for joy. Instead of celebrating with Allen, Wally went home took some pain medications and went to sleep.

Wally received a large, engraved silver plate and two thousand dollars. He gave half of the winnings to Allen. The entire community and our family were stunned that he had entered and won this road race. There was an article in the local paper and a photo of him holding up his silver-plated trophy with a cast on his hand.

After the race, Wally sold his car and lost all interest in cars and racing, much to the dismay of Allen, who, after initial success, wanted to continue and go on to larger venues. As in so many undertakings Wally was involved in, after being initially successful, he quit midstream and got involved in something completely different. His interests then led him into the arts.

When Wally moved to Santa Fe, he seemed to change into the person he really was meant to be. Instead of a an intense and sometimes aggressive man, he transformed to a philosophical, outgoing, and kind person. He said that he felt a freedom that can happen only when there is a self-realization. It was a feeling that he had never experienced before, as if a heavy weight had been lifted from his shoulders that he was constantly carrying and now he was ready to fly.

Santa Fe seemed to draw not only artists but people who were part of the counterculture. Wally became well known among this community as a person who was "Cool," and amazingly talented. Wally was looked upon as a fun-loving priest, guru, or father figure by some. Many people viewed him as their clinical psychologist or their life coach to whom they would seek advice, wisdom, and emotional support. Many were psychologically and emotionally damaged, without a firm foundation in life. Many came from seriously dysfunctional families and harbored deep-seated insecurities.

Wally talked of life and philosophy. He professed peace, tolerance, and love for one another. Wally's personal attitude was so positive that some of his aura would inevitably rub off on people. While sitting in a beautiful setting, Wally would frequently come close to the person he was speaking to and stare deeply into their eyes with understanding and empathy. He would calmly smile and impart his way of seeing things. He occasionally would hold people's hands when they appeared emotionally fragile. He convinced people that their lives mattered and that they were loved. When he spoke, Wally would make you feel like you were the most important person in the world. Many of the things he spoke about were teachings of Jesus but were never acknowledged as such. Some people would follow him around like puppies, just waiting for a treat of philosophical wisdom. He frequently had to tell them nicely to go home. It was not uncommon for friends on motorcycles or old, dilapidated cars, filled with people to come driving up Wally's dirt road to his house unannounced. Wally would always give a hearty greeting, a big smile, and offer his unexpected guests coffee or some herbal tea. They would "shoot the breeze" as they sat in lawn chairs overlooking the Santa fe Basin and the mountains beyond. When people left his house, they always left smiling and uplifted. His house became a popular place to visit by many.

One young writer who knew Wally wrote a chapter in a book about him. He didn't use Wally's name but used the pseudonym "Sunny" since Wally took the darkness out of the hearts of troubled people. He seemed to loosen people up with humor and laughter and then give them a little wisdom to build their confidence and fragile egos.

I recall being present with a couple of young hippies, listening to Wally by a campfire. He went on and on about the universe and how we are all one with it. He said we are all made of stardust. The key was to find the inner oneness that everyone had with the universe, and we would experience peace and harmony. This talk was more effective while everyone was looking at the stars and the Milky Way on a clear, moonless summer night in New Mexico. The two hippies' eyes were wide open and their mouths agape.

They both said, "Yeah, I get it. Wow, that's amazing, Wally. I never saw it that way. Far out!" They left inspired.

After they were gone, I said to Wally, "That was a bunch of crap you fed those two fools."

He said, "I know, but it made them feel good."

———

O nce Wally took me into the mountains to a commune near Taos, New Mexico, where he visited friends and traded or bought goods. He was invited to put on a musical show on the evening of our arrival. He had done this before, and they wanted a repeat performance. My impression was that his performances were payment for work and materials given by commune members to help build one of his houses.

So, Wally and I headed off to the remote mountains of northern New Mexico with his acoustic and electric guitar and an amplifier placed in the back of his old pickup truck.

I asked Wally, "It doesn't sound like there will be much electric power out there. Are you going to plug that amplifier into a tree? "I was curious to visit this place, but a little apprehensive too. I was thinking it may be a little weird especially if we were stuck there in the middle of nowhere.

He laughed and said, "It's fairly primitive, but we'll make do. You'll see; it'll be fun and definitely interesting. They're really good people."

It was a long drive on a winding single-lane dirt road to get to the place. It took about an hour from the nearest paved state road. The scenery was beautiful with multicolored rock mesas, deep ravines, and small rivers. No sign of human presence marred this vast, unspoiled area. We encountered pine forests as we gained altitude. We drove into a large valley beyond the forest. As we entered the valley, we could see the dirt road extending into an area of human-made structures.

When we drove into the village, Wally gave a characteristic honk of the horn that everyone associated with him. People thronged around the truck as Wally and I got out of the vehicle. The people gave him hugs and high fives. Wally was animated and exuberant. Obviously, these people knew him well and had a long history with him. Many of them I know had helped with the building of his house, most notably obtaining the large pine-log vegas for the construction of the roof, which had been no small task. This small village was an abandoned farm that these people had taken over for their own use.

The leader of the commune, Mishra, gave Wally a hug and a clasped handshake. Mishra said, "How are you doing, brother? Good to see you." He barely acknowledged me and almost seemed dismissive. My impression was that I didn't look like a person who should be there. I guess I was not "hip" enough. Mishra was a very tall, thin American man with a long mixed-gray beard. He had a long braided ponytail and was bald on top. He was shirtless and deeply tanned. He wore blue jeans with a colorful handmade beaded belt. He had a commanding, confident presence. No one seemed to know his real name or anything about his past. Rumor had it that he was initially from the Haight-Ashbury district of San Francisco in the 1960s but had dropped out to become a leader in the "commune scene."

The commune was in a picturesque mountain valley with a stream nearby. Multiple old cars and machinery in various states of disrepair were scattered about. Parked on the side of the road was a large yellow school bus that was used when the group went on outings. Flowers, peace signs, and other colorful psychedelic art were painted on the sides of the bus in vivid colors. There was an extensive, well-kept garden with multiple rows of corn, beans, squash, and other vegetables. This garden covered several acres and had some type of irrigation from the nearby stream. A large patch of sunflowers grew on one side of the garden. At least one hundred chickens roamed about the area. The chickens had a large coop to stay in at night next to the garden. My impression was that a large source of the people's dietary protein was likely eggs.

The people's dwellings were varied. They ranged from cabins, tepees, and plywood shacks to long houses that had once been barns and now sheltered multiple families. Mishra had a very nice house, distinct from the others, with a small porch. It was the only house that had running water from a well beneath the house. It also had a stone fireplace and a cast-iron wood-burning stove. My impression was that this had been the previous owner's house, since it was much better built and in better condition than the other structures. Four families were living in one large house that had previously been a barn and had been renovated to accommodate the people living there. The structure was crowded and messy. Dust was everywhere, since the floor was made of packed dirt. Old clothes and apparel were bunched in corners. Dirty cookware and dishes were piled on a table in a makeshift kitchen since there was no running water. Several children ran naked through the house.

There were around fifty people in the commune. Clothing was varied and obviously optional. There was a stream nearby with large smooth boulders that was used for water and bathing. Half of the people I saw were hard at work in the garden or doing other chores, while the remainder were just hanging around. One bunch was playing soccer with a ball and two small makeshift goals.

Wally knew everyone there, so he and I made the rounds, talking to various people as we walked through the village. He introduced me to everyone as his brother visiting from Kansas City as he put his arm around my shoulders. Everyone was overjoyed to see Wally. However, I got pretty much the same reaction that I had from Mishra—a pretty cold reception for Wally's younger brother. Most people were polite but standoffish despite my efforts at conversation. It seemed that people made snap judgments about me without even bothering to learn what I was about. I imagine their opinions were based on my appearance alone.

After a couple of hours, Wally became involved with some of the people, and I grew bored. I walked down to the small soccer game to see if they needed an extra player. They clearly didn't. I attempted to engage several people in conversation about life in the commune, but none wanted to talk, and they brushed me off. I went over to the garden and volunteered my help, whether it be pulling weeds or whatever I could do to pass the time. The people there said they would rather I not get involved in their work, but thanks anyway. I had the feeling of an unwanted outsider despite my brother being the super-cool artist guru that he was. My next stop was the mountain stream. It was beautiful. Just by its appearance, I thought there was a high likelihood that trout lived in the waters. I was greatly disappointed that I hadn't brought my fly rod. I doubted if any of the people there fished. After walking closer to the stream, I noted several naked men and women bathing and do-ing laundry in the stream. I didn't feel like joining them, so I decided to take a long hike up a nearby mountain to burn some time before Wally's musical performance that evening.

The hike to the top of the mountain was amazing. The vista from the summit of the surrounding mountains and valleys was breathtaking. I could see the village far below, nestled in the valley close to the stream where I had just been. I picked up some nice agate, rose quartz, and jasper along the way. The hike up this mountain was worth the whole trip for me.

To join the commune, you were expected to give all of your money to the communal bank managed by Mishra. The money would be used to buy necessities for the commune. Wally told me that Mishra did invest some of the money for the commune in mutual funds and bonds that he managed under his name. People could stay on a trial basis for two months before making a commitment to join. There were frequent transient guests in addition to the long-standing permanent group. I heard that the commune had once been unexpectedly visited by a predatory and violent motorcycle gang, who caused a lot of destruction, strife, and turmoil until they finally left. The police or sheriff couldn't be called because of the remote location and because the commune stored a significant number of illegal drugs that the members didn't want exposed to the law. It was my impression that they were not on the greatest of terms with local law enforcement, since their term for police were "pigs" or some other derogatory expression.

On Sundays and Wednesdays, the people would gather in an open field, sitting cross-legged on the ground in a large circle with Mishra in the middle. He would then give a talk and the ceremony would begin. Participation in the event was mandatory. The talk was mainly Eastern mystic philosophy, such as reincarnation, with every plant and animal having a soul with energy.

Mishra said, "There is so much ignorance and hypocrisy in the outside world. People out there live their lives divorced from the land and its bounty, filling their bodies with chemicals and poisons every day. They worship a so-called messiah who vanished two thousand years ago, and they've been looking for him ever since." (Speaking of Jesus Christ).

He spoke of how materialism was corrupting the world and how every life-sustaining element should be shared equally. This included not only food and material goods but relationships with one another. Mishra was known to have relationships with multiple women in the commune, despite the women having long-term connections with other men. He spoke of free love without inhibition for everyone. There was no private property; everything was for the group. Mishra criticized people's previous upbringing, family, and friends as misguided, corrupt, and even evil. He attempted to break down past family relationships and establish a new family with the commune and its values as its core.

What Mishra was saying was out of the teachings of Karl Marx mixed with new age Eastern mysticism. Any problems, questions, or controversies were brought to Mishra for judgment. It seemed to me that this was the totalitarian state of Mishra. At the end of the talk, the people would close their eyes and meditate. They would do breathing exercises using their diaphragm, while relaxing their bodies with their eyes closed. Then they would hold hands and chant simultaneously, "Oom, oom, oom," for several minutes before raising their hands in the air and looking at the sky. All would then take a deep breath and exhale, which concluded the ceremony.

Most of the people appeared dirty and mildly malnourished. They had goats for milking and chickens for eggs. Most, if not all, were veg-etarians. They made goat cheese, candles, and other products that they sold in town at the farmer's market. Occasionally they would go to town as a group in the yellow school bus and other cars for music festivals or other special events, but this was infrequent.

Some type of entertainment was scheduled for the group every Saturday night. Since the "farm" was so isolated, there was no TV or radio. The people therefore had to entertain themselves. Sometimes they had skits, plays, or music productions with guitars, drums, and flutes. Occasionally they had an outside musician such as Wally come in. These were very special events that they looked forward to. The people were particularly excited by the upcoming event during the evening that included Wally. He had obviously played this venue before to great acclaim.

The evening of our arrival, Wally put on a real show with his guitar. The electric guitar was plugged into a generator that ran on propane with an extra-long extension cord that Wally had brought with him. I suspected that the only person allowed to use the generator and the propane was Mishra, since he stored both in his house.

Two men accompanied Wally with one large and one smaller drum. A third man had a wooden flute and was quite an accomplished musician. Wally started his performance with the acoustic guitar and played a highly unusual conglomeration of jazz, blues, rock, and Spanish flamenco. All enjoyed this immensely. I had never heard anything like it. I was amazed that I liked it as well as I did. The music really made you want to get up and move. I likened it to a James Brown concert, where the rhythm and energy made it impossible to sit still, even if you were not a fan of soul music.

The setting was almost primitive. People were dancing around a large bonfire, while Wally and the others played with reckless abandon. Wally was really into it. His head was moving up and down and side to side, his feet keeping rhythm with the beat. A great part of the excitement generated was not only the music itself but the outward display of energy and emotion by Wally and the other musicians. With his exuberant spirit, Wally seemed to energize everyone.

Periodically he would shout along with the guitar chord he was playing. He would occasionally verbalize words along with the music, such as "Dig it! Break on through! Oooh yeah!" This elicited a loud vocal response from the crowd in the same chord. Wally became the leader of a unified and highly unusual chant. With his guitar, he occasionally traded riffs with the flute, which followed the guitar lead. At one time, he stopped playing and let the drummers play a long solo. The flute then came in loud and strong backed by the drums. Wally temporarily walked away. He then switched to his electric guitar, plugged it into the amplifier, and turned the amplifier up to its maximum volume. He came back and literally jumped in with a more vibrant guitar riff than before. The sound coming out of the guitar was almost shockingly loud but clear. The notes were fast but concise, flowing like rapid water coming over a waterfall. The sound echoed through the valley off of the canyon walls like a natural amphitheater. This little show of musical theatrics set the audience on fire with yelling, whistling, and clapping. The music was continuous with no set songs. The performance ebbed and flowed continuously for several hours, leading to a big crescendo at the end. Wally threw both arms in the air, followed by a huge audience response of jumping and screaming.

A lot of pot and other drugs were floating around, and almost everyone seemed to be in an altered state. This was their chance to party and let off steam from the previous week of hard boring physical labor. Mishra was front and center, clapping his hands and encouraging participation in the festivities.

Most of the men danced in a mechanical, uncoordinated, nearly spastic manner, waving their arms around stiffly. Some had their mouths open, shaking their heads with their long, ill-kept hair. Occasionally they kicked their legs in a stiff, absurd gallop. One man with long hair and a beard wore a striped necktie with no shirt. My guess was that he had gotten dressed up for the big dance.

The majority of the women, on the other hand, seemed much more coordinated. They moved their entire frames smoothly and rhythmically. Both arms were frequently raised, as they slowly moved and intertwined them like two rhythmic snakes. Most wore very loose-fitting, thin dresses and blouses that were transparent against the light of the fire. They frequently closed their eyes and slowly moved their heads with the music. Their long hair swayed from side to side along with their hips, which undulated slowly and sensually. Each person, it seemed, was dancing in a solitary, individual manner. Only a few couples were dancing together but not touching.

When the music began to slow down, two women who had been dancing came over to me and sat down. They were attractive and much more well-groomed than most of the others. Both had been at the "farm" for less than a month. I was surprised at how friendly, intelligent, and articulate they were. They were both around twenty-three, my age. One was from Philadelphia, Pennsylvania, and knew Wally well. The other was from Austin, Texas. I was grateful for the company since no one had gone out of their way so far to make me feel welcome. They were both impressed that I was Wally's little brother. It seemed that Wally had attained near rock-star status. He was "So cool!"

The conversation was easy and effortless. Both girls were energetic and seemed to want the evening to continue. They playfully fingered my hair, stroked my hands, and softly rubbed my knee. The philosophy of this group of people was that whatever you felt like doing was okay, and free love was a big part of this worldview. I remembered many stories from my youth of love in the wrong situation winding up in disaster.

The stories of David and Bathsheba, Samson and Delilah, and Joseph and Potiphar's wife, as well as my uncle John, had all ended in catastrophic situations after just one episode of love under the wrong circumstances. The situation reminded me of fishing, where the fish saw a flashy lure, but beneath the attractive flash was a barbed hook and a future in the frying pan. One never knew if there would be a jealous boyfriend, the contraction of a disease, pregnancy, or a beautiful woman turned stalker with insane drama. I think both women were looking for fun and adventure. I couldn't see them sticking around the "farm" for very long. That night reminded me of a lyric in an old Creedence Clearwater Revival song: "Barefoot girls dancing in the moonlight."

Wally and I stayed overnight. We were offered places to stay in various shelters, but the conditions were crowded, and there were mice and other creatures that the people there had gotten used to. Wally and I spent the night on a small hill under a tree away from the village. It was a beautiful and memorable evening, sleeping in the open with the brilliant stars above.

I got the feeling that most of the people in the commune were city kids with utopian aspirations to build a new society. Most hadn't anticipated the amount of work and sacrifice that would be required for them to carve out a new life in the middle of nowhere. Most knew nothing about farming or communal living. Many had changed their names, such as Brother Bear, Moonglow, and Earth Pig, to mention a few. I thought this was silly. It seemed that these people had switched from being independent to being guided by a guru authority figure, giving up their freedom to be told what they could and could not do. These people had discarded all previous societal traditions and were trying to find another way without experience or rational consideration of the consequences. The basic rules of Judeo-Christian society were discarded for being "free" but under the authority of a guru to tell them what was right and wrong. Suffice it to say that interpersonal relationships, especially between men and women, were frequently volatile and chaotic, with extreme emotional consequences.

There were frequent conflicts regarding the delegation and amount of work. Some people were lazier than others. Drugs frequently reduced the amount and quality of the work done on the "farm." Wally said that many people just wanted to be taken care of and told what to do instead of truly being free and independent. It takes hard work to be free, and freedom can sometimes be frightening. Unfortunately, many people are like sheep. This is why America is such a unique experiment in governance. Aside from ancient Athens, Greece, it is the first nation in human history to maintain a democracy. The remainder of people throughout history have been ruled by despots and authoritarian dictators.

Whenever there is more than one person, there must be rules to live by. In American society, the social rules are based on the Ten Commandments and the Constitution of the United States. The people in the commune, although they claimed to be free, were really under closer scrutiny with their own rules than they would have been in "straight" society. Wally recognized this and called these people "beautiful sheep" following the pied piper to future chaos.

Many of these people were trying to find meaning in their lives. Most had grown up in middle-class or even wealthy families and had all of their material and educational needs met. Many were college graduates. However, they were looking for meaning in life. Material things were of little importance in their quest. For most Americans until this generation, the need for meaning had been met by family, religion, community, and country. All of these sources had been discarded by these people. Most had misguided notions that America was essentially a racist, genocidal, and imperialist country.

Without meaning in life, most felt lonely and empty despite having all the money they needed. They used the country and the government as scapegoats for their own unhappiness, in which they grew to hate America and "Straight" society. Most of the people had broken off their relationships with their previous family and friends, which was encouraged by Mishra.

This search for the meaning of life is as old as humankind. The Bible clearly states that humans will always be empty and unfulfilled unless they accept a personal relationship with God. King Solomon, considered one of the wisest men ever, came to this conclusion. He had all the riches, women, and power in the world, but still he was unfulfilled and empty. Only through a relationship with God was he satisfied. He described this search for the meaning in life in a book of the Bible, Ecclesiastes, which he wrote. Jesus said, "It is written that man shall not live by bread alone, but by every word that comes from God." Jesus also said, speaking of spiritual fulfillment, "I will give you living water to where you will not thirst again." Unfortunately, these misguided people had the truth in front of them, but they discarded Judeo-Christian beliefs along with the traditional family values that are the foundation of American society. They replaced these beliefs with extreme left-wing idealism (i.e., communism, hedonism, and mystic Eastern thought). These beliefs became their religion.

Many of the people living in the commune thought people in straight society were racists, or fascists, basically bad people. They ostracized others in an "us-against-them" philosophy, where anyone who didn't think like them was evil, which was encouraged by Mishra. In the commune, they all thought of themselves as nonconformists; however, they had traded one conformity for another. They were now conforming to their own exclusive society.

I suspect that some of the people in the commune were undergoing a transient rebellion, trying to find their individuality and break away from their parents. Such people will usually come to their senses later and return to regular society. I think that the two girls who talked with me after the music were likely in this group.

Wally recognized the hypocrisy of Mishra and with many people in society, however he tried to show others the truth by his own actions. I showed Wally the lyrics of a song, called "Laughing," written by David Crosby that summed up the situation regarding these people looking for truth and winding up into a dead end. Wally thought it outstanding and "Right on!"

Wally was always hospitable to newcomers and family alike. He relished showing people Santa Fe, touring around the area, and having a good time. The day usually ended with a big spaghetti dinner at the large round table in the "kiva room" in his house. The kiva room was a large, circular room with a skylight at the top, similar to a castle tower. Afterward, there would be a campfire outside with good conversation and marveling at the bright stars above or looking out over the valley to the city below with its myriad of sparkling lights. My family took a yearly trip to Santa Fe to ski and eat great New Mexican food laced with hot red and green chili.

Wally was an expert skier. He skied incredibly fast but with great skill and control, as in his car racing days. His favorite skis were Head 220s that were much longer and stiffer than the usual ski. They were built for speed. When skiing, Wally would make few turns, just run straight down the slope, hitting the tops of bumps on the way down, but always in control. He drove his car the way he skied, fast but always in control. Wally's main car, in addition to his work truck, was an old beat-up machine with no heat or air conditioning. Two windows were absent, and the doors were fused so that they couldn't be opened. To enter the car, one would crawl through one of the open windows. The floor was rusted out in areas where you could see the street pavement below. Old Mexican blankets covered the back seat with an ample amount of residual dog hair. Despite the body of the car being a disaster the engine worked extremely well. For some reason he had a real emotional attachment to that od machine.

I received a call from Wally one night. He told me he was stuck in a position bent over a chair and couldn't change his position without pain. He said that his pain was mainly in the right lower quadrant of his abdomen, and he had had a fever of 103 for several days. He said, "I'm getting some amazingly colorful visuals" (i.e., hallucinations). He was describing the perfect natural history of a perforated appendicitis with sepsis. Wally was always one to joke or make fun of even serious situations. I told him, "Wally, get to the hospital immediately!" The next day, the surgeon spoke with me and described what had been done. The appendix had been removed and a large abdominal abscess drained.

However, most of the conversation related to Wally's personality. The doctor said, "Wally is really an amazing guy. I don't think I have ever met anyone quite like him. He is an enjoyable patient, and the entire hospital staff loves him." I thanked the surgeon for taking such good care of Wally and told him that Wally had that effect on people.

Wally had great empathy for nearly all people whoever they were, or station in life. However, he showed exceptional kindness to those with disabilities. He and my son Andy, who has Downs syndrome, had a special relationship. Wally would carry Andy on his shoulders on long hikes through rugged territory. Andy loved it. Wally would perform crazy antics to make Andy laugh. Whenever Wally entered the room, Andy would respond with a big smile and laugh. When Andy was born, despite myself being a physician, it was a time of great sadness and despair for me and my wife because of his permanent disability and extensive medical problems requiring surgery. My mindset in life had always been goal and achievement oriented, which is not an uncommon trait among physicians. I was mentally and emotionally unprepared for a handicapped son. Wally was immediate in his support and instrumental in changing our point of view. He made us realize that Andy is a beautiful human being with a future of love that can be a light and positive force to the entire family. Wally gave us hope and light when there was none. He lifted our spirits when no one else could. He turned out to be so right! Wally couldn't wait to see Andy and hold him in his arms.

I think Wally was one of many people in search for a meaning to life. For some reason when he moved to Santa Fe, it seemed he had a transformative experience. I notice a marked change in his personality. He seemed to almost glow with love, happiness, and self contentment. He tried to impart this to others around him, whoever they were, and give them a little bit of his happiness. This is why people flocked to him for years. He showed people understanding, and kindness, with the zeal of a true Christian, although he never professed to being religious. He had a great gift of charisma and the ability to influence people for the good.

Wally always believed that what you did in life for a job, or a profession was merely a vehicle to get you where your spirit could flourish. What was important in life was your character, not your position, status in society, or your wealth. All of the trappings a person had in life meant nothing. It was what your inner soul was like, which was all important and the key to happiness.

Like all human beings we are imperfect creatures, and we all have our demons. As time progressed, Wally began drinking and using marijuana heavily. His burning, exuberant positive energy along with his creativity seemed to slowly dim. Nonetheless, women seemed to be attracted to Wally, with resultant affairs or, as he would call it, "adult fun." These factors led to his divorce from Char. As Wally came to realize, free love is never free. There is always a price to be paid eventually, and there are always strings attached, even if there is a supposed "understanding". The affair may be a onetime event or a long relationship. Even in the most discreet of circumstances, affairs never work out well, and all have unintended consequences.

Wally became more reclusive and began having difficulty walking.

He ate very little food and lost a significant amount of weight. Most of his calories came from alcohol. He was hospitalized several times for complications of alcoholism. It was sad to see such a creative, energetic, and gifted talent slowly deteriorate. On repeated occasions my sister, his ex-wife Charlene, and I, tried to pull him out of a slow spiral downward, but nothing helped. It was as if I could see Wally under water slowly sinking with his hand outstretched to mine just out of my grasp, continuously sinking lower beyond my helping hand.

Wally was a bright shinning light of hope to so many. Although the light of his gift slowly dimmed, it left a lasting burning ember in the souls of so many, including myself. Whenever I have talked about Wally to others who knew him, it always evoked an immediate big smile, and good feeling, along with a good Wally story. I think that's the way Wally would've liked it after leaving this earth.

There was a large get-together at Wally's house after his death. A large circle was formed, and each person shared an experience he or she had had with Wally. The event was touching and meaningful. His daughter did a masterful job at managing the event. Charlene was there and related the good times they had together. After I spoke, I read the lyrics to a song written by Carol King, that Wally always liked, "I wasn't Born to Follow," sung by Roger McGuinn and the Byrds. The title of the song seemed to fit Wally perfectly.

9.

Play by
the Rules

The Dartmouth College baseball team was at the end of a long road trip covering the East Coast. They were on a real winning streak. Dartmouth had had a winning season and wanted to go out on a winning note since it was the last game of the season. For Jerry Foote, it was not only the last game of the season but more than likely the last game of his outstanding baseball career. He was a senior and had played on the team for four years.

Jerry Foote was a level-headed, dedicated player and an above-average hitter. One thing that set him apart from the other players was his unique ability to get base hits in critical situations with men on base, making him a so-called clutch hitter. This is an innate and rare talent that cannot be taught or coached. A player just has it or doesn't. For a baseball team, this ability is an enormous asset because baseball is a game of getting the right hit at the right time. Jerry was not an extraordinary athlete by any means. He had average speed and above-average fielding ability. He had found a niche for himself at first base, which he played well. All through high school, most of his friends were better players than he, but because of his extraordinary work ethic and determination, he became an asset to any team.

In addition to being a clutch hitter, he had an ability to spark the whole team to play better. Some would call this leadership. On every team he ever played for, it seemed that Jerry became the glue that held things together. When Jerry was not playing, the team just didn't do as well and seemed not to play as a cohesive unit. Jerry simply had this natural leadership ability. Tony Lupien, the Dartmouth coach, recognized what a valuable asset Jerry was and made him team captain. Everyone liked his easygoing but determined, nonjudgmental style.

Their final game would be against Holy Cross College. Earlier in the season, Dartmouth had lost a game to them. Holy Cross was one of the best teams in college baseball, well on the way to winning their conference—if they could beat Dartmouth in today's game. Needless to say, both teams had a big incentive to win. Tony Lupien gave a rousing pregame speech. Fired up, Jerry and his teammates climbed out of the dugout and took the field determined to win.

It was a beautiful spring day. The field was well maintained with thick, soft green grass. The smell of recently cut grass pervaded the area. The field had been well manicured by someone who was obviously a professional. The recently placed chalk base lines were so bright white that they were nearly blinding. The canvas-covered base pads were so clean and white that someone might have had second thoughts about stepping on them. The partisan crowd filled the stadium, ready to cheer on their home team. By all accounts, it was a wonderful day and place to play baseball.

Jerry took his usual position at first base. He looked at each of his teammates in the infield and nodded, giving a sign of confidence. It was a knowing glance between brothers, a nonverbal connection based on years of shared trials and experience.

The first batter came to the plate. With a booming voice heard around the stadium, the umpire called, "play ball!"

The infielders crouched in a ready position; their gazes fixed on the batter. The pitcher for Dartmouth was their ace. He was a good, reliable performer but not a superstar. Everyone was hoping he would put on the performance of his life today. Jerry took a look at the pitcher's face, and he appeared to be dead serious in his focus.

The pitcher went through his windup and then the pitch. The batter swung. Jerry heard a loud crack from the bat and saw the ball sail into the outfield. The center fielder turned, ran back to the stadium wall, and caught the ball on the run. It was a great catch. "Good!" Jerry thought. "One down."

The second batter hit a blistering ball down the third base line, which was handily retrieved by the third baseman and then thrown to Jerry at first base. They had practiced this play thousands of times to perfect their speed and accuracy. Jerry snagged the ball in his glove with his foot on the bag long before the runner got to first. Jerry put two fingers up so all could see, signifying the second out.

The next batter was a left-hander who was known to be an excellent hitter. Jerry knew he needed to be extra sharp at first base. The batter hit several high foul balls deep into the stands, where the spectators scrambled for the balls. Jerry became a little concerned that the batter might be starting to figure out their pitcher. The pitcher strolled around the mound, thinking about his next pitch. He picked up the rosin bag at the base of the mound to dry his already sweating hands. The pitcher wound up and then delivered a fastball down the middle of the plate. The batter swung, and Jerry heard a loud crack from the bat. The ball instantly came right at Jerry, a line drive in fair territory. Then it began taking off higher, rocketing above Jerry's head. With an instantaneous reflex, Jerry leaped into the air, stretching his arm and glove as high as he could. He didn't know if he was going to catch this one. Just as that thought crossed his mind, he felt a solid hit in his mitt and heard the thwap of contact. Somehow, he caught the ball in the tip of the webbing of his glove. He wasn't sure how he had done it, but he felt great relief because that ball had extra bases written all over it.

Whew! Out number three. Jerry threw the ball to the umpire and jogged in as if nothing had happened, as did the other players. As he entered the dugout, a bit of unease came over him regarding his team's pitcher. Although no one had gotten on base, there had been significant contact with the ball, requiring a lot of defense to get out of the inning. He was hoping the opposing team did not have their pitcher figured out.

For collegiate baseball in the 1960s, Holy Cross was renowned for their excellent pitching staff. Their ace, Gene Malinowski, was big and strong—six feet six inches tall and weighing about 240 pounds. With only one loss in the season and several no-hitters to his record, Malinowski was considered nearly unhittable, although no one on the Dartmouth team would have openly said so. His fastball was consistently nearly one hundred miles per hour. But there was more. He had a full repertoire of other pitches, all with great accuracy. It was well known that he was being scouted by the major leagues. In fact, it was rumored that professional baseball scouts would be in the stands during today's game. The success of Holy Cross during the season was attributed largely to Malinowski.

Malinowski was somewhat of a character. He frequently taunted the opposing team with verbal abuse and hand gestures. This may have been by design to upset the opposing players so that they would lose their composure and focus and try too hard to slam the ball. Whatever the reason, he was known to have a huge ego. Unfortunately, he was good enough to get away with all the bravado. During the previous game between Holy Cross and Dartmouth, Malinowski had pointed his finger at a batter he had struck out and laughed. At the end of the same game, he had given an obscene hand gesture to the Dartmouth coach, Tony Lupien. This had infuriated the entire Dartmouth team and staff, but Tony had just laughed. The team had just had to take it and wait for the next game with Holy Cross.

Sports reporters from the local newspaper frequently wrote stories lauding Malinowski's spectacular skills and showmanship, giving Malinowski near hero status among local residents. Many people in the town of Worcester, Massachusetts, went to games just to see him play and watch his antics.

Out came Malinowski with the rest of the Holy Cross team. There was a big cheer from the home team crowd. Malinowski looked into the stands, smiled, tipped his hat, and waved to the fans.

"Oh, brother, is this guy cocky! We've just got to take him down," thought Jerry. Jerry yelled out in the dugout, "Let's go get 'em, boys!" He went out to the on-deck circle; he was batting second.

The first batter was one of the team's most reliable hitters. Malinowski wound up and delivered the first pitch. Swing and a miss, fastball down the middle. Malinowski was daring the hitter to take his best shot at it. Two more fastballs painted the corners of the strike zone. The umpire yelled, "Strike three, out!" Malinowski smiled at the batter and waved goodbye, which prompted laughter from the partisan crowd.

When the teams had met earlier in the year, Jerry had hit one single, but it hadn't been a solid hit, and he felt lucky to have gotten on base. He was determined to do better this time. He picked up his old reliable Louisville Slugger bat and took a few practice swings to loosen up. Jerry slowly stepped into the batter's box, took his stance, and stared at Malinowski.

Malinowski gave Jerry a mocking look. Jerry wanted to clobber the ball in the worst way, but he knew he needed to stay cool and relaxed, ready for an immediate explosion of energy and accuracy toward the incoming ball. He tried to put all his emotions about Malinowski out of his mind.

Malinowski looked at his catcher and nodded. He wound up and delivered the pitch. Fastball down the middle, strike one. Jerry could barely see the ball. It was the fastest pitch he had ever seen in his life. He knew he needed to start the swing before the ball even left the pitcher's hand in order to make contact.

The next pitch came. Jerry swung and missed before the ball even got to the catcher's glove. Jerry had anticipated another fastball, but it turned out to be an off-speed changeup. The ball came in slowly, causing Jerry to swing too early and miss the ball completely.

Jerry stepped out of the batter's box, took a deep breath, and collected his thoughts. He stretched his arms and then resumed his batter's stance. Malinowski walked around the pitcher's mound, taking his time to deliver the next pitch, most likely hoping to cause Jerry to "tighten up." Malinowski had noticed Jerry stretching his arms possibly indicating muscle stiffness. Malinowski, in a bent-over position, stared into Jerry's eyes. The wait was too long, and Jerry stepped out of the box again. He thought, "This Malinowski guy is trying to play games with my mind." After taking a few practice swings, he stepped back into the box and resumed the batter's stance. Malinowski began his windup, then the follow-through.

The pitch was a curveball barely in the strike zone, down and away. "you're out!" yelled the umpire. Those words seemed to sting sharply, like a slap in the face.

Malinowski grinned at Jerry as he walked back to the dugout. Jerry realized that Malinowski was even better than the last time they had met. He'd brought his best stuff today. Jerry showed no emotion, but he was thinking, "I can't stand that guy! I'll get him next time."

As the game progressed, Malinowski really put on a show. Jerry managed to get three singles, but again, they were lucky shallow hits, with two made on errors. Jerry was the only offense Dartmouth generated. While sitting on the bench Jerry briefly thought of a previous teammate who was an outstanding hitter, and all of the past years events that had led up to this point.

Probably the best overall player on Jerry's team was Peter Benzo, who had a tremendous amount of natural talent. He was by far the best hitter on the team and an exceptional fielder. There was a problem, though; he was not a team player in a team sport. He had a huge ego and was spoiled. He came from a very wealthy and prestigious Boston family. Jerry and some of the other team members nicknamed him "Hotshot." Benzo didn't seem that smart and at times appeared downright dumb. Jerry always wondered how he had even gotten into Dartmouth.

Benzo refused to do wind sprints and calisthenics during the pre-season workouts. When forced by the coach, he would act silly and move spastically for attention. He frequently made stupid and some-times derogatory comments to his teammates. However, he could re-ally play baseball. Many times, he single-handedly won games with his offensive and defensive skills. However, Benzo was a clear detriment to team morale and unity.

On road trips, he was difficult to control. He was usually late to team meetings. He frequently broke curfew. He once pulled a fire alarm at a hotel where the team was staying, creating chaos and trouble for the team. Jerry pulled him aside on numerous occasions for serious talks about these problems, but his words fell on deaf ears. Benzo usually laughed off Jerry's advice.

One night prior to a game the next day, Benzo sneaked out, break-ing the curfew, to party with some friends and got drunk. The next morning, he overslept. It was afternoon when he woke up, and he was hungover. He missed the bus to the field. When he finally pulled him-self together, he took a cab to the field and arrived just as the game began. Jerry looked at him and just shook his head. The coach told Benzo that he wasn't playing; he was benched. Benzo began yelling and generally making a scene. He picked up a bat and forcefully threw it to the ground. He then threw his mitt into the dugout. Everyone just stared at the childlike behavior of their most talented player.

Benzo got in coach Lupien's face and said, "If I don't get to play, I might as well quit!"

The coach replied, "If that's what you want, then fine, you're out of here."

Benzo stormed out, swearing as he went into the locker room. The coach told Bill, the second-string player, to get out in center field. Bill was thrilled at the chance he had been waiting for so long.

After the game, Benzo tried to apologize to Lupien and wanted to get back on the team. Lupien refused, telling him that he was not worth the trouble. Lupien said, "There are some things more important than winning games."

Jerry was impressed with his coach's integrity. Benzo was a potential major league professional-level prospect, which meant winning games and even championships with him in the lineup. However, the coach stuck to his guns because it would dishonor the whole team if Benzo remained. Benzo then went to Jerry and asked him to talk to the coach. Benzo knew that coach Lupien respected and listened to Jerry. Jerry said, "Pete, you've got to play by the rules. Life and this team don't revolve around you, no matter how good you are. Rules are there for a reason. You've just broken them too many times. What if everyone acted like you? Tony was a lot easier on you than I would have been. Even if Tony was wrong and you felt he was being unfair, he's still the coach, and he's someone you don't mess with. You have to respect his position. The coach is the coach! You never mess with the coach! Pete, there's nothing I can do for you."

Benzo cleaned out his locker, slammed it shut, and left. Jerry never heard from him again.

The Dartmouth defense was keeping the team in the game, making one great play after another. The outfielders were running all over the field, making many diving and leaping catches. Great throws back to the infield were preventing the runners from advancing and scoring. The infield was putting on a spectacular defensive performance. There were several exceptional double plays and even two pickoffs at first base. Two players that Jerry had worked with in the pre-season were now showing tremendous fielding skill. Jerry was not only the appointed captain of the team but a true leader to his teammates. He was always encouraging and supportive to all the players, even those who were primarily sitting on the bench.

Bill was an outfielder who was a tremendous hitter, but he made a lot of fielding errors and had only average speed and thus was second string. The first-string player ahead of Bill was Peter Benzo who was the most talented player on the team. This caused Bill to become discouraged. After two years, he felt that he was going nowhere and that he would never get off the bench. He considered quitting the team since he didn't see any chance for advancement. Bill decided to talk to Jerry before going to the coach to resign. Jerry encouraged him and told him to give it at least one more year. Jerry said, "If you're going to quit, never do it during the season or you'll be labeled a quitter."

Jerry then went to Tony Lupien and told him that he thought it would be beneficial to keep Bill on the team. He asked the coach to talk to Bill to see if he could motivate him and convince him that all of his work was not for nothing. Bill was ready to begin his junior year and had little playing time except for occasional pinch hitting. To obtain a Dartmouth school athletic letter jacket, the policy was that a player had to play a certain number of games on first string level. Tony decided to expand the criteria for lettering to include more players. He gave Bill a letter jacket to encourage him to give his best effort and continue on the team. This gave players like Bill an incentive to stay on because it gave them a sense that they were truly members of the team. Jerry was pleased that the coach had taken his advice.

No player tried harder to improve his skills than Bill. Jerry saw potential in him and admired his perseverance. Jerry encouraged him to keep working. Bill asked Jerry to help him. Jerry repeated an old saying that he had heard from one of his coaches: "The only thing more important than the will to win is the will to prepare to win."

During the preseason, Jerry and Bill met after class at the baseball field, where Jerry would hit balls to Bill in the outfield. Jerry taught Bill not to commit too quickly until he could determine the trajectory of the ball first. This technique prevented Bill from letting the ball go over his head. Jerry hit ball after ball, some deep, some shallow, some to either side. They practiced like this for several months.

The coach knew Jerry was spending time helping Bill, and he thanked and encouraged Jerry. The coach approached Jerry one day and said, "Since you're working with Bill on fielding, could you help out Dave for infield practice?" Dave was thrilled at the chance to work with Jerry after class. He was a solid shortstop with good potential, but like Bill, Dave needed to develop his skills to a higher level. Dave was a senior and had been on the team for three years. This was his last chance to be on the varsity squad. Both Bill and Dave had noticed that some of the players who played on first string were talented but sometimes erratic. They wanted to improve their game for a better chance to get out on the field and play. So far, neither had received a significant amount of playing time on the varsity level.

Now, Jerry had Bill in the outfield and Dave in the infield, fielding balls hit to them. Nearly every afternoon prior to the baseball season,

Jerry would be behind the backstop with several buckets of baseballs at his side, hitting balls to the two second stringers. Both Bill and Dave were grateful to Jerry; they worked hard and never complained. Jerry noticed that when Dave joined the practice sessions, Bill's playing improved even more. Bill and Dave seemed to feed off each other, each trying to out do the other. Jerry got a real kick out of hitting barely catchable balls to them. He would chuckle at the sight of the two diving and jumping for balls and then seeing them roll and sprawl on the ground after a tremendous catch. He thought a little competition was a good thing. In reality, all three were having fun doing the extra practice. They all looked forward to the afternoon practice sessions. After Peter Benzo left, Bill filled the outfield position nearly as well. The starting shortstop got injured early in the season leaving the position open for Dave who did an outstanding job. The Dartmouth team did better with the two new players than before.

Jerry yelled his support to his teammates after each great play: "way to go! great play! that's it! keep it up, guys!"

Holy Cross had multiple base hits but just couldn't score. They left men stranded on base in scoring position every inning. Malinowski continued to shut down the Dartmouth offense putting on a real pitching performance. He would occasionally make a fist and direct it toward home plate and then elevate it up in the air after a batter had struck out, simultaneously giving a yell out, "Yeah!" He then walked around the pitcher's mound and swing his throwing arm around like a windmill ending in a wave to the crowd and the professional baseball scouts who were in attendance. The hometown partisan crowd loved his over-the-top bravado and cheered on his exuberant antics. The Dartmouth team was disgusted with his "showboat" acting of this "Hot-dog" pitcher. Jerry seemed to sense that Malinowski and his crazy behavior was starting to affect his team's moral. Malinowski seemed to be putting salt in an already painful wound of striking out time and again. This lunatic pitcher began to seem like a superman.

The game went on and on, scoreless, into extra innings. Malinowski was still looking strong and delivering great pitches. However, the Dartmouth pitcher was starting to waver. He was putting tremendous effort into keeping his team in the game. A relief pitcher was eventually called for in the thirteenth inning. This only increased Jerry's anxiety because he knew the Dartmouth relievers were the weakest part of the team. The relief pitcher who was coming in was the best reliever they had but was less consistent and less accurate than their starting pitcher.

It was now the fifteenth inning. Jerry came up to the plate once again. He thought, "How can this Malinowski guy keep going like this? He's got to be tiring out; he's only human." Jerry raised his bat and positioned himself. He took a deep breath and relaxed, telling himself not to focus on the pitcher but just to follow the ball in. Malinowski gave him another smirk. Jerry just focused on the pitcher's arm.

Malinowski pitched a scorching fastball. It rocketed directly toward Jerry's head, causing him to rapidly fall to the ground to avoid being hit. "ball," yelled the umpire. "That was close," Jerry thought as he stood up and dusted himself off. It was also a little scary since being hit by a hundred-miles-per-hour fastball would be painful, if not dangerous. Malinowski stared at Jerry and gave a big toothy grin. It was Jerry's belief that the pitch had been intentional, since Malinowski was too accurate a pitcher to throw such a wild pitch. "So far, I'm the only player on the team to get a hit off Malinowski. He wants me damaged or out of the way," Jerry thought.

Undaunted, Jerry shook it off, took a practice swing, and stepped back into the batter's box. He thought, "I'll bet he thinks that I'm shook up after that close call, nearly being hit. I'll bet his next pitch is a fastball because he thinks I'm now intimidated and can be bullied. He thinks he's going to put the icing on the cake with me, so I'll be an ineffective hitter from here on. That's not going to happen!" Jerry took a final practice swing to loosen his slowly tightening muscles, then got into position, eyes fixed on Malinowski's arm.

Malinowski gave the windup and pitch. Jerry knew instantly, fastball! He was like a tightly coiled spring ready to be triggered. He unleashed a mighty and lightning-fast swing. He felt an immediate pop in the middle of the bat and heard the loud crack, followed by cheering from the Dartmouth dugout. The ball flew into the deep right field corner. Jerry took off toward first base. He rounded first and noticed that the right fielder was having trouble getting the ball as it bounced off the wall into a tight angle of the corner. Jerry headed for second. It was going to be an easy stand-up double. However, Jerry thought, "No one has been able to hit off of Malinowski the entire game, and our pitcher is questionable. I'm going to take the risk and go for third."

Without hesitation, Jerry rounded second base as fast as his legs would take him. As he approached third base, he went into a slide. He sensed the ball flying past him and for a moment thought he was too late and was going to be out. However, the ball was too widely thrown, and the third baseman couldn't catch it as it flew out of bounds.

This was his chance! He immediately popped up from the slide and sprinted for home plate. He saw the catcher with his face mask off in a crouched position like a wrestler, standing over the plate. Jerry went into a slide for the second time with as much force and velocity as he could muster. He had a fleeting thought that he may be sliding into a brick wall with the appearance of this stocky muscular catcher just ahead of him. He felt the ball whiz past him, and saw the ball enter the catcher's glove. The catcher immediately turned to him. Still in his slide, Jerry stretched his leg out and touched home plate just before he was tagged with the ball.

"Safe!" the umpire yelled as he stood over Jerry and the catcher, who was sprawled over him. Jerry had scored an inside-the-park home run! Dartmouth won in a walk-off. Jerry glanced back at the pitching mound as his cheering teammates crowded around him. Malinowski took his glove off and threw it violently to the ground as he kicked the dirt. Jerry smiled but didn't say a word to him.

Lupien greatly respected Jerry, not only as a player but as a young man with accurate and helpful insight. He looked upon Jerry almost as a second coach. Throughout the years, he and Jerry kept in touch. Jerry frequently made trips back to Dartmouth to see Lupien. The coach was a mentor to Jerry, teaching him not only about baseball and leadership skills but about how to be a gentleman and have a successful life. Jerry went on to medical school at the university of Missouri. He became a respected dermatologist and a well-known pillar of the community in Columbia, Missouri.

———

Jerry was married to my sister Heather. However, he was more like a brother to me than a brother-in-law. Jerry's main goal in life was to be a good father and husband and to have a stable, comfortable life. He certainly accomplished this. He was one of the most capable people I have ever known, yet he maintained great humility. He had the capacity to do anything he wished to do, yet he was unwavering in his commitment to his life goal and succeeded at it.

I think the greatest joy in any person's life is a stable and loving family. Jerry believed this to be true as well. It is uncommon for any job or employment to achieve the profound sense of contentment and happiness that a family can bring. Having a successful family life requires deep commitment and constant work that can be difficult and at times painful, but it is the most important thing that a person can do in life.

Jerry took great pride in his family, school, state, and country. He became a benefactor and contributor to the Dartmouth baseball program and to the University of Missouri medical school. There was no greater patriot and loyal person than Jerry Foote.

Jerry was a mentor and an example for me as a youth, as well as for many others. He once told me, "Life is a lot like baseball. It is a team sport, but individuals can make a big difference in the game and with others. Remember that you are on a team and no better than anyone else. You must respect others, no matter what their ability. If you conduct yourself with distinction, you can be an inspiration to others and thereby bring out the best in them. Most people have some type of untapped potential. It can be amazing what a little maturity, hard work, and persistence can do. Many times, these efforts can overcome a lack of natural ability.

"A baseball game, or for that matter any sporting event, teaches life lessons. All the achievements, disappointments, thrills, mistakes, hard work, adversity, setbacks, and resilience that play out in a lifetime can unfold within a single game. You practice and compete against someone who has practiced and is competing just as hard against you. This process builds toughness and resilience. This can be applied to any business or profession that you may have in the future. Sports are a good teacher for life.

"Baseball, like life, requires resilience to succeed. You cannot allow a failure or setback to deter you from your goal. Everyone in life will experience failure. Resilience, the ability to adapt, and determination will get you out of that setback. Resilience is something that is learned. Like a muscle, the more you use it, the stronger it becomes. If you get knocked down and get up time and again, it becomes a habit. You get through adversity by being resilient. You cannot build resilience if you are coddled or shielded from failure and adversity.

"Excellence withers without an adversary. The stronger your opponent, the stronger you become after preparation and then final success over that adversary. You must not be intimidated by the strength of an adversary. Look at your opponent as an opportunity to improve your game. Just as repeated heavy resistance builds a stronger muscle, it also makes you think about different ways to succeed that have not been considered before, thereby improving your mental acuity and resourcefulness. Sometimes cleverness, skill, and guile can win the day over brute strength or physical ability alone. These things again can be used not just in sport but in your own life and business.

"Baseball has certain rules. If you don't follow the rules, trouble will be ahead. If you don't follow the straight and narrow early in life, later, you'll get further and further away from success and any goal you may have. It could also possibly get you into trouble if you stray too far. Baseball requires concentration and focus on the situation at hand. Anxiety and emotional upset impair your ability to perform, just as clarity of mind is key to success. In baseball, there are times of inactivity followed by dramatic surges of extraordinary power and energy. As in life, you have to know when to 'turn on the gas' and when to relax."

Jerry's advice to me when growing up was to focus on my goals, stay on the straight and narrow, and follow the rules.

I have certainly found that it was good advice.

In great deeds, something abides. On great fields, something stays.

Forms change and pass, bodies disappear but spirits linger to
consecrate ground for the vision place of the soul.

And reverent men and women from afar and generations that know
us not and that we know not of, shall come here to ponder and
dream and the power of the vision shall pass into their souls.

—Joshua Lawrence Chamberlain
1828–1914

John W. Graham (Happy Jack)
Notice Union Army Military Unit
Designation painted at base:
Company D. 8th Kansas Infantry

Sod House on Kansas Prairie 1868

Cheyenne War Club

Medal given to John W. Graham
(Happy Jack)

Honorable Military Discharge paper for
John W. Graham (Happy Jack) from Civil War

Dr. J.W., wife and son, Highland, Kansas

J.W. Graham (Far Left) Professor of Anatomy
and Surgery in Anatomy Lab: University of Kansas

Dr. J.W. Graham MD

Stanley Hill and Family:
Velma, Edna, Harrel

Municipal Auditorium,
Kansas City, Missouri

Baptist Hospital,
Kansas City, Missouri

Wallace Graham, MD

Wallace Graham's Combat Helmet.
Notice bullet damage left lower brim

P .38 German Officer's pistol

Sergeant Gorsky having a smoke after a firefight, France 1944

Copy of Hitler's last will and testament

Wallace Graham with King Ibn Saud

Gold plated sword given as gift by King Ibn Saud

President Harry Truman with
Wallace Graham MD

President Harry Truman and General Douglas MacArthur
Note: Wallace Graham in the center background

President Harry S. Truman

Velma (2nd from the left) with nursing students and friends

Velma Hill Graham

Velma Graham in Vienna, Austria

Wallace and Velma skiing in
Bavarian Alps

Velma Graham on one of
many spontaneous outings

Velma and Andy

Wally Graham with Jazz Guitar

Wally Graham at the commune

Wally and Son on Mexican beach

Abstract Form, Wally Graham

Jerry Foote MD with wife Heather Graham Foote

Jerry Foote middle Lower Row fourth from right

ABOUT THE AUTHOR

Bruce D. Graham M.D. is a board certified General and Colon Rectal surgeon who lives in Shawnee, Kansas. He is married and has three children. He received a B.A. at the University of Missouri where he was also a collegiate wrestler. He received an M.S. at the University of Arkansas and an M.D. at the University of Missouri. His General Surgery and fellowship in Colon and Rectal Surgery training was at Michigan State University. He has been in private practice in the Kansas City area for over thirty years. He is an associate clinical professor at the University of Kansas. He has published numerous scientific papers. He is an amateur historian, an avid fisherman, and gardener.